Sankey
MY LIFE &
SACRED SONGS

IRA D. SANKEY

CRIMOND
HOUSE

CRIMOND HOUSE PUBLICATIONS

© Copyright 2018 Crimond House Publications

Published in 2018 by
Crimond House Publications
A division of
Ards Evangelical Bookshop
"Crimond House"
48 Frances Street
Newtownards
Co. Down
BT23 7DN
www.ardsbookshop.com

Printed in Belfast by J.C. Print Ltd

ISBN: 978 1 908618 20 7

Foreward

Of the half-dozen or so leading streams from which we receive so many of our beloved hymns, perhaps the most interesting and treasured is the source of well-known hymns which were made famous by the campaigns of Moody and Sankey.

In Psalm 40, the Psalmist says, "He hath put a new song in my mouth, even praise unto our God: many shall see it, and fear, and shall trust in the LORD." In Acts 16, Paul and Silas are singing and we are told "the prisoners heard them." It has ever been a feature of Christian testimony that the preaching of the gospel has been accompanied by song to the blessing of the audience. Many of the most famous preachers of the last century had their singer to accompany the preaching. R.A. Torrey had Charles Alexander, Billy Sunday had Homer Rodeheaver, and, most famous of all, Billy Graham had George Beverly Shea and Cliff Barrows. Ira Sankey may have been the most influential of them all. A keen student of hymnology, he was always on the look-out for new songs and it was through him that many of the hymns which we treasure today were made well known.

In this book, Sankey gives his own life story, and then goes on to tell the background of many of these hymns and how they have been used by God. These hymns, mostly from American and British writers, have become so familiar to us and we trust that learning of their origins will deepen our appreciation for them. On these pages there will be encouragement for the downcast, light for the sinner, material for the preacher and a note of song for the heart of every believer.

We have republished this book, and commend it to you, so that the stories of these hymns may be preserved. Our prayer is that you will find encouragement in reading this book, and you will gain a fresh appreciation of our heritage of hymns. Believers in the Lord Jesus should be a singing people and these "old-time" hymns have a timeless value. We trust that their use among us may be long preserved.

Ricky McCoubrey
November, 2018.

Introduction

The deep interest I have always taken in the subject of hymnology, and my warm personal affection for the author of this volume, are my warrant for be speaking for it a warm and hearty welcome. If ever a man was raised and endowed for a special work by our Divine Master, that man is Ira D. Sankey.

His work has been of a twofold character. Before his day psalms and hymns and spiritual songs had always been an important part of the services of religious worship throughout Christendom.

But he introduced a peculiar style of popular hymns which are calculated to awaken the careless, to melt the hardened, and to guide inquiring souls to the Lord Jesus Christ. In the next place, he sang these powerful revival-hymns himself, and became as effective a preacher of the gospel of salvation by song as his associate, Dwight L. Moody, was by sermon. The multitudes who heard his rich and inspiring voice in "The Ninety and Nine," "Jesus of Nazareth Passeth By" and "When the Mists Have Rolled Away" will testify to the prodigious power with which the Holy Spirit gave him utterance. While he has had many successors, he was the pioneer.

This position which our beloved Brother Sankey holds before the whole Christian world fitted him to prepare such a volume as this valuable addition to hymnology. It is the simple but sublime story of the quickening, converting and sanctifying power of sacred song. It adds a new and thrilling chapter to the triumph of the Cross. It is a precious legacy by a faithful veteran of Jesus Christ to his fellow-soldiers in all lands who are battling for the cause and crown of the glorious Captain of our salvation, and who "wait for his appearing."

Theodore L. Cuyler
Brooklyn, New York.
November, 1905.

Preface

Since Moses and the children of Israel, on the shore of the Red Sea, sang of their deliverance from the hand of Pharaoh, saying: "I will sing unto the Lord, for He hath triumphed gloriously; the horse and his rider hath He thrown into the sea," there has never been any great religious movement without the use of sacred song. Luther set all Germany ablaze with religious enthusiasm as he sang his magnificent hymn, "Ein Feste Burg," in which Melanchthon and multitudes of Christian soldiers joined. In later years the church of God was thrilled by the sermons of John Wesley and the songs of his brother Charles, whose hymns are more extensively used throughout Christendom than any others. After the Wesleys came Charles G. Finney, who, although he did not use the service of song as much as others, yet as a preacher was one of the mightiest men of his day. Later came E. P. Hammond, the children's evangelist, who gave the praise service an especially important place in his work.

Then, in 1873, God was pleased to send Mr. Moody and myself to Great Britain, where a work of grace was begun that has continued until the present day. About the same time Whittle and Bliss were doing a remarkable work in the United States, Bliss becoming one of the greatest song-evangelists of that age. For the last two or three years we have had the splendid campaign of Torrey and Alexander in Australia, Great Britain and America. In their work the prominent feature has been the use of praise, their most popular hymn being "The Glory Song."

We all agree with what Dr. Pentecost has said regarding the power of sacred song: "I am profoundly sure that among the divinely ordained instrumentalities for the conversion and sanctification of the soul, God has not given a greater, besides the preaching of the Gospel, than the singing of psalms and hymns and spiritual songs. I have known a hymn to do God's work in a soul when every other instrumentality has failed.

I could not enumerate the times God has rescued and saved my soul from darkness, discouragement and weariness by the singing of a hymn, generally by bringing one to my own heart and causing me to sing it to myself. It would be easy to fill many pages with interesting facts in connection with the use of hymns in the public worship of the house of God. I have seen vast audiences melted and swayed by a simple hymn when they have been unmoved by a powerful presentation of the Gospel from the pulpit."

For many years past I have been collecting and writing up the history of hymns, and incidents connected with their composition and their use by Mr. Moody and myself, as well as by others; but in 1901, when the manuscript of these stories was almost completed, it was unfortunately destroyed in the fire that devastated the great Sanitarium at Battle Creek, Michigan, where I was at that time a guest of my friend Dr. J. H. Kellogg. In view of the regret which was expressed by my friends over this loss, and the interest taken by the people who sing our hymns, I decided to rewrite the story from memory, as far as I was able. The present is the result.

I am indebted to the Rev. John Julian, the Rev. S. W. Duffield and the Rev. E. S. Lorenz, from whose works I have collected some dates and incidents; also to my faithful secretary, Mr. Charles G. Rosewall, for aid in compiling and writing this book. In the preparation of the old original manuscript I was especially indebted to my friend, Mr. Oliver H. Shiras, for his able assistance.

Ira D. Sankey
Brooklyn, New York
January 1906

Sankey's
STORY OF MY LIFE

I was born in the village of Edinburg, on the Mahoning River in Western Pennsylvania, August 28, 1840.

The first hymn I remember having heard was from the lips of my beloved mother, when, as a child, she sang me to sleep with the strains of that sweet old hymn:

"Hush, my dear, lie still and slumber, Holy angels guard thy bed."

As a boy, it was one of my chief joys to meet with other members of our family around the great log fire in the old homestead, and spend the long winter evenings singing with them the good old hymns and tunes of the church, which was the only music we had in those days. When at home, my father would frequently join us in these evenings of sacred song, singing a splendid bass, while other members of the family carried the other parts. In this way I learned to read music, and when I was about eight years old I could sing correctly such tunes as St. Martin's, Belmont, Coronation, etc.

The church to which I belonged was situated several miles from our home, but my fondness for singing led me to be a regular attendant.

I received the usual school privileges which fell to the lot of boys and girls of those days. The very first recollection I have of anything pertaining to a holy life was in connection with a Mr. Frazer. I recall how he took me by the hand and led me with his own children to the Sunday-school held in the old schoolhouse. I shall remember this to my dying day. He had a warm heart and the children all loved him. It was not until some years after that I was converted, at the age of sixteen, while attending revival meetings at a church known as The King's Chapel, about three miles from my home, but my first impressions were received from that man when I was very young.

In 1857 our family removed to New Castle, where my father assumed the presidency of the bank. Here I attended the high school, where every opportunity was given to study such of the higher branches as the student might have a taste for, and later I took a position in the bank. On arriving at New Castle I joined the Methodist Episcopal Church. Soon I was elected superintendent of the Sunday-school and leader of the choir.

When I first took charge of the singing it was thought by many of the church members that the use of an organ, or any kind of musical instrument to accompany the voices of the singers, was wicked and worldly. The twanging of an old tuning-fork on the back of a hymnbook was not objected to, nor the running of the whole gamut in subdued voice to find the proper key, nor the choir trying to get the proper note to their respective parts in the never-to-be forgotten, "Do, Mi, Sol, Mi, Do," before beginning the hymn. For several years we kept on in this way, but by and by we found that the majority were in favour of having an organ in the choir. I shall never forget the day on which the organ was first introduced. I had the honour of presiding at the instrument, and I remember well how carefully I played the opening piece. Only one or two of the old members left the church during the singing. It was reported that an old man who left the church on account of the introduction of the organ, was seen on his dray the next day, driving through the main street of the town, seated on the top of a large casket of rum, singing at the top of his voice:

"A charge to keep I have," etc.

It was here that I began to make special use of my voice in song, and in this way, though unconsciously, I was making preparation for the work in which I was to spend my life.

When about twenty years of age I went to Farmingtown, Ohio, to attend a musical convention, conducted by Mr. Bradbury. On my return home, my father said to mother: "I am afraid that boy will never amount to anything; all he does is to run about the country with a hymn-book under his arm." Mother replied that she would rather see me with a hymn-book under my arm than with a whisky bottle in my pocket.

In the spring of 1860, on the call of President Lincoln for men to sustain the Government, I was among the first in New Castle to have my name enrolled as a soldier. My company was sent to Maryland. Religious services were held in the camp, and I often led the singing. I soon found several other young men who could render the same service. In a short time the people around us also learned that there were some singers in the Union camp, and we were frequently invited out by families who had heard of the singing of the "boys in blue."

I remember with what astonishment the Southern people heard some of our soldier boys play the piano in their beautiful homes. The singing of some of the old-time "home songs" seemed to dispel all feeling of enmity. We were always treated with the utmost hospitality and kindness, and many friendships were formed that lasted until long after the war was ended.

I organized a male choir in the company to which I belonged, and we would frequently be called upon to assist the chaplain in conducting the religious services of the camp.

At the expiration of my term as a soldier I did not re-enter the army, but returned to New Castle to assist my father, who had been appointed by Abraham Lincoln as a collector of internal revenue.

In 1863, on the 9th of September, I married a member of my choir Miss Fanny V. Edwards, a daughter of the Hon. John Edwards. She has been a blessing and a helpmate to me throughout my life and in all my work.

My services as a singer were utilized in Western Pennsylvania and Eastern Ohio for Sunday-school conventions and political gatherings. In 1867, when I was twenty-seven years old, a branch of the Young Men's Christian Association was organized at New Castle, of which I was at that time elected secretary and later president. The first meetings were held in a small hired room. From that modest beginning, by the help of God, I was later enabled to give to the city a Young Men's Christian Association building, including gymnasium, library and bathrooms, in all costing more than $40,000, by means of money realized from the sale of "Gospel Hymns." Not far from this building, on Jefferson street, I bought a beautiful lot for my old church, on which to erect a new structure, and later I assisted Bishop Vincent to raise the necessary funds, so that the new church was dedicated without any debt. My father and mother were members of this church until they passed away.

In 1870, with two or three others, I was appointed a delegate to the International Convention of the Association, to be held at Indianapolis that year.

For several years I had read in the religious press about Mr. Moody, and I was therefore pleased when I learned that he would be at the convention, being a delegate from the Chicago Association. For a couple of days I was disappointed in neither seeing nor hearing him. At several of the annual conventions prior to this occasion, it had been the custom to select Moody as chairman, but now it was decided that someone else should occupy the chair, and Moody therefore took a seat among the other delegates on the floor. However, late on a Saturday afternoon, it was announced that Moody of Chicago would lead a six o'clock morning prayer-meeting in the Baptist Church. I was rather late, and therefore sat down near the door with a Presbyterian minister, the Rev. Robert McMillan, a delegate from my own county, who said to me, "Mr. Sankey, the singing here has been abominable; I wish you would start up something when that man stops praying, if he ever does." I promised to do so, and when opportunity offered I started the familiar hymn, "There is a fountain filled with blood." The congregation joined heartily and a brighter aspect seemed to be given to the meeting.

At the conclusion of the meeting Mr. McMillan said to me: "Let me introduce you to Mr. Moody."

We joined the little procession of persons who were going up to shake hands with him, and thus I met for the first time the man with whom, in the providence of God, I was to be associated for the remainder of his life, or nearly thirty years.

Moody's first words to me, after my introduction, were, "Where are you from? Are you married? What is your business?" Upon telling him that I lived in Pennsylvania, was married, had two children, and was in the government employ, he said abruptly, "You will have to give that up."

I stood amazed, at a loss to understand why the man told me that I would have to give up what I considered a good position. "What for?" I exclaimed.

"To come to Chicago and help me in my work," was the answer.

When I told him that I could not leave my business, he retorted, "You must; I have been looking for you for the last eight years."

I answered that I would think the matter over; but as yet I had no thought of giving up my position. He told me about his religious work in Chicago, and closed by saying that the greatest trouble in connection with his meetings was the matter of the singing. He said he could not sing himself, and therefore had to depend upon all kinds of people to lead his service of song, and that sometimes when he had talked to a crowd of people, and was about to "pull the net," someone would strike up a long meter hymn to a short meter tune, and thereby upset the whole meeting. Mr. Moody then asked me if I would go with him and pray over the matter, and to this I consented out of politeness. After the prayer we parted, and I returned to my room, much impressed by Mr. Moody s prayer, but still undecided.

The next day I received a card from Mr. Moody asking if I would meet him on a certain street corner that evening at six o clock. At that hour I was at the place named, with a few of my friends. In a few minutes Moody came along.

Without stopping to speak, he passed on into a store near by, and asked permission to use a large store-box. The permission was granted; he rolled the box into the street, and, calling me aside, asked me to get up on the box and sing something.

"Am I a soldier of the cross?" soon gathered a considerable crowd. After the song, Mr. Moody climbed up on the box and began to talk. The workingmen were just going home from the mills and the factories, and in a short time a very large crowd had gathered. The people stood spellbound as the words fell from Moody's lips with wonderful force and rapidity. When he had spoken for some twenty-five minutes he announced that the meeting would be continued at the Opera House, and invited the people to accompany us there. He asked me to lead the way and with my friends sing some familiar hymn. This we did, singing as we marched down the street, "Shall we gather at the river." The men with the dinner pails followed closely on our heels instead of going home, so completely were they carried away by the sermon from the store-box.

The Opera House was packed to the doors, and Moody first saw that all the workingmen were seated before he ascended to the platform to speak. His second address was as captivating as the one delivered on the street corner, and it was not until the delegates had arrived for the evening session of the convention that Mr. Moody closed the meeting, saying, "Now we must close, as the brethren of the convention wish to come in to discuss the question, How to reach the masses!" Here was a man who could successfully reach the masses while others were talking about it.

When Mr. Moody again brought up the question of our going into the work together, I was still undecided. After a delay of over six months, and much urging on Mr. Moody's part, I consented to spend a week with him.

I arrived in Chicago one bright morning about daylight, and after a hasty breakfast proceeded at once to Mr. Moody's home, on the north side of the city. Immediately on entering the house, and without any preliminaries or introductions to such members of his family as were present, he asked me if I would not sit down at the organ and lead the singing for the family devotions. After the services were over and I had been introduced to his family, he said: "I am going to spend the day in visiting a lot of sick people, and I want you to go with me and sing for them." In the first home we visited we found a sick mother with a very large family, who were all very glad to see Mr. Moody, who at once took a seat by the bedside, saying: "I am going to read a few words from the Bible, but first I want my friend, Sankey, to sing a little hymn for you" I sang "Scatter Seeds of Kindness," which was quite popular in those days. This hymn, which was the first one I sang for Moody, on joining him in Chicago, in 1871, was the last one I sang for him, twenty-eight years later. This was at the last public meeting we held together, which was in Brooklyn, in the church of the Rev. Richard M. Storrs, D. D., in September, 1899.

Besides visiting the sick, we spent the week in holding a number of meetings in the Illinois Street Church, of which Moody was the founder and leader, noon prayer-meetings in the business part of the city, some evangelistic services in different churches, and concluded the week with a mass meeting in Farwell Hall. This meeting he opened with a congregational hymn, and while it was being sung, he said to me: "I am going to speak on The Prodigal Son, and I want you to sing one of the songs I heard you sing at Indianapolis, Come home, O prodigal child!" I replied: "But I have no organ with which to accompany myself." Pointing his finger over his shoulder at the great three thousand dollar organ at the rear of the platform, he said: "Isn't that enough for you?" I replied that it was too large, and too far away, and that if I used it, I would have to turn my back to the audience while singing, and that the song so rendered would not amount to anything, nor did I think that the German gentleman who had been playing the organ could accompany me in the way in which I should like to render the hymn. Moody then said: "Give him a book, and tell him how you want it played." This I did. Later on when Moody suddenly finished his address, which was one of great power, he looked at me and said: "Mr. Sankey will now sing a solo for us, and let it be perfectly still while he sings." I arose quickly, and turned around to indicate to the organist that I was ready, but to my horror, he had not yet returned from the quiet smoke which he was in the habit of enjoying in a back room while Moody was preaching. I stepped to the front of the platform and sang the song as best I could without any musical accompaniment. I have always remembered that song, as being the first sacred solo sung by me in one of Mr. Moody's large evangelistic meetings.

As I was about to leave the city for my home the next morning, Mr. Moody said: "You see that I was right; your singing has been very helpful in all the meetings, and I am sure you ought to come to Chicago at once, and give up your business."

When arriving home, I consulted my pastor, rather hoping that he would advise me not to go, but when he, as well as all my friends, was of the opinion that it was my plain duty to go, I sent my resignation to Mr. Hugh McCullough, at that time Secretary of the Treasury, and the position which I had held was, at my request, given to a "bucktail" soldier who had escaped from Libby Prison.

We thus commenced work together in Chicago in the early part of 1871, singing and praying with the sick, speaking and singing at the daily noon prayer-meetings, and other work, until Mr. Moody's church was destroyed in the Chicago fire.

Sunday evening, October 8, 1871, we were holding a meeting in Farwell Hall, which was crowded to the doors. At the close of his address Mr. Moody asked me to sing a solo, and standing by the great organ at the rear of the platform I began the old, familiar hymn,

> Today the Saviour calls:
> For refuge fly;
> The storm of justice falls,
> And death is nigh.

By the time I had reached the third verse, "Today the Saviour calls: For refuge fly; The storm of justice falls, And death is nigh," my voice was drowned by the loud noise of the fire engines rushing past the hall, and the tolling of bells, among which we could hear, ever and anon, the deep, sullen tones of the great city bell, in the steeple of the old court-house close at hand, ringing out a general alarm.

Tremendous confusion was heard in the streets, and Mr. Moody decided to close the meeting at once, for the audience was becoming restless and alarmed. As the people dispersed, I went with Mr. Moody down the small back stairway leading into the old Arcade Court, and from our position there we watched the reflection of the fire, half a mile away, on the west side of the city, as it cast its ominous glare against the sky. After a few moments we separated, I to go over the river to where the fire was raging, and he to his home on the North Side. We did not meet again for more than two months.

On reaching the scene of the fire I found a whole block of small frame buildings burning fiercely, and I assisted in tearing down some board fences, to try to keep the fire from spreading to the adjoining territory. While thus engaged, the wind from the southwest had risen almost to a hurricane, and the flying embers from the falling buildings were quickly caught up and carried high upon the roofs of the houses adjoining, which were soon in flames. Thus the fire spread from building to building, and from block to block, until it seemed evident that the city was doomed. All this time the fire was moving towards Farwell Hall and the business centre of the city.

I now gave up the fight, and made haste to re-cross the river, hurrying back to my quarters my living room and office in the Farwell Hall Building. The fire followed so rapidly that several times I had to shake the falling embers from my coat. Arriving at the hall, I gathered up a number of belongings which I especially wished to save, and, placing them close to the door of my office, went out to find a conveyance so as to transfer them to a place of safety. It was now between one and two o'clock in the morning, and not a carriage or truck could be found.

While still looking for a conveyance I saw in the distance, coming up Clark Street, a horse attached to an express wagon, running at full speed, without a driver, and ten or fifteen men running after it trying to capture the animal. I made a dash for the flying steed, but in turning from one street into another he slipped and fell, and in a moment a crowd of men were on top of him, each claiming the right of possession. Not caring to share in the contest, I returned to the hall, and commenced the task of carrying my effects toward Lake Michigan, half a mile distant.

On the way to the lake I passed the present location of the Palmer House, then being erected, the foundation of which had only been built to the level of the street. Believing that the rooms and underground passages would afford a temporary place of security for some of my things, I walked on a plank down into the cellar, and hid two large valises in the darkest corner I could find. As yet, only a few people were moving out of their homes in this section of the city, and, as I noticed the seeming indifference of those who had come to the windows of their houses, I called out to them to escape for their lives, as the city was doomed to destruction. Some became alarmed; others only laughed.

I returned to the hall for another load of my belongings, and after securing all I could carry, started in a more direct route for the lake, the streets being lighted up by the glare of the oncoming conflagration. After getting about half-way to the shore, I stopped and deposited my burden on the front steps of a fine residence I was passing, thinking I would soon return and find them there. Again, for the third time, I went back to my rooms, and, gathering up a few more articles, started for the stone steps. I found, however, on reaching the house, that the things I had left there were covered several feet deep with other people's belongings, and I never saw them again.

By this time the people were fully awake, rushing about the street, or anxiously looking out of their windows and from the tops of their houses in the direction of the fire. I could not help thinking of the Bible story of the destruction of the Cities of the Plain in the long ago, as many still made light of those who said the city would be destroyed. The air was filled with flying sparks of fire, resembling a spring snowstorm, when the sky is filled with huge, falling flakes.

As I pressed on, two men carrying a sick man on a stretcher overtook me. After passing a short distance ahead, they stopped and laid him by the side of the street, as the invalid, being quite sure the city would not be destroyed, did not wish to be carried farther. As soon as the carriers had been paid off and discharged I employed them to assist me in carrying my effects to the lakeside; but before we reached our destination, in looking southward, they saw that the fire was sweeping through the southeastern section of the city, where they lived. Dropping my goods in the middle of the street, and without waiting for compensation, they rushed away to secure their own homes.

Again I secured help, and at last reached the lake, where I deposited my trunks and possessions close by the edge of the water, with the thought that if the flames came to the edge of the lake I would walk into the water and be saved from the heat. Remembering my first attempt at carrying my goods away from Farwell Hall, I returned to the Palmer House block, to secure, if possible, my first cargo, very much fearing that the things would not be there when I reached the place, as I thought some night wanderer might have noticed my leaving them and appropriated them to his own use. Much to my joy, I found them still there, and carried them away to the lake.

By this time I was greatly exhausted, and almost famished for want of water, that along the shore not being fit to drink. I asked another refugee, who was in like case with myself, watching his little store of precious things, if he would look out for mine while I returned into the city to get some water to drink. The man consenting, I went back to Wabash Avenue, one of the finest residential streets in the city, and, entering one of the large houses, asked if I might have some water. I was told to go into the rear of the building and get all I wished. I found a faucet, but, on attempting to draw water, air rushed out instead. This was my first intimation that the water works, two miles to the northward, had been destroyed. A few minutes later I heard a terrific explosion, which seemed to shake the city, and was told that the city gas works had blown up.

Things began to look very desperate no water, no light in the houses, and the city in flames! I made my way back again to the lake and, wrapping myself in a great overcoat, lay down behind one of the large trunks which I had saved. Thus sheltered from the wind, I slept for an hour. On awaking I could hear the rush and roar of the fire coming nearer and nearer. The sun, slowly rising out of the waters of the lake, seemed like a red ball of fire. The wind had not fallen, and huge waves were breaking on the shore at my feet.

I now felt that I must have water to drink, and, after wandering along the shore for some distance, found some small rowboats, and asked a man near by, who seemed to be their owner, if I might have one to go out into the lake for fresh water. "Yes," he said; "if you can manage the boat you can have it, as we are not likely to have much more boating in this section for some time to come." So I took possession of one, and rowed down to where my goods were deposited. Rolling them on board, I made my way out into the lake, passing through the piling on which the railway was built, in front of the city. After getting my boat through the piling, I rowed out far enough to find fresh water. Then, tying my boat to some timbers that were being used for the erection of a new breakwater, I climbed up on the pile of lumber and for several hours watched the destruction of the city. Every few minutes a loud explosion was heard. I afterwards learned that these were caused by the blowing up of buildings by order of General Sheri dan, who was in the city at the time so as to form a barrier against the fire and prevent its spreading to the southward.

It was interesting to watch the tramps and thieves carrying away on their backs large bales of silk and satin goods which they had taken from the burning stores in the wholesale district. Most of them followed the railway track southward, not knowing that at the place where the track reached the land a company of fire insurance agents were waiting with open arms to relieve them of their burdens.

The day wore away, but the city was still burning, and, as the sun was sinking in the west, a song came into my mind which I had been singing a few days before in Mr. Moody s large Sunday-school on the North Side, and I sang it through as I sat there, with the waves beating about me. The first verse was as follows:

> Dark is the night, and cold the wind is blowing,
> Nearer and nearer comes the breakers roar;
> Where shall I go, or whither fly for refuge?
> Hide me, my Father, till the storm is o'er.

I finally determined to get back to land, but was not aware of the fact that the riding of my boat upon the waves had almost sawn asunder the line with which it was attached to the timber. As I jumped into the boat the line broke, and I was swept out into the lake, the waves sweeping over my little craft. For a moment I was in real danger of being lost, but I soon had the boat under control, and, after a few moments of hard work, reached the shore in safety.

I then secured a drayman, who for the sum of ten dollars agreed to carry me and my effects to the unburned end of the Fort Wayne & Chicago Railway if he could find it. He succeeded. I checked my goods for my home in the East, secured some refreshments at a near-by restaurant, and went back into the burnt district. Farwell Hall was gone, and every building in that part of the city had disappeared. The paved streets, covered with hot bricks and long coils of burnt and twisted telegraph wire, told something of the awful story. Most of the substance of these great buildings had actually been carried away by the hot air into the water of Lake Michigan.

After seeing something of the fearful destruction wrought by the conflagration, I made my way through the heated streets to the railway, and took an outgoing train for my home in Pennsylvania. As we left the city it seemed as though the whole country was on fire; in all directions we could see huge banks of flame sweeping across the prairies, and the air was filled to suffocation with smoke.

I was soon able to telegraph home of my safety and speedy return. It seemed as though this would end my work in Chicago, but two months later Mr. Moody telegraphed me to return and help him in the new temporary "Tabernacle," which had by that time been erected. On my return to Chicago I learned that Mr. Moody, after reaching his home on the North Side, had aroused his sleeping neighbours, assisted men and women into conveyances, and urged them to flee for their lives. As the billows of fire came nearer and nearer, Mr. Moody, with his wife and children, made his way into the northwestern district to a place of safety beyond the fire line. Before leaving her home Mrs. Moody took down from the wall an oil painting of her husband and asked him to carry it with him; but he declined, saying that he did not think it would look well for him to be running through the streets of Chicago with his picture in his arms at such a time! Speaking of the fire to a friend some time later, Mr. Moody remarked:

"All I saved was my Bible, my family and my reputation."

We continued to hold services and to help the poor and needy who had lost everything in the fire. We slept together in a corner of the new Tabernacle, with nothing for a bed but a single lounge, and frequently the fierce prairie winds would blow the drifting snow into our room.

During these busy months Mr. Moody was always soliciting help from his friends, for the purpose of rebuilding the church which had been destroyed by fire. I mention the following, as a characteristic incident of his skill in securing money: While walking with him one day along one of the principal streets of the city, we met one of his old acquaintances, and abruptly Moody said to him: "Look here, my friend, I am glad to see you, and I want one thousand dollars from you to help rebuild my church on the North Side." The man looked at him in amazement, and retorted: "I can't give it to you; I haven't got a thousand dollars." Mr. Moody quickly replied: "Well, you can borrow it." The gentleman was so amused and impressed with the earnestness of the petitioner that he at once said: "All right, Mr. Moody, I'll send you a cheque tomorrow," which he did.

In October of 1872 I moved my family to Chicago, and in the same year Mr. Moody went on his second trip to England, leaving me in charge of the work at the Tabernacle, assisted by Major Whittle, Richard Thain, Fleming H. Revell, and others. There were conversions in the church and Sunday-school every week.

After Mr. Moody's return we accepted an invitation to go to Springfield, Illinois, to hold services, which were attended with great blessing. Indeed, it seemed that if we had remained and thus worked in our own country a great revival would have taken place. On our way to Springfield the train stopped at a station near Chicago, where a great crowd was assembled on the platform. Mr. Moody sat by an open window. Near by stood a tall, gaunt-looking countryman, with his hands in his pockets, looking at Mr. Moody through the window. Mr. Moody asked him what the crowd meant, and the man replied:

"Oh, the folks have just come down to see the cars."

"Did you know that General Grant was on the train?" Mr. Moody inquired.

"Oh, is he?" the man exclaimed.

Mr. Moody, with a smile, told him that he was not. Quite nonplussed, the man walked down the platform a little way, but returned in a little while and said:

"Hello, Mister! We had a great time in town last night."

"How was that?" asked Mr. Moody.

"There was a woman here, and they wouldn't bury her."

"Why wouldn't they bury her?" Mr. Moody asked.

"Because she wasn't dead," the man smilingly answered, to the great amusement of his friends.

Mr. Moody turned to me and said: "Sankey, put that window down!"

About this time my friend Philip Phillips returned from Europe, where he had been singing for one hundred nights in succession. He came to

Chicago and stopped with me. He made a very enticing offer, including a large salary and all expenses, if I would go with him to the Pacific coast and there assist him in his services of song. I wouldn't promise anything until I had spent some hours in consultation and prayer with my friend, Mr. Moody; the result was that I remained with him.

In June, 1873, we sailed for England, Mr. Moody taking his wife and children with him, and my wife accompanying me, having left our two children with their grandparents.

The only books that I took with me were my Bagster Bible and my "musical scrap-book," which contained a number of hymns which I had collected in the past years, and many of which, in the providence of God, were to be used in arousing much religious interest among the people in the Old Country. The voyage was uneventful, but of great interest to our little party. Mr. Moody, shortly after leaving Sandy Hook, for good and sufficient reasons retired to his berth, where he remained for the larger part of the voyage. I had the good fortune to escape seasickness, and was able to partake of my regular three meals a day. Mr. Moody would frequently send his ship steward over to my side of the ship to ascertain how I was getting on, and suggesting a large number of infallible remedies for seasickness.

On arriving at Queenstown, the vessel stopped for a short time, to land and receive mail. Among some letters which Mr. Moody received was one informing him that both the men who had invited us to come to England, the Rev. William Pennefather, a minister of the Established Church of London, and Mr. Cuthbert Bainbridge, a Wesleyan, and a prominent merchant of Newcastle-on-Tyne, were dead.

Turning to me, Mr. Moody said, "Sankey, it seems as if God has closed the door for us, and if he will not open it we will return to America at once."

The next day we landed in Liverpool, strangers in a strange country, without an invitation, without a committee, and with but very little money. The situation was anything but cheerful. I have always felt that God was, by this strange providence, calling upon us to lean wholly upon him in any work in which we might be permitted to engage. We had no friends to meet us, and at once we made our way to the North western Hotel, where we spent the night.

As Mr. Moody was looking over some letters which he had received in New York before sailing, and which had remained unread, he found one from the secretary of the Young Men's Christian Association at York, asking him if he ever came to England again, to come there and speak for the Association. "Here is a door," said Moody to me after reading the letter, "which is partly open, and we will go there and begin our work."

The next morning we left Liverpool, Mr. Moody taking his family to London, where Mrs. Moody, being born in England, had a sister. I, with my wife, went to Manchester, to the home of my greatly beloved friend, Henry Morehouse, whom I had met in Chicago.

After three days stay in London Mr. Moody went to York, where I joined him. On arriving there I went to the home of Mr. George Bennett, Honorary Secretary of the Young Men's Christian Association, who had invited us to come to York, and, on inquiring if Mr. Moody had arrived, was told that he was in the room directly overhead. When Moody saw me he said, laughingly: "Our friend here is very much excited over our arrival, and says that he did not expect us so soon, and that he does not think this will be a good time to commence meetings, as all the people are away at the seaside." I was struck with the fact that notwithstanding these unpropitious circumstances, Mr. Moody did not show the slightest sign of disappointment or anxiety. After talking over the situation for a while, we called for Mr. Bennett, who was busy dispensing his medicines in his drug store below, and asked him if he could get the use of a chapel for our meetings. He at once secured permission to use an Independent Chapel. On his return he requested me to write out the following notice:

EVANGELISTIC SERVICES

D. L. Moody of Chicago will preach, and Ira D. Sankey of Chicago will sing, at 7 o clock P. M. tomorrow, Thursday, and each succeeding evening for a week, in the Independent Chapel. All are welcome. No collection.

The first meeting was attended by less than fifty persons, who took seats as far away from the pulpit as possible. I sang several solos before Mr. Moody s address, and that was my first service of song in England. It was with some difficulty that I could get the people to sing, as they had not been accustomed to the kind of songs that I was using.

Although this, the first meeting of the long campaign, was not especially well received by the congregation, it gave Mr. Moody an opportunity to announce his noonday prayer-meetings and Bible meetings, which were to follow. The noonday prayer-meetings were held in a small upper room (reached through a dark passage-way), where the Y. M. C. A. held their meetings. Only six persons attended the first of these meetings. But these meetings were the beginning of days with us the rising of the cloud of blessing, not larger than a man's hand, but which was soon to overshadow us with plenteous showers, and often with floods upon the dry ground.

It was at one of these noonday meetings that a young minister, pastor of the leading Baptist church of the city, his face lighted up with a light which I had not often witnessed before, rose and said: "Brethren, what Mr. Moody said the other day about the Holy Spirit for service is true. I have been preaching for years without any special blessing, simply beating the air, and have been toiling hard, but without the power of God upon me. For two days I have been away from the meetings, closeted with my Master. I think he has had the victory over my arrogance and pride, and I believe I have made a full surrender of all to him, and today I have come here to join you in worship, and to ask you to pray for me."

This confession and testimony was the rod in God's hand that smote the rock in the desert of doubt and unbelief at York. From that day the work took a new start, and soon there were hundreds of souls crowding the inquiry rooms. We were invited to hold services in this young pastor's chapel, and a large number were taken into his church. From that day on marvellous success has attended his preaching, and his name has become almost a household word in the Church at large. He has visited the conventions at Northfield for many years, and has conducted meetings of ministers in many of the leading cities of this country. His books have had an enormous circulation, and together with his addresses have been most helpful, not only to ministers of the gospel, but to Christian workers of all denominations. This young preacher, the Rev. F. B. Meyer, B. A., will ever be held in grateful remembrance by tens of thousands in this and other lands.

On his way from London to Northfield this year (1907), Dr. Meyer paid me a most delightful visit on a Sunday afternoon. We talked over the old times at York, London, Leicester and other places, and I sang for him, "There'll be no Dark Valley When Jesus Comes," and after praying with me, he promised to call and see me again.

From that small beginning in York the attendance at our meetings continued to increase, until not less than twenty thousand persons attended the meetings at the Agricultural Hall, London.

The first public mention of our arrival in England was as follows:

"Mr. D. L. Moody has just arrived from Chicago with his family, and is accompanied by a Christian brother, who leads the singing at the meetings after the manner of our friend, Philip Phillips.

Last Lord's Day he preached in Independent and Wesleyan Chapels, in York, and we believe that he intends to continue a while in the north of England, and then go to Scotland…"

Our sacred songs continued to grow in popularity, and I was continually beset with requests for the loan of my "musical scrap-book," in which alone could be found the songs that were then being sung as solos at our meetings. For a while I permitted many of my friends to have them, but soon found that it would be impossible to continue doing so, as persons having my book failed to return it in time for the meetings, thus preventing me from using the desired hymns at the services. To overcome this difficulty I had the words of a number of hymns printed on small cards. I hoped that these cards would supply the demand for the song, but as soon as the congregation observed that the cards were given out free to applicants, a rush was made for the platform, and the supply was exhausted the first day. I could not afford to continue this plan, and it was evident that something else had to be done. Having received a number of complaints from persons who had purchased copies of the "Hallowed Songs," which we were using in the meetings, that that book contained but a very few of the solos the people so much desired, I made an effort to have the publishers of that book print a few of the most popular pieces and bind them in the back of future editions of that book. This offer the publishers respectfully declined, saying that Philip Phillips, the compiler of the book, was in California, and that they did not care to make any alterations without his permission. I wrote them again, saying that I was an intimate friend of Mr. Phillips, and that I was sure he would be very glad to have this addition made to his book, but again the offer was declined, and here the matter rested for a while.

Among the many requests we had by this time received from towns in the vicinity, was a very urgent one from a large watering place on the north shore of England. We accepted the invitation and expected to go, but a few days before the time appointed for our start, a deputation of ministers called upon us, asking if they might not recall their invitation, giving as the reason, that the attendance at our meetings was so very large, it would no doubt interfere somewhat with the "penny collections," which they were in the habit of receiving from visitors during the summer season, and on which they relied very largely for the necessary funds to carry on the work for the balance of the year. Notwithstanding that Moody was well aware that they were making a mistake, he allowed them to withdraw the invitation, as we had many others in hand, and there was lost to that town an opportunity which never returned. A number of petitions were brought to us from this place, urging us to come and hold meetings, but we were never able to do so.

Among other invitations was one from a minister at Sunderland, the Rev. A. A. Rees. Mr. Moody, fearing that in this case there might also be some trouble in regard to "penny collections," sent me to the place to learn the situation. Mr. Rees met me at the station, and I remained with him over night. During the evening he made a number of inquiries about Mr. Moody, and said that a year or so ago he had met a man in Ireland with the name of Moody, and that if this was the same man, he desired very much to have him come and preach in his chapel. His reason for this was, that in the home of a Mr. Bewley, he had been assigned to share a bedroom with Mr. Moody, and before retiring Moody suggested that they have evening devotions, and that he had never heard anything that equalled Mr. Moody's prayer and burning desire for a greater knowledge of God's Word and power to preach it. On assuring him that this was the same man, it was at once settled that we should come the next week, and that there should be no "penny collections" to interfere with the work.

Almost immediately after arriving Mr. Rees requested me to go with him to the home of Mr. Longstaff, treasurer of Mr. Rees chapel, and the man who many years afterward wrote the hymn, "Take time to be holy." On entering the parlour I discovered an American organ in a corner of the room, which, I was told, had been used by Philip Phillips in his service of song in that city. I was requested to sing, which I did, not knowing that the minister was strongly opposed, not only to solo singing, but to organs and choirs as well, never allowing anything of the kind in his church. Among the songs that I sang on this occasion I recall the following: "Come home, O Prodigal." "Free from the law." and "More to follow." The minister made no comments, but seemed much interested in the singing. A few days after our arrival in the city we were surprised to see the walls and billboards placarded with enormous posters, containing the following notice: "D. L. Moody of Chicago will preach the gospel, and Ira D. Sankey of Chicago will sing the gospel in Bethesda Chapel every afternoon and evening this week, except Saturday, at 3 and 7 o'clock. All are welcome." Thus the phrase, "sing the gospel" originated with one of the most conservative ministers in England.

We soon learned that we were in the hands of a pastor who was known throughout that section as "the pope of the north," and that none of the other ministers had been asked to join in the services. For the first time in the history of that chapel a small cabinet organ was not only brought in, but given conspicuous place in the large pulpit, from which place I was better able to command the galleries and lead the singing than would have been the case had the organ occupied a place on the floor below.

Up to this time we had not organized any choirs to assist in the singing, but the people were learning the American tunes very fast, and the singing was becoming a marked feature of the meetings.

The hymn most used by our congregations in those days was, "Sun of my soul," to the tune "Hursley," which was almost the only distinctively English tune with which I was familiar up to that time, and finding that it could be adapted to "Rock of Ages," and many other hymns, we used the tune in almost every meeting.

During our stay at Sunderland we occupied "lodgings," ordering from the market such provisions as we desired, having the cooking done for us by those in charge of the house. On one occasion Mr. Moody was requested to order some fish, and, going through the market that day, he discovered a beautiful salmon, weighing not less than fifteen pounds, which he immediately purchased and had sent to our home. A fish of four or five pounds would have been abundantly large for our temporary wants, but Mr. Moody's generosity kept us in salmon during the remainder of our stay in that city. This was only a small indication of the large things always devised by Mr. Moody.

While here Mr. R. C. Morgan, of London, editor of "The Christian," having heard of the work that, was going on in the north, visited us for the purpose of writing up an account of the meetings for his paper, and while seated one day at the dinner table, I remarked to him that I was afraid what I had heard about the English people being slow and conservative was all too true. I spoke with considerable animation on the subject, and he inquired what I meant. I then told him of my attempt to give away my sacred songs, which were in such demand by the people, and that I could get no one to take them. He at once remarked that as he had been printing musical leaflets for a number of years, he would be glad to take some of mine with him to London and publish them in a small paper-covered pamphlet. So I cut from my scrap-book twenty-three pieces, rolled them up, and wrote on them the words, "Sacred Songs and Solos, sung by Ira D. Sankey at the meetings of Mr. Moody of Chicago."

Mr. Morgan returned to London the next day, and in about two weeks we received 500 copies of the pamphlet, which was first used at an all-day meeting, held near the close of our mission in Sunderland. The little book was sold at sixpence per copy, and before the day was over every book had been purchased. We immediately telegraphed for a still larger supply, which was also soon exhausted, and a few days later copies were seen not only in the windows of book stores, but grocers, dry-goods establishments, etc. Thus began the publication and sale of a book which, together with the edition of words only, has now grown into a volume of twelve hundred pieces.

During all our campaigns abroad it was our custom to rest on Saturdays, and to make excursions into the country on that day, whenever it was convenient. While at Sunderland, one Saturday, we took a cab and drove a few miles northward along the seashore. Coming to an almost perpendicular cliff rising hundreds of feet above the level of the sea, we descended by a stairway to the beach below. For a while we enjoyed ourselves by walking along the shore, examining the beautiful shells left exposed by the tide, which had gone out before we arrived. Our attention was soon arrested by someone shouting from the top of the cliff. We saw a man wildly beckoning to us to return. On looking around we discovered that the tide had risen and had filled a deep channel between us and the stairway. It was clear that we had no time to lose. Mr. Moody suggested that I should plunge in and lead the way to the cliff as quickly as possible, and while I did so he stood looking on, convulsed with laughter at my frantic strides through the water over the slippery stones. But I reached a place of safety. Then the tables were turned, and it was my opportunity to enjoy a sight not soon to be forgotten, as my friend slowly and with considerable difficulty waded through the constantly rising water to the place where I stood. We were to hold a Bible reading that after noon at three o'clock. Not having time to go to our lodgings for a chance of clothing, we at once proceeded to the place of the meeting, and we held the service in our wet clothes and shoes.

The experience which we had just passed through suggested to me the hymn, "Pull for the shore, sailor, pull for the shore, and I sang the hymn at this meeting for the first time in England.

Many interesting incidents occurred at the Sunderland meetings, of which I recall the following: One evening at the conclusion of a very earnest gospel address, I was requested to sing a hymn which had hitherto been greatly blessed in bringing wanderers into the fold, "Come home, O prodigal, Come home!" A deep hush prevailed during the singing, and just before its conclusion a cry was heard through the building: "Oh, father, will you forgive me?" while a young man rushed from the back part of the room down the middle aisle to where his father was seated. Throwing his arms around his neck, and with the deepest emotion, he begged forgiveness for some great wrong that he had done. The father rose from his seat and said: "My boy, I forgive everything; come now, let us go into the vestry and ask God to forgive us both, even as I have forgiven you." This incident made a profound impression upon the whole congregation, and that night hundreds of penitents retired to an adjoining room for prayer and consultation. From this time on the spirit of anxious inquiry deepened throughout the city, and in a few days Victoria Hall, the largest in the city, seating 3,000, was engaged for our meetings, and was crowded to the doors during the remainder of our stay.

While here a prominent Christian gentleman of Newcastle-on-Tyne, Mr. Richard Hoyle, who had heard of our work, came over, and, after attending some meetings, asked if we would come to his city. Mr. Moody told him that if the ministers of Newcastle would unite in requesting us to come we would gladly do so. Mr. Hoyle returned to his city and, calling the ministers together, told them what he had seen and heard at Sunderland. As a result of this meeting a petition was at once signed by a large number of non-conformist ministers, together with a few prominent laymen, and forwarded to Mr. Moody, who immediately accepted the invitation. On August 25 we arrived at Newcastle. It was a dark, gloomy night, the town being enveloped in a dense fog. At the chapel which had been selected for our opening meeting that night we found very few present. In the small audience I was impressed with the radiant countenance of one of the ladies, who sat near the front. From the opening hymn to the close of Mr. Moody's address, the expression on her face seemed to show that she fully understood and appreciated the message that was being proclaimed, and at the close she came forward, thanking the preacher and the singer for what she had heard, and predicting that before many days a great blessing from God would be poured out upon that community. How truly this prophecy of Hannah Swinburn was fulfiled is now known to all. Shortly afterward I was invited with my wife to this lady's home, and with her delightful family we spent some of the happiest hours in the Old Country.

In a few days the evening meetings became so crowded that overflow meetings had to be held in near-by halls and chapels. A remarkable impression was made at this place upon some of the people known as Quakers, or Society of Friends. It was not only by Mr. Moody's stirring addresses and Bible lectures, but also by the new hymns and tunes, the like of which had never been heard in the city before. It was not an uncommon sight to see an aged Quaker lady, dressed in the garb of her sect, as soon as it was announced that I would sing in the overflow meeting, get up and follow me to the place of the meeting, and take a place near the platform, where she could hear the new songs. It was at this place that I first began singing the new songs, "The Sweet By and By!" "That will be Heaven for me," and "Christ Arose," which soon became so popular all over Great Britain, also such hymns as "Come to the Saviour," "When He Cometh," etc. It was most interesting to notice how quickly the people took up these songs; they sang them in the ship-yards on Tyneside, on the streets, in the railway trains, and in the market-places. It was the beginning of a revolution in Great Britain in the matter of popular sacred songs, and now, though over thirty years have rolled by, it is said they are still in great favour with the people. It was while in this city that we organized the first "Moody and Sankey" choir.

As the mission here was nearing its close, we went to the town of Walker to hold a meeting, and addressed a large number of workingmen connected with the shipbuilding industry at that place. At the close of the meeting, as we were about to leave the hall, and while I was on the platform gathering up my hymn-books, a very refined-looking gentleman, with a strong Scotch accent, came up to me and said: "Do you think Mr. Moody would go to Edinburgh if he had an invitation from the ministers there?" This canny Scot had been attending our meetings for the past ten days, and was reporting what he had witnessed to his ministerial friends in Scotland. He was somewhat disguised, for he wore an old, soft white hat, while at home he wore a very proper high silk hat. I told him that I thought Mr. Moody would be very glad to go to Scotland, but that he had better speak to him about it. At the close of the meeting this gentleman, who proved to be the Rev. John Kelman, of Leith, who afterward became chairman of our general committee in Edinburgh, took from his pocket a petition, largely signed by ministers and prominent laymen, asking us to come to Edinburgh for a series of meetings. He handed the paper to Mr. Moody, who at once accepted the invitation.

Before going to Scotland we visited Bishop Auckland, Middleton, Darlington and Carlisle. In many of the smaller places we found considerable difficulty in securing small cabinet organs, it being inconvenient and expensive to carry our own instrument from place to place. I shall never forget an experience in Bishop Auckland. The organ, which had been supplied by the committee, was placed in a high pulpit, where there was room for both speaker and singer. The organ did fairly well, till near the close of the meeting. While Moody was in the vestry speaking to the inquirers, I remained with one of the ministers in the large hall, conducting a service of prayer. While thus engaged, the organ suddenly became disorganized and proceeded to give forth a number of discordant sounds, which I was utterly unable to suppress, and in despair I rushed into the vestry, where Moody was speaking to a number of inquirers. He asked me why I had left the prayer-meeting in the other room. I took him to the door of the chapel and asked him to listen. The organ was still pouring forth its shrill and inharmonious notes, and the prayer-meeting was brought to a rather abrupt conclusion.

We went to Carlisle on November 15, 1873, on the invitation of a prominent Christian worker with whom we had no acquaintance whatever, but who proved to be one of the leading Plymouth Brethren of that place. But one minister and the pastor of the chapel where we held the meeting attended the first service. For a few days there was no power in the meetings, and Moody decided to call together all the ministers of the place to see what was wrong. When assembled he asked them if they knew what was the cause of the lack of interest in the meetings. One minister arose and said that he had not attended, because he did not believe in "sheep stealing." Others expressed the same sentiment, saying that as we had come to the place by invitation of one who was not in sympathy with the ministers and their work, as carried on in the churches and chapels, they had decided not to have anything to do with this mission. Mr. Moody at once arose and said that he had never before been accused of "sheep stealing," or of working to either build up or tear down any one denomination of Christians; that he had come to Carlisle to preach the gospel, and that he desired the co-operation of all the ministers of the place, and asked them if they would not join him in prayer over the subject. He asked that each one present lead in prayer, and when this was done there was established the most kindly and brotherly feeling, and all promised to be present at all the meetings which were to follow.

It was a dismal night in November, 1873, when our train rolled into the station in the city of Edinburgh. Desiring to avoid the formality of a reception at the hands of the committee and friends who had invited us to conduct a series of evangelistic meetings in their city, we had refrained from notifying them as to the hour of our arrival. Securing public cabs from the numerous array massed about the station, we were soon rattling along the well-lighted streets to the places where we were to abide.

I had selected a hotel on the principal street, not far from the Walter Scott monument, and after being assigned my room walked out on the crowded thoroughfare for a stroll. I had not proceeded half a block when a hand was laid on my shoulder, and a voice said, "Ah, Mr. Sankey, is this you? When did you arrive, and where is Mr. Moody?"

I gave the desired information in a few words and then made bold to ask, "And, pray, who are you?"

"The chairman of your committee," he responded. "And I've been waiting for days to hear when you would arrive. Come away. You're not to be stopping at a public hotel when there are a hundred homes ready to receive you."

So, hurrying me into a cab, and arranging with the hotel-keeper to release my room, I was soon welcomed into one of the most delightful homes in all Edinburgh. It was while abiding in this house that I wrote the music of my first Gospel song, "Yet there is room."

Our first meeting in Edinburgh was advertised to be held on Sunday evening, November 23, and long before the hour for commencing the service arrived the whole building was densely packed to its utmost corners; even the lobbies, stairs and entrance were crowded with people, while more than two thousand were turned away.

The first announcement made was a sad disappointment to the congregation, for it was that Mr. Moody could not be present, he having contracted a severe cold the day before, while on the train en route from Carlisle. It was further announced that Mr. Sankey would conduct the service of song, and the Rev. J. H. Wilson would preach.

This was indeed a trying hour for the singer. Much had been said and written in Scotland against the use of "human hymns" in public worship, and even more had been uttered against the employment of the "kist o' whistles," the term by which they designated the small cabinet organ I employed as an accompaniment to my voice.

A goodly number of ministers and prominent lay men were present. After the opening prayer I asked all to join in singing a portion of the One Hundredth Psalm. To this they responded with a will, as it was safe and common ground for all denominations, and no questions were raised as to Mr. Rouse having introduced anything "human" into David's version as found in the Bible. This was followed by reading the Scriptures and prayer.

The service having been thus opened in regular order, we now faced the problem of "singing the gospel" a term first devised and used by the Rev. Arthur A. Rees, of Sunderland, England, some months before, in advertising our meetings in that city, and since then much discussed in Scotland. The song selected for my first solo was "Jesus of Nazareth passeth by."

The intense silence that pervaded that great audience during the singing of this song at once assured me that even "human hymns," sung in a prayerful spirit, were indeed likely to be used of God to arrest attention and convey gospel truth to the hearts of men in bonny Scotland, even as they had in other places.

After a powerful address by Dr. Wilson, and a closing prayer, I was requested to sing another solo. Selecting "Hold the Fort," then comparatively new in Edinburgh, the audience was requested to join in singing the chorus, "Hold the fort, for I am coming," which they did with such heartiness and such power that I was further convinced that gospel songs would prove as useful and acceptable to the masses in Edinburgh as they had in the cities of York and Newcastle in England.

In our meetings held prior to entering Scotland, it had been our custom to have the committee in charge of the various meetings often three and four, in different localities, in a day see that organs were placed in the halls and chapels ready for use. In Edinburgh we failed to inform the committee that upon them would devolve the matter of placing the organs in each hall and church as needed. The consequence of this oversight was that at our second meeting, held in Barclay Free Church, there was no organ provided, and therefore we could have no solo singing or gospel hymns.

When the committee discovered, about the hour for commencing the service, that the organ was not present, but away off at the Music Hall, they sent after the missing instrument, which was brought with great speed.

They hoped to arrive at the meeting in season for the closing exercises, and this end they certainly would have attained had not the Jehu in charge been over zealous in the use of his whip. In whirling round a corner near the church at too great a speed he overturned the vehicle, rolling both deputation and "kist o' whistles" into the middle of the street.

The "kist" was in a sadly demoralized condition, and its appearance now strangely suggestive of its Scotch name. The outcome of the disaster was that Mr. Moody had to conduct the second meeting alone, as I had led the first alone.

These occurrences evidently greatly pleased some of the Scotch folks, as they were heard to say: "It had a fine tendency to break up any scheme the evangelists might have had in their working together."

The third meeting was held in the same church, and great interest was manifested by the citizens. The question of the solo singing, as to its propriety and usefulness, was not as yet fully understood or admitted; hence it was with much fear and trepidation that we thus really entered, this third night, upon our three months campaign.

As I took my seat at the instrument on that, to me, most memorable evening, I discovered, to my great surprise, that Dr. Horatius Bonar was seated close by my organ, right in front of the pulpit. The first gospel-song music I had ever composed, written since coming to Edinburgh, was set to words which he wrote "Yet there is room."

Of all men in Scotland he was the one man concerning whose decision I was most solicitous. He was, indeed, my ideal hymn-writer, the prince among hymnists of his day and generation. And yet he would not sing one of his own beautiful hymns in his own congregation, such as, "I heard the voice of Jesus say," or, "I was a wandering sheep," because he ministered to a church that believed in the use of the Psalms only.

With fear and trembling I announced as a solo the song, "Free from the Law, oh, happy condition."

No prayer having been offered for this part of the service, and feeling that the singing might prove only an entertainment, and not a spiritual blessing, I requested the whole congregation to join me in a word of prayer, asking God to bless the truth about to be sung.

In the prayer my anxiety was relieved. Believing and rejoicing in the glorious truth contained in the song, I sang it through to the end.

At the close of Mr. Moody's address, Dr. Bonar turned toward me with a smile on his venerable face, and reaching out his hand he said: "Well, Mr. Sankey, you sang the gospel tonight."

And thus the way was opened for the mission of sacred song in Scotland.

At one of the meetings here a young man anxious to gain admittance to the already over-crowded hall, cried out to Mr. Moody: "I have come twenty miles to hear you, can't you make room for me somewhere?" Moody calmly replied: "Well, if we push the walls out you know what the roof will do."

On another occasion, as we were holding meetings in the Free Assembly Hall, while I was singing a solo a woman's shrill voice was heard in the gallery, as she made her way toward the door, crying: "Let me oot! Let me oot! What would John Knox think of the like of yon?" At the conclusion of the solo I went across the street to sing at an overflow meeting in the famous Tolbooth Church. I had just begun to sing, when the same voice was again heard, "Let me oot! Let me oot! What would John Knox think of the like of yon?"

Professor Blaikie said in the Edinburgh Daily Review at this time: "It is almost amusing to observe how entirely the latent distrust of Mr. Sankey's "kist o' whistles" has disappeared. There are different ways of using the organ. There are organs in some churches for mere display, as someone has said, "with a devil in every pipe; but a small harmonium, designed to keep the tune right, is a different matter, and is seen to be no hindrance to the devout and spiritual worship of God."

In 1874 my father visited Scotland, bringing with him my two children. He frequently said to his friends that he never enjoyed anything in his life as much as this visit to Scotland.

In London, a little later, Gladstone, accompanied by Lord Kinnaird, visited one of the meetings we were holding at Agricultural Hall. At the conclusion of the address Mr. Moody was introduced to the Grand Old Man of England by Lord Kinnaird. "You have a fine body for your profession," remarked Mr. Gladstone. "Yes, if I only had your head on it," Mr. Moody replied, and then hurried away to an inquiry meeting. The Princess of Wales and other members of the royal family attended a number of our meetings at Her Majesty's Theatre, occupying their private box. I was told by the Duchess of Sutherland that the Princess was very fond of "Sacred Songs and Solos," a copy of which I had the pleasure of presenting to her. When the weather was not propitious and she remained at home from her church service, she would gather her children around the piano and sing by the hour.

We remained in Great Britain this time for two years, holding meetings in many of the leading cities of England, Scotland and Ireland.

We found but little opposition to the use of hymns and organs in Ireland, and our choirs contained many people of the higher walks of life. It was in the Exhibition Palace in Dublin that I first sang, "What shall the harvest be?" I was surprised when Moody requested me never to sing it again in the meetings, and for a while he took the precaution personally to announce the solos that he wished to have sung. I afterwards learned that his reason for not wanting this hymn sung at his meetings was that a prominent minister, after having heard the hymn the first time I sang it, had remarked to Moody that if I kept on singing such hymns I would soon have them all dancing. However, when Moody did not announce the solos he wished me to sing, I would start up, "Sowing the seed in the daylight fair," and after some time he began to give it out himself occasionally, and, hearing no further criticism, the hymn was from that time onward always sung in connection with Moody's address on "Sowing and Reaping."

Another instance of Mr. Moody's being influenced against certain hymns, was in the case of the hymn "Memories of Galilee." I first introduced this hymn at one of our meetings at Newcastle-on-Tyne, at which service a very prominent and distinguished lady was present. She expressed herself as not approving of these kind of hymns, and Mr. Moody at once requested me to leave it out of "Sacred Songs and Solos," which I was just then preparing. I told him that I thought the song would certainly become popular, and that I very much needed some new solos, and that I had already sent it on to the publishers. A few months later this lady again heard me sing the song, and after the meeting she told Mr. Moody that she thought it was one of the most beautiful songs she had ever heard. The song from this time became a great favourite of us all.

Some of the comedians at the theatres tried to make hits by changing our hymns and using our names on the stage. This was always resented by the audiences.

In imitation of the popular song, "He's a Fraud," an actor one evening sang at the Royal Theatre in Manchester some doggerel beginning, "We know that Moody and Sankey are doing some good in their way." It received both cheers and hisses from the audience at first, but on a repetition of the words the displeasure was so great that the comedian had to leave the stage. At a circus in Dublin, on one occasion, one clown said to another, "I am rather Moody tonight; how do you feel?" The other responded, "I feel rather Sankey-monious." This by-play was not only met with hisses, but the whole audience arose and joined with tremendous effect in singing one of our hymns, "Hold the fort, for I am coming."

While holding meetings at Burdett road, London, in 1874, Mr. Moody and I one Saturday took a drive out to Epping Forest. There we visited a gypsy camp. While stopping to speak to two brothers who had been converted and were doing good missionary work, a few young gypsy lads came up to our carriage. I put my hand on the head of one of them and said: "May the Lord make a preacher of you, my boy!"

Fifteen years later, when Gypsy Smith made his first visit to America, I had the pleasure of taking him for a drive in Brooklyn. While passing through Prospect Park he asked me:

"Do you remember driving out from London one day to a gypsy camp at Epping Forest?" I replied that I did. "Do you remember a little gypsy boy standing by your carriage," he asked again, "and you put your hand on his head, saying that you hoped he would be a preacher?"

"Yes, I remember it well."

"I am that boy," said Gypsy Smith.

My surprise can better be imagined than described. Little had I thought that the successful evangelist and fine gospel singer of whom I had heard so much, and whom I had so much admired, was the little boy I had met in the gypsy camp. Truly God has granted my wish of fifteen years before, and has made a mighty preacher of the gypsy boy.

During our meetings in Her Majesty's Theatre at Pall Mall a Mr. Studd, who had a great many fast horses and fox-hounds, gave them all up and became a follower of Christ. Mr. Studd's son was attending Eton College, at Windsor, near the Queenscastle. He and Mr. Graham, of Glasgow, a member of Parliament, invited us to go to Windsor and hold meetings for the young Lords in the college. When it was rumoured that we would accept the invitation, the subject was taken up and discussed in Parliament.

Although we were accustomed to devote Saturdays to rest, we decided to give one Saturday to Eton College. When we arrived at Windsor Station we were met by Mr. Studd and Mr. Graham, and taken to the home of a merchant. As there was so much excitement in the town because of our coming, it was decided that it would be best to hold the meetings in this gentleman's garden. Mr. Graham gathered about fifty of the students under a large apple tree in the garden. There Mr. Moody gave a short address on John 3:16, and I sang a number of solos, including "Pass me not, O gentle Saviour." We also distributed copies of "Sacred Songs and Solos" among the students, who took an enthusiastic part in the singing. Mr. Studd's son, who afterward became known as one of the chief cricketers of England, was converted at this meeting.

On one of our subsequent visits to Great Britain this young man got up a large petition, inviting us to Cambridge. The invitation to Cambridge we gladly accepted, and arrived there on Guy Fawkes night. When we entered the Corn Exchange, which was the largest meeting room in town, we found it filled with students. It was the largest religious meeting that had ever been held in Cambridge. On reaching the platform we found Mr. George E. Morgan, of "The Christian," London, who was then a Cambridge student, conducting the singing. Mr. Moody asked one of the Dons to lead in prayer, after which he called upon me to sing "The Ninety and Nine." The students listened to the first verse in perfect silence, but at its conclusion they vigorously beat the floor with canes and umbrellas, and cried, "Hear, hear!" This demonstration followed each verse to the end. Mr. Moody's address for half an hour held the undivided attention of his congregation. At the conclusion some of the students attempted to stampede the meeting, but a large majority remained and gathered around us, saying: "These men must have fair play while they are in Cambridge." Thus began a great revival in that town. Hundreds of young men dated their conversion from that time.

The news of the religious work at Cambridge naturally spread to Oxford, and we were invited to hold meetings there. We had hoped that the success of our meetings at Cambridge would make the way easier at Oxford. But a similar process had to be gone through there. We stopped at the Bull's Head Hotel, and held meetings for two weeks in a large hall connected with that building, and eventually a large number of students took their stand on the Lord's side.

One day as I was making some purchases in a bookstore in London, a sailor came rushing in, saying: "Give me a dozen little Sankeys, quick!" The hymn book "Sacred Songs and Solos" was usually called "Sankeys."

While holding meetings at Campbeltown, on a subsequent visit to Scotland, a drunken man staggered into the meeting one evening, while Mr. Moody was preaching. He had not been seated long before he arose and said: "Mr. Moody, will you please stop a bit, I want to hear Mr. Sankey sing The Ninety and Nine." Moody, with his marvellous tact, said: "All right; sit down, my friend, I will ask Mr. Sankey to sing for you." Those sitting near him said he was visibly affected by the song. Later on when the invitation was given to retire to the inquiry room the man sitting next to this drunkard brought him in. I sat down beside him and talked and prayed with him. He said he was the black, as well as the lost sheep of his family, and that he wanted to sign a pledge to stop drinking. We did not use the pledge in those days, but to please this man we hunted up a copy, under which he signed his name, John McNeil. He declared his intention to give up drink forever. For many evenings he came to our services, and always went into the inquiry meetings. He told me that to get away from temptation he used to take his mother's Bible and his lunch, and for many days go into the hills in the country. I corresponded with him for over a year. He was said to have been one of the most wicked men of his town, and had given the police more trouble than any other man there, but he became a humble follower of Christ.

On the 3rd of August, 1875, a great farewell meeting was held for us in Liverpool. Several addresses were made, one of some length by Mr. Moody. As we took our departure on the S.S. Spain we left with the most enthusiastic applause and evidences of good will, the great crowd on the shore singing several of our hymns as the vessel moved out of sight.

After our return to America, the first meeting held was at Northfield, on the 9th of September, 1875. There, among many others, Mr. Moody's mother, who was a Unitarian, stood up for prayer. At this meeting I first sang "The Ninety and Nine" in this country.

One day while crossing the Connecticut River on a ferry, which was pulled across by a line stretched over the river, Mr. Bliss and I were singing, "Pull for the shore, sailor, pull for the shore," when we noticed that the boat pulled unusually heavy, and on investigating, found that Mr. Moody, who was sitting in the rear, was pulling back on the line with all his might, so as to delay the trip, and give him a chance to listen to the singing. This illustrates Mr. Moody's fondness for singing. Although himself not a singer, he used the service of praise more extensively and successfully than any other man in the nineteenth century.

Brooklyn was our next place to visit. Although the first meeting, held in Clermont Avenue Rink, October 24, was at half past eight in the morning, the hall, which had chairs for five thousand persons, was packed full, and thousands were turned away for want of room. I was assisted in the singing here by a choir of two hundred and fifty voices. My first solo was, "Rejoice and be glad! the Redeemer has come!" At the second meeting, in the afternoon, fifteen thousand persons had to be turned away for lack of accommodation. From two to three hundred requests for prayer would often be announced at these meetings.

At one of them a fine-looking young man came into the inquiry room along with a number of others. I asked him if he was willing to accept Christ as his only Saviour. He bowed his head in his hands as he sat by my side. With great earnestness, while his whole frame shook with deepest feeling, he replied:

"Jesus will not accept me."

"Why not?"

Because I have been an infidel for many years, a follower of Charles Bradlaugh, and for the last eight years have not ceased to speak in private and public against Christ. I have travelled over nearly all the world, and have spoken everywhere against Him and all those who professed to be Christians; now I fear He will not forgive me for what I have done."

"Do you want Him to forgive you?" I asked.

"Well, sir," he said, I do not know what is the matter with me or why I am here tonight. Some power that I do not understand has been working upon me for the last two days, and I am in a despondent state of mind."

I lifted my heart in prayer that I might make no mistake in dealing with this man. I waited for a moment, and then said, "My dear friend, what you need tonight is Christ; He will dispel your gloom and sorrow."

"But," he exclaimed, arousing himself from what seemed to be a deep reverie, "I have fought against Him all my life, and I thought I was right, too."

"Did you have peace in your heart when you were preaching against Christ?"

He looked up at me. "No, I was a coward," he confessed. "I remember, while coming home from a long journey on the sea, we were one night driven by the storm near the rocks off a certain cape, and when I thought we were sure to go to the bottom of the sea, I got down on my knees and prayed to God to save us. The storm died, and with it went my prayers. For as soon as I thought we were safe, like a coward I went back to my old ways, and denied that there was a God."

"Well," I said, "let that go. What brought you here tonight?"

"I don't know," he replied. "I have not been in church for eight years; I have not spoken to a Christian in that time, as I have lived entirely among infidels and sceptics. But about a year ago I received a letter from my poor old mother, away over in Dundee, Scotland. She asked me to make her one promise, that when Mr. Moody and Mr. Sankey came back to America I would go to hear them, if they came to the place where I was. I answered her that I would. When you came here I thought I would have to keep my word to my mother, so I went to the Rink two nights in succession. Since that time I have had no rest. Yesterday and today I have had to close up my office. I am a civil engineer. I have been walking the streets all day, thinking, thinking. Not being acquainted with any Christians to whom I could speak, I thought I would go once more to the Rink. And now here I am, talking to you."

"My dear friend," I said, "it is an answer to your mother's prayer. She may be praying for her wandering boy this very night. Now, do not delay any longer. Yield to Christ and he will receive you."

He bowed his head, while his trembling form told how deeply his heart was moved. After a hard struggle he took my hand and said: "By the grace of God I take Jesus Christ as my Saviour now!"

After a word of prayer I asked him if he would not write to Scotland at once and tell his mother all about it, and he promised that he would. A few evenings later I met him at the door of the Rink. As he came up to shake hands and bid me good bye I asked him if he had written to his mother.

"Oh, yes," said he, "but not until I had sent her a cable dispatch first."

"What did you say in the dispatch?" I asked.

"Well, I just said, I've found Jesus, and signed my name to it."

"Thank the Lord," said I.

"Yes," he exclaimed, "that is just what my dear old mother cabled back to me, Thank the Lord, O my soul."

Our first meeting in Philadelphia was held on November 24, in the old Pennsylvania Railroad Depot, which John Wanamaker fitted up for our use. It had a seating capacity of more than ten thousand persons. Here, as in Brooklyn, the leading ministers gave their hearty support to the work and in every way expressed their approval of the effort. On one occasion the meetings were attended by President U. S. Grant, several Senators, and members of the Supreme Court. During my stay in Philadelphia I often visited the home of Henry Clay Trumbull, then the editor of "The Sunday School Times," who gave us his heartiest support in every way. Among the laymen who were very efficient helpers at our meetings were John Wanamaker and George H. Stuart. Mr. Wanamaker's special meetings for young men were largely attended. Under Moody's powerful preaching many conversions took place in Philadelphia.

A number of Princeton students attended the meetings, and an invitation was extended to us to go to Princeton to hold meetings there for the college men, which we were glad to accept. In the Princeton meetings we had the warm sympathy and co-operation of President McCosh. Among the converts at Princeton was Wilton Merle Smith, now one of the leading ministers of New York City.

The old Hippodrome in New York, located where Madison Square Garden is now, was the scene of our next meetings, in February, March, and April of 1876. It was the largest place of assembly in the city, though a very unattractive structure. The building had never been used for religious meetings before, but was a place for sport and gaiety. The hall which we used, the largest in the building, seated eight thousand. A monster stage was built, large enough to hold the choir of six hundred voices, and still to leave room for at least four hundred visiting clergymen and guests. Here for the first time I sang "Waiting and Watching," which afterward became a great favourite. Thurlow Weed, who frequently attended the meetings and occupied a seat at the reporter's desk, would often have written requests laid on my organ asking me to sing this hymn. The New York meetings were very successful. One day, near the close of the ten weeks campaign, an audience assembled which numbered more than four thousand persons, all of whom confessed that they had been converted at these meetings.

Our next large meetings were held in Chicago during the fall of 1876, in a large Tabernacle erected for the occasion by John V. Farwell. It was capable of seating more than eight thousand. At one of these meetings Mr. Moody's attention was attracted by an usher with a wand in his hand, seating the people as they came in. Mr. Moody did not like the man's appearance. He asked the chairman of the committee, Mr. Harvey, who the usher was. Mr. Harvey replied that he did not know, but would go and see. Taking the man out into the inquiry room, Mr. Harvey learned that his name was Guiteau the man who afterward shot President Garfield. So great was Mr. Moody's power in reading character.

At the close of the three months mission in Chicago, a farewell service was held for those alone who professed to have been brought to Christ during the meetings, and it was attended by six thousand persons.

Then, for six months, we conducted meetings in Boston. On an average, three meetings a day were held, in a large temporary building erected for the occasion by a committee of wealthy gentlemen. Here also we had the hearty co-operation of many prominent ministers and laymen, among whom Dr. A. J. Gordon, Dr. Joseph Cook, Phillips Brooks, and Henry

M. Moore may be mentioned. Among those who professed conversion at these meetings was H. M. F. Marshall, who afterward removed to Northfield, and there, under Mr. Moody's direction, erected a number of the school buildings.

New Haven was our next field of labour. Many of the Yale University students were here converted, and afterward became useful ministers of the gospel throughout the country.

At Hartford, which we next visited, Mark Twain attended several of our meetings. On one occasion P. T. Barnum, the famous showman, attended and remained for an inquiry meeting, where it was my privilege to speak to him in regard to his spiritual condition. In our conversation he said: "Mr. Sankey, you go on singing "The Ninety and Nine" and when you get that lost sheep in the fold we will all be saved." I afterward learned that he was a Universalist.

For the next six months we conducted meetings in the churches of St. Louis. Able assistance was, rendered by the Rev. J. H. Brookes and other eminent ministers. At one of the inquiry meetings I asked a fine-looking man as he was leaving the meeting, if he was a Christian. "No," he replied, "I am a Missourian."

On our first visit to California, we stopped at Ogden, so as not to travel on Sunday, and went to Salt Lake City on Saturday afternoon. As soon as it became known that we were in the city, we were invited by the Presbyterian minister to hold services in his church, which we did. The interest at once became so great that we decided to change our plans and stay here for a couple of weeks. The church soon became too small for the great crowds, and we were invited to the Methodist Church, the largest in the city. Many Mormons attended the meetings, and one night two daughters of President Taylor went into the inquiry room and professed conversion. The solo singing was of great interest to the Mormons. A gentleman from England, who had become a Mormon, and who was collector of tithes, took a great fancy to Mr. Moody, of whom he had heard much from friends in England, and invited us to hold meetings in the Mormon Tabernacle. This, however, we declined. The Englishman said to Moody: "You are all right, only you don t go far enough." When Moody asked what he meant he said: "You do not have the revelation of Joseph Smith in your Bible." Moody answered that he was thankful for it; that he had no gospel of man, and that if Joseph Smith could have a revelation, D. L. Moody could have one also. This closed their discussion. A great crowd of people, among whom were many Mormons, came to the station to bid us goodbye. Mr. Moody never visited Salt Lake City again.

Our work spread out in all directions, and hundreds of cities were visited, not only throughout the United States, but in Canada, and even in Mexico, much blessing attending all the services.

At a meeting in Norfolk, as Mr. Moody was about to begin his sermon, after I had sung a number of hymns, the minister of the church stepped up and said: "I want to make a little explanation to my people; many of my members believe that Moody and Sankey are one man, but brethren and sisters, this man is Mr. Moody, and that man at the organ is Mr. Sankey; they are not one person, as you supposed."

At Chattanooga the black people boycotted our meetings, the black ministers taking offense because they were not invited to take seats on the platform. We arranged a special meeting for the black people, and were surprised to find the church nearly empty when we arrived. But Moody was not to be defeated in this way. He went out into the street and gave personal invitation to hundreds of black people, and no further difficulty was experienced.

On one occasion, when I was leaving Chicago for New York on an evening train, a gentleman took his seat beside me. For some time nothing was said, but after a while we got into a general conversation. After discussing the weather and politics, we entered upon the subject of religion. This finally led to the discussion of Moody and Sankey. The stranger said that he had never had the pleasure of hearing either of them. When I told him that I had often heard Moody preach and Sankey sing, he seemed much interested and asked:

"What kind of folks are they?"

"Oh, they are just common folks like you and me," I replied.

His daughter, he said, had a cabinet organ and they were all very fond of the "Gospel Hymns," and he was sorry that he had not had the opportunity to hear Sankey sing The Ninety and Nine before he died. I told him I was much surprised, and asked him what proof he had of Sankey's death. He replied that he had seen it in the papers.

"It must be true if you have seen it in the papers," I said.

By this time we were nearing the station where my friend was to get out. Hearing the whistle blow, he looked out of the window and remarked: "I have enjoyed your company very much, but will soon have to leave you now."

"I hardly think it is fair that we should part without telling you that I am one of the men we have been talking about," I said.

"Why, who are you?" he asked.

"I am what is left of Sankey."

At this he reached for his gripsack, and giving me a quizzical look he said: "You can't play that on me, old fellow; Sankey is dead." Then he rushed for the door, leaving me to continue my journey alone.

During the years which followed, we made several trips to Great Britain and held meetings in hundreds of places. In the campaign of 1881- '84 we held meetings in ninety-nine places in Scotland alone. Mr. Moody was once asked if he had kept any record of the number of converts at his meetings.

"Records!" he exclaimed, "why, they are only kept in heaven."

In one of the recent revival meetings at Sheffield, conducted by Torrey and Alexander, a man gave the following testimony: "I found Christ in this hall in 1882, when Moody and Sankey were preaching the gospel; I was brought face to face with God, and in the after-meeting Mr. Sankey led me to Christ, and I am happy in Him today."

"Well, now, that is refreshing," commented Mr. Alexander. "When anybody asks you if revival converts stand, you can speak of that one; he looks as if he is going to stay, too. As we have gone around the world we have found that the best workers, as a general rule, are either workers or converts of the Moody and Sankey meetings. We have found them in India, in Tasmania, and everywhere we have gone."

Lord Shaftesbury, speaking at a meeting in Exeter Hall, London, in the interest of evangelical work in Ireland, said: "Therefore go on circulating the Scriptures. I should have been glad to have had also the circulation of some well-known hymns, because I have seen the effect produced by those of Moody and Sankey. If they would only return to this country they would be astonished at seeing the influence exerted by those hymns which they sung. A week ago, when in Paris, I went to Belleville, the very nest of the communists, and even in this quarter I heard their hymns being sung. If we could get something like that in Ireland a mighty influence would be exerted."

"These American laymen," said another prominent man, "have wrought a work in Great Britain which the Church of England itself feels in its inmost heart. They are not, it is true, graduates of any university; they are men of the people, speaking the language and using the methods not of the refined, but of the generality. Yet they have probably left a deeper impress of their individuality upon the men and women of Great Britain than any other persons that could be named."

One of the most delightful experiences of my life was a trip to the Holy Land in 1898. I was accompanied by my wife, one of my sons, my brother, and a few friends. One of the most genial members of the company was the late Roswell P. Flower, with whom we had the pleasure of traveling for more than three months. We sailed from New York in January, made a short stop at Gibraltar, and dropped anchor at Alexandria. Cairo we reached by rail. We saw the pyramids, the Gizeh Museum, and the Howling Dervishes; made an excursion to Heliopolis, and took the trip up the Nile to the First Cataract, visiting the usual places, such as Luxor and Karnak. At the latter place we met the old Arab who discovered the mummy of Rameses II. We asked him if he would allow us to take a snapshot of him. This he at first refused, but the glint of the bright Egyptian sun on the proffered piece of silver secured his consent.

After spending about forty days in Egypt we started for Palestine in March by a provokingly slow train from Cairo to Port Said, and thence by one of the regular mail steamers to Jaffa. In the Holy Land we followed much the usual round exploring Jerusalem, Bethlehem, Jericho, Bethany and other historic spots, and sharing the profound emotions that forever stir the hearts of Christian tourists in Palestine. On our way home we visited Constantinople, returning via Athens, Naples and Rome and, of course, taking in Mt. Vesuvius.

All through this trip here so briefly outlined I had occasion to sing the "Gospel Hymns" many times. The first evening in Cairo I visited the American Mission. I found the building well filled with Americans, Egyptians and English. A man on the platform was giving an address on temperance. The room was divided by a partition about two feet high, separating the natives from the foreigners. I made my way to a seat among the Americans, and had not been there long when a missionary beside me leaned over and said: "Are you not Mr. Sankey?" When I replied that I was he said he hoped that I would sing for them. I told him that, although I had come for rest, I would gladly sing if they had a small organ or piano on which I might accompany myself. There being no instrument in the church, the matter was dropped. A few minutes later a lady pressed her way into the pew behind me and, leaning over toward me, said: "I am delighted to see you here tonight, and I hope you will sing for us."

She proved to be a woman from my own county in Pennsylvania. Being told that there was no instrument in the church, she declared that she would soon get one. She beckoned to four Egyptian soldiers to follow her. In a few minutes they returned with a small cabinet organ, which they placed on the platform. At the conclusion of the address I gave a service of song, lasting for a half hour, after which I said good-night. But they refused to be satisfied, and demanded more songs. Again a number of pieces were rendered, and the service was finally closed.

While returning down the Nile I was often prevailed upon by missionaries along the way where the steamer stopped to give services of song. At several of these services I found that the natives already knew a number of our hymns.

In Jerusalem I started early one morning to visit the Tower of David, which was located only a few rods from the hotel. I was stopped by one of the Sultan's soldiers, who informed me by signs and gesticulations that I could not ascend the tower without a permit from the captain of the guard. I secured the desired permit by the use of a little bakhsheesh, and was escorted up the winding stairway by a savage-looking soldier carrying a gun. From the top of the tower may be seen one of the grandest and most interesting scenes in the world. I determined to have at least one song in honour of King David before descending. Selecting one of the most beautiful psalms, the 121st, "I to the hills will lift mine eyes," I began to sing at the top of my voice, using the grand old tune, "Belmont." The soldier, not acquainted with that kind of performance, and perhaps never having heard a sacred song in his life, rushed up to where I stood, looking quite alarmed. I knew that he could not understand a word of what I was singing, so I kept right on to the end of the psalm. Coming to the conclusion by this time that I was not likely to do any special damage either to him or to myself, the guard smiled and tipped his cap as I finished. By tipping him I returned the salutation, and then we passed down into the Street of David.

A few hours later our party visited that portion of the city called Mount Zion, where we entered the fine school erected by an English bishop for the children of Jerusalem. We were greeted by the principal, who proved to have been a member of my choir at the meetings in London. I was invited to sing for the children, and consented to do so if they would sing for us first. I was much surprised to hear them sing some of my own songs, as well as their native songs in Arabic. I sang "The Ninety and Nine" and other songs, much to the delight of the children.

Standing on the summit of the green hill far away, outside the city wall, I sang the fine old gospel hymn: "On Calvary s brow my Saviour died." While at Constantinople I visited Robert College, where I sang several hymns and gave an address to the Turkish students; and also at the American and English missions in that city I rendered my service of song. In Rome I had the same pleasant experience, where I held a number of services, both speaking and singing in the English, American and Scotch churches.

On returning to America I visited the soldiers in camp at Tampa, Florida, where I held several services. I was here invited by Theodore Roosevelt, then Colonel of the Rough Riders, to conduct services at his camp, but a previous engagement prevented my accepting.

The following year I again visited Great Britain, where I held services of "Sacred Song and Story" in thirty cities and towns. The result was that my health broke down. Later I lost my eyesight.

My friend, Dwight Lyman Moody, was born February 5, 1837, at Northfield, Massachusetts. His father, who was a stone mason, died when the lad was about four years old. Many years later Mr. Moody was laying the corner-stone of the first building at Northfield. His friends had secured a silver trowel for him, but he refused to use it. He had been at his mother's home, and in the garret he had found one of his father's old trowels with which he had earned bread for the family.

"You may keep the silver trowel," Mr. Moody said; "this one is good enough for me."

Mr. Moody used to tell of how he earned his first money by driving the neighbours cows to and from pasture at two cents a day. When he was eight years old a man who owned a mortgage on his mother's little farm came to the house one day and told the widow that she must pay the mortgage or get out of the house. The poor woman was sick at the time. She turned over in the bed and prayed that God would help her. Then she wrote to her brother, and he helped her by paying the interest on the mortgage for several years. At last, by economy and industry, the family was able to clear off the mortgage and retain the home. Many years afterward, by God's blessing, young Dwight was able to secure the farm belonging to the man who had once held the mortgage, and on that farm is now located the school of Mount Hermon, established for the education of young men.

At the age of nineteen young Moody left the farm and went to Boston, where he entered a shoe store owned by his uncle. In Boston he was converted through the preaching of Dr. Kirk, at the Mount Vernon Church. After remaining in Boston for some time, Moody went to Chicago, where he found employment in a shoe store owned by a Mr. Henderson. He made a good record in business, and sold more shoes than any other clerk in the establishment. And whenever Mr. Henderson heard of the failure of any of his customers in the towns about Chicago, he would always send Moody to collect the debts, as he invariably arrived there ahead of all other creditors.

While he was thus engaged Mr. Moody did not lose zeal in religious matters. He was very active in the work of the Young Men's Christian Association, and was soon elected president of the branch located at Farwell Hall. He also became much interested in Sunday-school work, hiring a saloon for use on Sundays.

In his Sunday-school was a wicked and unruly young man, who constantly disturbed the exercises. Mr. Moody remonstrated with him a number of times, but to no avail. Finally, taking the young man into an adjoining room, he gave him a severe chastising.

When Moody returned, flushed with excitement, he said to his assistant superintendent: "I think I have saved that young man." And truly he had, for from that time the young disturber became an earnest Christian, and was one of Moody's warmest and best supporters for many years. Mr. Moody's Sunday-school work grew until he had one of the largest schools in Chicago, in what was known as the Illinois Street Church. There I joined him in 1871, acting as his chorister until we went to England in 1873, after which we continued to work together for about a quarter of a century.

Dwight L. Moody was the greatest and noblest man I have ever known. His strongest characteristic was common sense. The poor heard him gladly, as they did his Master of old; the rich and learned were charmed by his simple, earnest words. He will not only be remembered for his extended evangelistic work, but also for the two noble schools which he founded.

Those schools at Northfield and Mount Hermon, Massachusetts, originated in this way: One day, in the early seventies, Mr. Moody drove up into the mountains near his mother's home. Stopping at a much dilapidated farmhouse, he hitched his horse to the fence and went in. The man of the family was sick in bed; the mother and two daughters were making straw hats, by which to support the family. Moody said to them:

"What are you going to do? This old farm is unable to maintain your family."

The girls answered that if they could obtain an education in some way they might afterward be able to earn sufficient money for the support of their parents.

"Well, let us pray about it," said Moody. After the prayer he gave them a little money, got into his carriage, and started back down the mountain to the village. I met him on his return, and he said to me: "I have made up my mind to start a school for poor girls in New England." Later it was proposed to utilize the royalty received from our hymn-books for the erection of buildings.

To this I heartily agreed, and this was the beginning of the now famous Northfield schools. The first students in the school were the poor girls who were making the straw hats. The story of these two girls, and of Mr. Moody's visit to them, I told some years afterward to a number of summer guests at Lake Mohonk. The proprietor of the hotel, Mr. Smiley, being much impressed, took his hat and collected among the guests $1,500 for the school. On receiving the offering next day, Moody said to me that it was the most providential thing, as they were just that amount short in making up the annual accounts of the school.

Some time after the establishment of the girls school a wealthy gentleman from New Haven was visiting Northfield. He sought Mr. Moody's advice concerning the making of his will, and Mr. Moody said: "Be your own executor and have the joy of giving your own money."

He then asked Mr. Moody to suggest a worthy object, and Mr. Moody outlined his plan for a boys' school.

"I will give $25,000 to commence with," said the old, white-haired man.

The offer was gladly accepted. It was this money which Mr. Moody used for buying the farm of the man who had ordered his widowed mother from her home. On this farm, situated four and a half miles from the girls' school, across the Connecticut River, are now located a number of buildings, in which young men from all over the world are educated. About a thousand students attend the schools every year. One hundred dollars a year is charged for each student, but pupils are expected to do whatever work they can to help along.

After forty-four years of faithful and consecrated labour for his Master, Mr. Moody passed on to his reward December 22, 1899.

The last meeting Mr. Moody and I held together was in Dr. Starrs church, in Brooklyn. His subject at this time was "Mary and Martha." I had often listened to him speaking on these two friends of Jesus before, but never with greater pleasure than on this occasion. His heart seemed very tender, as he talked in a quiet and sympathetic way about Mary, Martha, and their brother Lazarus, and the love and sympathy that existed between them and Jesus. The hearts of all present seemed deeply moved, and many strong men, unused to tears, were unable to hide their emotion. Hundreds tarried after the meeting to shake hands, many recalling memories of blessings received in the meetings in this city twenty-five years before. Mr. Moody seemed to have just as much power and unction upon him in this meeting as I had ever witnessed during all the long years of our united labours. Little did I think that this was to be our last service together. A few weeks later I spent a Sunday with him in New York, walking with him to Dr. Hall's church and back to the hotel, where we parted for the last time.

On my way from Canada I stopped over one night in Rochester to hold a service of "Sacred Song and Story," and there I received the last letter from him, It was dated at Northfield, November 6, 1899, containing nine pages, in which he spoke of his work in Northfield and Chicago. He also told me he was due in New York at 3.30 on Wednesday, and asked if I could meet him at the Murray Hill Hotel. I at once telegraphed that I would come down on the night express and see him the next morning.

When I arrived he had gone. I learned later that he went to Philadelphia on Wednesday evening, spending an hour with friends there, and took the night train for Kansas City, where he fell in the front of the battle, as brave a soldier of the cross as ever won a victor's crown.

Before sending forth this book on its mission I wish to express my thank fulness to Almighty God for having permitted me to live, move and have my being; for the promise which He hath given of eternal life through His name; and for the confidence that I shall be with Him by and by in the land where there is no more pain, sorrow or death, and where He shall wipe all tears from our eyes.

Ira D. Sankey

Dwight L. Moody

Ira D. Sankey with Fanny J. Crosby

Free Church Assembly Hall, Edinburgh

Bingley Hall, Birmingham

Mr. Sankey at Northfield

Mr. Sankey's last appearance in the Metropolitan Tabernacle, 1901

The Story of
SACRED SONGS AND SOLOS

A Mighty Fortress

Words by Martin Luther   Music by Martin Luther

A mighty fortress is our God,
A bulwark never failing.

Martin Luther, the great leader of the Reformation, is the author of both the words and music of this famous hymn, probably written in 1521. Two of the most popular English translations are by Dr. F.H. Hedge and Thomas Carlyle.

During the prolonged contest of the Reformation period "A Mighty Fortress" was of incalculable benefit and comfort to the Protestant people, and it became the national hymn of Germany. Gustavus Adolphus, the hero of the Thirty Years' War, used it as his battle-hymn, when he led his troops to meet Wallenstein.

While Luther was still living his enemies in the Roman Catholic Church declared that the whole German people were singing themselves into Luther's doctrines, and that his hymns "destroyed more souls than all his writings and sermons."

The first line of this hymn is inscribed on Luther's monument in Wittenburg. Luther himself found great comfort in his hymn. When dangers thickened around him he would turn to his companion, Melanchthon, and say: "Come, Philip, let us sing the 46th Psalm" – and they would sing it in this characteristic version.

In 1720 a remarkable revival began in a town in Moravia. Jesuits opposed it, and the meetings were prohibited. Those who still assembled were seized and imprisoned in stables and cellars.

At David Nitschmann's house, where a hundred and fifty persons gathered, the police broke in and seized the books. Not dismayed, the congregation struck up the stanza of Luther's hymn,

> And though this world, with devils filled,
> Should threaten to undo us;
> We will not fear, for God hath willed
> His truth to triumph through us.

Twenty heads of families were for this sent to jail, including Nitschmann, who was treated with special severity. He finally escaped, fled to the Moravians at Herrnhut, became a bishop, and afterwards joined the Wesleys in 1735 in their expedition to Savannah, Georgia.

A Shelter in the Time of Storm

Words by V.J. Charlesworth   Music by Ira D. Sankey

> The Lord's our rock, in Him we hide,
> A shelter in the time of storm.

I found this hymn in a small paper published in London, called "The Postman." It was said to be a favourite song of the fishermen on the north coast of England, and they were often heard singing it as they approached their harbours in the time of storm. As the hymn was set to a weird minor tune, I decided to compose one that would be more practical, one that could be more easily sung by the people.

A Sinner Forgiven

Words by Jeremiah J. Callahan   Music by I.B. Woodbury

> To the hall of the feast came the sinful and fair;
> She heard in the city that Jesus was there.

"Mr. F. Markham, connected with a large and well-known piano factory, was leading an ungodly and heedless life," says a London periodical. "One day he saw an announcement that Moody and Sankey were to open a mission at St. Pancras that evening. Instantly he resolved to go and hear the singing. He and a companion reached the hall in good time, as they thought, only to find it crowded to the doors. "An overflow meeting was announced at a neighbouring church, and thither they went. By and by Mr. Sankey sang "To the hall of the feast came the sinful and fair.' As Markham listened, his past life seemed to rise before him;

the tears rushed into his eyes; his heart seemed broken. "Coming out, he asked his companion what he thought of it.

'Oh,' was the careless reply, 'he is a nice singer.'

'Is that all? It has broken my heart.'

Ere long he could say, in the words of the song, 'He looked on his lost one; my sins are forgiven.'

"When he got home his wife was amazed at what had come over him, and could not make out where he had been. She had been converted years before, but had backslidden. She accompanied him to the mission on the following evening, and was happily received. The man became a Christian worker, and is the founder and superintendent of the Tahhall Road Factory Lads' Home and Institution."

A Song of Heaven and Homeland

Words by Eben Rexford   Music by Ira D. Sankey

> Sometimes I hear strange music,
> Like none e'er heard before.

In the year 1901 Mr. Eben Rexford, editor of The Ladies' Home Journal landscape and gardening department, wrote me, asking a donation of fifty copies of Gospel Hymns for a poor church, saying he would give me twenty new hymns in exchange. I sent the books and received the hymns, among which I found "A Song of Heaven and Homeland," which I soon set to music, and which I consider one of my best compositions. It was first published in The Ladies' Home Journal.

Abide with Me

Words by H.F. Lyte   Music by William H. Monk

> Abide with me! Fast falls the eventide,
> The darkness deepens – Lord, with me abide.

Henry Francis Lyte wrote this hymn in 1847, in his fifty-fourth year, when he felt the eventide of life approaching. For twenty years he had ministered to a lowly congregation in Devonshire. He decided to spend the next winter in Italy, on account of rapidly declining health. On a Sunday in September – in weakness, and against the advice of his friends – he preached a farewell sermon to his much-loved people, and in the evening of the same day he wrote this immortal hymn. He died a few weeks later, his last words being "Peace, joy!"

One of the many instances of the power of this hymn has been recorded by Dr. Theodore L. Cuyler:

"During my active pastorate I often got better sermons from my people than I ever gave them. I recall now a most touching and sublime scene that I once witnessed in the death-chamber of a noble woman who had suffered for many months from an excruciating malady. The end was drawing near. She seemed to be catching a foregleam of the glory that awaited her. With tremulous tones she began to recite Henry Lyte's matchless hymn, 'Abide With Me! Fast falls the eventide.' One line after another was feebly repeated, until, with a rapturous sweetness, she exclaimed:

> Hold Thou Thy cross before my closing eyes,
> Shine through the gloom, and point me to the skies;
> Heaven's morning breaks, and earth's vain shadows flee!
> In life, in death, O Lord, abide with me.

"As I came away from that room, which had been as the vestibule of heaven, I understood how the 'light of eventide' could be only a flashing forth of the overwhelming glory that plays forever around the throne of God."

All Hail the Power of Jesus' Name

Words by E. Perronet   Music by Oliver Holden

> All hail the power of Jesus' name!
> Let angels prostrate fall.

The following remarkable story is related of the working of the Holy Spirit through the singing of this hymn to some savage heathens:

Some few years ago a missionary from a foreign land was seen in an American city leading a little boy of copper complexion. A Christian minister noticed him, and invited him home, and learned something of his history. "Converted to God in youth, I desired to consecrate myself to His service in a foreign land. While residing in an Oriental city, in Siam, there came to me a man of savage and awful appearance. I inquired concerning this dreadful looking man, and found he belonged to a tribe whose home was in the mountains, living in barbarism, entirely ignorant of the gospel. A desire to go among them and preach Jesus instantly filled my soul. My friends urged me not to go — it would be death to me — I should be killed — and why should I throw away my life?

"After praying God to direct me, and asking Christ to go with me, I seemed to hear His voice, saying: 'Go ye into all the world, and preach the gospel to every creature.' I was determined to go and tell these savages of 'Jesus and His love.' I started off with a scanty outfit, feeling that Christ was with me, for He has said: 'Lo, I am with you alway, even to the end of the world.' His sweet peace filled my soul, as I bade farewell to friends. Not long after reaching this tribe of savages, they surrounded me by hundreds, all armed with spears. I could not speak their language. As a lamb among wolves, there I stood. Christ was with me. In Him I trusted; He heard my prayer. Tuning my violin, I began singing and playing that precious hymn:

> All hail the power of Jesus' name,
> Let angels prostrate fall, etc.

I closed my eyes while singing, and on reaching the verse,

> Let every kindred, every tribe,
> On this terrestrial ball,

I opened my eyes, and every spear was dropped, tears were coursing down the cheeks of those warriors. They made signs, and took me home to their houses, and gave me food, shelter, and everything I needed. I learned their language, and preached to them Jesus; hundreds were converted to Christ. Broken down in health, I came home to rest, and must soon return, leaving this dear boy to be educated in America."

A man in England, who had been a happy Christian, began gradually to lose his faith, and at last boldly avowed the infidelity that had for a long time been quietly slumbering within. To his wife, who still loved and clung to the Saviour, this was indeed a blow, and her heart was torn at the thought that one she tenderly loved, and with whom she had often held sweet counsel, should now turn from the truth she held to be priceless, and overturn the faith he once sought to uphold. The husband was soon taken very sick, and it was evident to the anxious wife that the sickness was unto death.

She pleaded with and for the dying one that he might again confess Christ, in whom he had once been so happy, but no relief came to her distressed soul. One day the dying man was heard to utter a faint cry, and his wife caught the words, "Bring, bring." Thinking that he desired a cooling drink, she brought him what she supposed he wanted, but he waved his hand, and again uttered the words, "Bring, bring."

The wife was at a loss to understand what could be the meaning, when he, with a final struggle, as if he had gathered all the remaining energy into one last effort, exclaimed:

> Bring forth the royal diadem
> And crown Him Lord of all.

And he departed to join that company that wait that morning when the redeemed shall be gathered in.

All the Way My Saviour Leads Me

Words by Fanny J. Crosby   Music by Robert Lowry

> All the way my Saviour leads me;
> What have I to ask beside?

The gifted author of this hymn, to whom some reference is made in succeding pages, does not mourn over the fact that she is blind. On the contrary, she has frequently been heard to say that if the gift of sight were offered to her she would choose rather to remain as she is. At the early age of eight years she wrote the following statement of the situation as she viewed it:

> Oh, what a happy soul I am!
> Although I cannot see,
> I am resolved that in this world
> Contented I will be;
> How many blessings I enjoy
> That other people don't!
> To weep and sigh because I'm blind
> I cannot, and I won't.

She is firmly of the opinion that her blindness has proved a blessing. "If I had not been deprived of sight," she says, "I should never have received so good an education, nor have cultivated so fine a memory, nor have been able to do so good to so many people." This is her consolation and joy.

Fanny Crosby had been the recipient of a very unexpected temporal blessing, and while seated in her quiet room, meditating on the goodness of God to her and all his ways, this hymn flashed into her mind. It was written out and given to Robert Lowry, who wrote the fine tune which has given it wings, and carried it into millions of homes and hearts.

All to Christ I Owe

Words by Mrs. Elvina M. Hall   Music by John T. Grape

I hear the Saviour say,
Thy strength indeed is small.

"Our church was undergoing some alterations," writes Mr. Grape, "and the cabinet organ was placed in my care. Thus afforded a pleasure not before enjoyed. I delighted myself in playing over our Sunday school hymns. I determined to give tangible shape to a theme that had been running in my mind for some time – to write, if possible, an answer to Mr. Brandbury's beautiful piece, 'Jesus paid it all.' "I made it a matter of prayer and study, and gave to the public the music, now known as the tune to 'All to Christ I owe.' It was pronounced very poorly by my choir and my friends, but my dear wife persistently declared that it was a good piece of music and would live. "Time has proved the correctness of her judgment. "Soon after Mr. Schrick called on me to select anything new in music that I had to offer. On hearing this piece he expressed his pleasure with it, and stated that Mrs. Elvina M. Hall had written some words which he thought would just suit the music. I gave him a copy of it, and it was soon sung in several churches and well received. "At the suggestion of friends, I sent a copy to Professor Theodore Perkins, and it was published in 'Sabbath Chords.' Under the providence of God, it has been going ever since. I trust that it has not failed in the accomplishment of some good to my fellow-men, for the glory of God.

"On New Year's night, 1886, some missionaries were holding open-air services in order to attract passers-by to a near-by mission, where meetings were to be held later. "All to Christ I owe" was sung, and after a gentleman had given a short address he hastened away to the mission. He soon heard footsteps close behind him and a young woman caught up with him and said:

"'I heard you addressing the open-air meeting just now; do you think, sir, that Jesus could save a sinner like me?'

The gentleman replied that there was no doubt about that, if she was anxious to be saved. She told him that she was a servant girl, and had left her place that morning after a disagreement with her mistress. As she had been wandering about the streets in the dark, wondering where she was to spend the night, the sweet melodies of this hymn had attracted her, and she drew near and listened attentively. "As the different verses were being sung, she felt that the words surely had something to do with her. Through the whole service she seemed to hear what met her oppressed soul's need at that moment. God's Spirit had showed her what a poor, sinful and wretched creature she was, and had led her to ask what she must do. "On hearing her experience, the gentleman took her back to the mission and left her with the ladies in charge. The young, wayward woman was brought to Christ that night. A situation was secured for her in a minister's family. There she became ill and had to be taken to a hospital. She rapidly failed and it became evident that she would not be long on earth. One day the gentleman whom she met on New Year's night was visiting her in the ward. After quoting a few suitable verses of Scripture, he repeated her favourite hymn, "All to Christ I owe." On coming to the fourth verse –

> When from my dying bed
> My ransomed soul shall rise,
> Then 'Jesus paid it all,'
> Shall rend the vaulted skies,

She seemed overwhelmed with the thought of coming glory, and repeated the chorus so precious to her,

> Jesus paid it all,
> All to Him I owe.

Two hours afterward she passed away.

Almost Persuaded

Words by P.P. Bliss   Music by P.P. Bliss

> 'Almost persuaded,' now to believe;
> 'Almost persuaded,' Christ to receive.

"He who is almost persuaded is almost saved, and to be almost saved is to be entirely lost," were the words with which Mr. Brundage ended one of his sermons. "P.P. Bliss, who was in the audience, was much impressed with the thought, and immediately set about the composition of what proved to be one of his most popular songs.

One of the most impressive occasions in which this hymn was sung was in the Agricultural Hall in London, in 1874, when Mr. Gladstone was present. At the close of his sermon Mr. Moody asked the congregation to bow their heads, while I sang "Almost Persuaded." The stillness of death prevailed throughout the audience of over fifteen thousand, as souls were making their decisions for Christ.

"While engaged in evangelistic work in western Pennsylvania," writes A. J. Furman, "I saw the people deeply moved by singing. I had begun my preparation to preach in the evening, from the text, "Almost thou persuadest me to be a Christian,' when it occurred to me that if Mrs. B–, an estimable Christian and a most excellent singer, would sing, 'Almost Persuaded' as a solo, great good might be done. "At once I left the room and called on the lady, who consented to sing as requested. When I had finished my sermon, she sang the song with wonderful pathos and power. It moved many to tears. Among them was the principal of the high school, who could not resist the appeal through that song. He and several others found the Pearl of Great Price before the next day. After the close of the sermon, I spoke to Mrs. B– about the effect of her singing, and she told me that she had been praying earnestly all that afternoon, that he might so sing as to win sinners for her Saviour that night, and her prayers were surely answered."

"It was Sunday night, November 18, 1883," writes Mr. S.W. Tucker, of Clapton, London, "when I heard you sing 'Almost Persuaded' in the Priory Hall, Islington, London, and God used that song in drawing me to the feet of Jesus. I was afraid to trust myself in His hands for fear of man. "For six weeks that hymn was ringing in my ears, till I accepted the invitation. I came, and am now rejoicing in the Lord, my Saviour. How often, with tears of joy and love, have I thought of those meetings and of you and dear Mr. Moody, who showed me and other sinners where there was love, happiness and joy."

Said a young man to Mr. Young: "I intend to become a Christian some time, but not now. Don't trouble yourself about me. I'll tend to it in good time." A few weeks after, the man was injured in a saw-mill, and as he lay dying, Mr. Young was called to him. He found him in despair, saying: "Leave me alone. At your meeting I was almost persuaded, but I would not yield, and now it is too late. Oh, get my wife, my sisters and my brothers to seek God, and do it now, but leave me alone, for I am lost."

Within an hour he passed away, with these words on his lips, "I am lost, I am lost, just because I would not yield when I was almost persuaded."

Are you Coming Home Tonight?

Words by C.C.   Music by James McGranahan

> Are you coming Home, ye wanderers
> Whom Jesus died to win?

The original of this hymn was written by a young lady in Scotland, who signed herself "C.C." Falling into Mr. McGranahan's hands, he arranged the poem somewhat differently, and set the words to music. The song has brought blessing to many.

A wild young soldier was induced to attend a Gospel meeting in London. As he entered, the congregation was singing "Are You Coming Home tonight?" The song made a deep impression upon him. He came back the next night, and he continued to attend until he was saved. "I had to come," he said; "that hymn would not let me stay away. I could not sleep at night. All night long that question of the song, both in the words and music, kept returning to me, demanding an answer: 'Are You Coming Home tonight?'"

Arise, My Soul, Arise

Words by Charles Wesley   Music by Lewis Edson

> Arise, my soul, arise,
> Shake off thy guilty fears.

First published in 1742 under the title, "Behold the Man," this became one of the most useful of Charles Wesley's numerous hymns. In universal use in English countries, and translated into many languages, it has been the direct instrumentality in the conversion of thousands of souls. It has found expression in the exultant cry on the lips of many a dying saint.

"I have a record," said a Wesleyan missionary labouring in the West Indies, "of two hundred persons, young and old, who received the most direct evidence of the forgiveness of their sins while singing "Arise, my soul.' The conversion of the greater number of these persons took place while I was a missionary abroad."

Art Thou Weary?

Words by J.M. Neale, (translated)   Music by Henry W. Baker

> Are thou weary, art thou languid,
> Art thou sore distressed?

"Some years ago," writes Mr. James A. Watson, of Blackburn, England, "I often visited one of our adult Sunday-school scholars who had just been brought to the knowledge of the Saviour. She was formerly a Roman Catholic, but was brought to our church one Sunday evening by a fellow-worker in a cotton mill. She heard a Gospel of full and free salvation, embraced it, and gradually became a spirit-filled consistent Christian. "She was laid low with a serious illness, but it was always a pleasure to visit her.

"On one occasion she told me that the evening before, when she had been left alone for the night, a cloud came over her spirit, the sense of loneliness grew upon her, and she seemed forsaken of God. All looked black, and she dreaded the long, lone night. This was a most unusual thing and she wondered why it should be so. "Just then, in the quiet night, she heard steps on the flags of the foot-way. A man wearing the clogs of the factory operator was coming along, evidently returning late from some religious meeting. He was full of joy, for before he reached the house where my scholar was lying awake, he struck up in a joyful and loud song,

> Art thou weary, art thou languid?
> Art thou sore distressed?
> 'Come to Me,' saith One;
> And coming, be at rest!

The singer, 'an angel in clogs,' went on his way, singing aloud out of a full heart; but deep down into the heart of the lonely woman went the words, 'Be at rest!' "Again she cast herself upon the LORD; the cloud parted, peace and rest filled her heart, and she doubted no more."

Asleep in Jesus

Words by Mrs. Margaret Mackay   Music by W.B. Bradbury

> Asleep in Jesus! blessed sleep!
> From which none ever wake to weep.

"I had been driven in a friend's pony-carriage through some of the exquisite green lanes in Devonshire," wrote the author of this hymn the year before her death. "We paused at Pennycross, attracted by a rural burial-ground, and went in to look at the graves. It was a place of such sweet, entire repose as to leave a lasting impression on the memory. There were no artificial walks or decorations, but the grass was very green, and there were no unsightly signs of neglect. "On one of the stones were the words, 'Sleeping in Jesus.' It was in such entire keeping with the lovely and peaceful surroundings that it clung to my thoughts. On arriving at home I took a pencil and commenced writing the hymn, little thinking that it was destined to find so much favour, and that part of it would be inscribed on many tombstones."

Mrs. Mackay was born in Scotland, and died at Cheltenham, England, in 1887, at the age of eighty-five. Her husband was a distinguished lieutenant-colonel in the British army.

At the Cross

Words by Isaac Watts   Music by R.E. Hudson

> Alas! and did my Saviour bleed?
> And did my SOVEREIGN die?

"At the Cross" is the name of the new tune by R.E. Hudson for the old hymn by Watts, "Alas, and did my Saviour bleed." The words were first published in Watts' "Hymns and Spiritual Songs," in 1707, under the title, "Godly Sorrow Arising from the Sufferings of Christ." In "Sacred Songs and Solos" the new tune is used to the hymn "I'm not ashamed to own my Lord."

The children's evangelist, E.P. Hammond, credits this hymn with his conversion, when he was only seventeen years old.

Awake My Soul

Words by Joel Barlow   Music by A. R. Reinagle

> Awake, my soul! To sound His praise,
> Awake, my harp! To sing.

This is Joel Barlow's version of the 108th Psalm. In 1785, by the request of the General Association of Connecticut, he corrected and revised Watts' version of the Psalms, supplying such as had been omitted by Watts and adapting it to American thought and requirement.

Awake My Soul, To Joyful Lays

Words by Samuel Medley

> Awake, my soul, to joyful lays,
> And sing thy great Redeemer's praise.

This hymn with its fervent, joyful tone, its touching refrain and the peculiar old melody united to it, has been greatly esteemed in this country in days gone by. It first appeared in 1782, in Meyer's collection of hymns for use of Lady Huntingdon's church. Samuel Medley, the author of the hymn, was visiting at the house of a Mr. Phillips in London, and asked the daughter of his host to bring him some paper and ink. With these he retired to his room and presently came back with this hymn written. Mr. Medley was pastor of a Baptist Church in Liverpool for many years. He was born in 1738 and died 1799.

Beautiful Valley of Eden

Words by W.O. Cushing   Music by William F. Sherwin

> Beautiful valley of Eden!
> Sweet is thy noon-tide calm.

"One day in 1875 I was reaching up for a blessing," says the author of these words, "when suddenly there came down upon my heart a vision of the heavenly country. I seemed to look down upon a river that like a mighty tide rolled beneath me. "Across, on the other side of this river, I saw an enchanted land; its hills and valleys were sleeping in a heavenly calm. It was more beautiful than words can tell, and my heart seemed to be there. As I gazed on the scene, there came to my lips the words,

'Beautiful valley of Eden.' "The vision remained until I had written down the hymn; then it gradually faded from my sight. but I want to say that the beauty of the hymn is largely due to Mr. Sherwin, who, by his rich melody, has reached a deeper chord than any mere words could ever have reached."

Beulah Land

Words by E.P. Stites   Music by John R. Sweeney

I've reached the land of corn and wine,
And all its riches freely mine.

First sung at Ocean Grove, New Jersey, at a great gathering of Methodists, this hymn at once became very popular. It has been sung in every land where the name of Christ is known. The secretary of the Young Men's Christian Association at Plymouth, England, wrote me a beautiful story of a young lady, who sang it on her dying bed as she passed into the land that is fairer than day.

I sang this favourite song over the dead body of my friend, Mr. Sweeney, at the church of which he was a leading member, in West Chester, Pennsylvania, on the day of his burial.

Blessed Assurance

Words by Fanny J. Crosby   Music by Mrs. Joseph F. Knapp

Blessed assurance, Jesus is mine!
O, what a foretaste of glory divine!

"During the recent war in the Transvaal," said a gentleman at my meeting in Exeter Hall, London, in 1900, "when the soldiers were going to the front were passing another body of soldiers whom they recognized, their greetings used to be, 'Four-nine-four, boys; four-nine-four;' and the salute would invariably be answered with 'Six further on, boys; six further on.' the significance of this was that, in 'Sacred Songs and Solos,' a number of copies of the small edition of which had been sent to the front, number 494 was, 'God be with you till we meet again;' and six further on than 494, or number 500, was 'Blessed Assurance, Jesus is mine.'"

One of the most popular and useful of the "Gospel Hymns," this was sung by a large delegation of Christian Endeavours on the train to Minneapolis, some years ago. And it was often sung at night as the street-cars were crowded with passengers on their way to the Convention Hall, greatly to the delight of the people of that city.

Blest Be the Tie That Binds

Words by John Fawcett   Music by H.G. Nageli

> Blest be the tie that binds
> Our hearts in Christian love.

Dr. John Fawcett was the pastor of a small church at Wainsgate, and was called from there to a larger church in London in 1772. He accepted the call and preached his farewell sermon. The wagons were loaded with his books and furniture, and all was ready for the departure, when his parishioners gathered around him, and with tears in their eyes begged of him to stay. His wife said,

"Oh, John, John, I cannot bear this."

"Neither can I," exclaimed the good parson, "and we will not go. Unload the wagons and put everything as it was before."

His decision was hailed with great joy by his people, and he wrote the words of this hymn in commemoration of the event. This song, and "God be with you till we meet again," are the most useful farewell hymns in the world.

Mr. Moody used to tell of a Sunday-school teacher, to whom he had given a class of girls, who one day came to Mr. Moody's store much disheartened. He had suffered from hemorrhage of the lungs, and his doctor had ordered him to leave Chicago. He was sad because he felt that he had not made a true effort to save his class. At Mr. Moody's proposal that they go to visit each of the class members, they took a carriage and at once began the work, the young man in his feebleness saying what he could to each. At a farewell meeting where they were all gathered, they endeavored to sing "Blest be the tie that binds," but their hearts were full and their voices failed. Every member of the class yielded her heart to God.

Calling Now

Words by P.P. Bliss   Music by P.P. Bliss

> This loving Saviour stands patiently;
> Tho' oft rejected, calls again for thee.

I remember singing a song somewhat similar to this as a solo in Mr. Moody's Tabernacle in Chicago at the close of an evangelistic meeting in 1872. Mr. Bliss came in late and stood just inside the door, listening. At the close of the meeting he came up to the platform and spoke enthusiastically about the piece, and remarked that he also would try to write a hymn on "The Prodigal." Not long afterward I heard him sing this beautiful hymn, which he himself entitled "Calling Now." It has been especially useful in inquiry-meetings and at the close of evangelistic addresses. I have often heard it sung with great effect – very softly by a choir, while the workers were speaking to the anxious ones – and its soft, sweet, pleading tones were always blessed to the hearers.

Close to Thee

Words by Fanny J. Crosby   Music by S. J. Vail

> Thou my everlasting portion,
> More than friend or life to me.

This is another popular hymn, written by Fanny J. Crosby, and set to music by Silas Jones Vail, who was born at Southold, Long Island, N. Y., October 6, 1818. He was a hatter by trade, but wrote a large number of songs for Philip Phillips, who was the first to publish any of Vail's compositions, among which may be mentioned, "Gates Ajar," "Nothing But Leaves," and "Scatter Seeds of Kindness." He died in Brooklyn, N. Y., May 20, 1883.

The late Silas J. Vail, having composed this tune, brought it to Fanny Crosby, and requested her to write words for it. As he was playing it for her on the piano, she said: "That refrain says: 'Close to Thee; Close to Thee.'" Mr. Vail agreed that that was true, and it was agreed that it should be a hymn entitled "Close to Thee."

"Come"

Words by James G. Johnson   Music by James McGranahan

O word of words the sweetest,
O word, in which there lie

"Mr. Moody used to tell the follomng story relating to this hymn —
"In Baltimore, a few years ago, we held a number of meetings for men. I
am very fond of this hymn; and we used to let the choir sing the chorus
over and over again, till all could sing it.

"There was a man in one of the meetings who had been brought there
against his will; he had come through some personal influence brought
to bear upon him. When he got to the meeting, the audience was singing
the chorus of this hymn —

Come! come! come!

He said afterwards he thought he never saw so many fools together in
his life before. The idea of a number of men standing there and singing,
'Come! come! come!' When he started home he could not get this little
word out of his head; it kept coming back all the time. He went into a
public-house, and ordered some whisky, thinking to drown it. But he
could not; it still kept coming back. He went into another public-house,
and drank some more whisky; but the words kept ringing in his ears:
'Come! come! come!' He said to himself, 'What a fool I am for allowing
myself to be troubled in this way!' He went to the third public-house;
had another glass of spirits; and finally got home.

"He went off to bed, but could not sleep; it seemed as if the very pillow
kept whispering the word, 'Come! come!' He began to be angry with
himself 'What a fool I was for ever going to that meeting at all!' When he
got up he took the little hymn book, found the hymn, and read it over.
'What nonsense!' he said to himself; 'the idea of a rational man being
disturbed by that hymn.'

He set fire to the hymn book; but he could not burn up the little word
'come!' Heaven and earth shall pass away: but My word shall not pass
away.'

"He declared he would never go to another of the meetings; but the
next night he came again. When he got there, strange to say, they were
singing the same hymn. 'There is that miserable old hymn again,' he
said; 'what a fool I am for coming!' I tell you, when the Spirit of God lays

hold of a man, he does a good many things he did not intend to do. To make a long story short, that man rose in a meeting of young converts and told the story that I have now told you. Pulling out the little hymn book — for he had bought another copy — and opening it at this hymn, he said: 'I think this hymn is the sweetest and the best in the English language. God blessed it to the saving of my soul.' And yet this was the very hymn he had despised!

Come Believing

Words by D.W. Whittle ("El. Nathan")   Music by James McGranahan

> Once again the Gospel message
> From the Saviour you have heard.

A lawyer from the West sank so low as to become a tramp in the streets of New York. He was fifty-four years old and a homeless, penniless wretch. As he stumbled by the Florence Mission one night the windows were open and he stopped a moment to listen to the singing. They sang:

> Once again the Gospel message
> From the Saviour you have heard;
> Will you heed the invitation?
> Will you turn and seek the Lord?

It came like the voice of God to him. His early training had been Christian, and he thought he would go in. He did so, and as he took his seat they were singing the second verse:

> Many summers you have wasted,
> Ripened harvest you have seen;
> Winter snows by spring have melted,
> Yet you linger in your sin.

He realized that his was a truthful picture of his own life, and listened to the third verse, ending:

> While the Spirit now is striving,
> Yield, and seek the Saviour's side.

Deeply convicted, he jumped to his feet and said, "I will yield, I will seek the Saviour's side." He was converted, and attended the meetings regularly. He secured good employment, wrote to his family and becoming reconciled to his wife and children, he returned West to the old home, where he lived as an earnest Christian.

Come, Great Deliverer, Come

Words by Fanny J. Crosby   Music by W.H. Doane

> O hear my cry, be gracious now to me,
> Come, Great Deliv'rer, come.

"Some time ago, about twelve o'clock one frosty Saturday night, when the keen winter wind was driving all indoors who had a home, a poor woman, in utter misery and despair, was pacing up and down along the Thames," writes a friend in England. "She had wandered into a mission hall during the evening and had restlessly come out, carrying no remembrance of anything that had been said; but these lines from a hymn still sounded in her ears:

> I've wandered far away o'er mountains cold
> I've wandered far away from home;
> Oh, take me now, and bring me to Thy fold,
> Come, Great Deliverer, come.

"She cried aloud: 'But there is no deliverer for me.'" "Very soon she was met by some Christian workers, who were spending the night in seeking to gather in such outcasts as she. They took her to a home. The human tenderness revealed to her the divine love. If strangers had thus received her and cared for her, would not her Heavenly Father, whose love she had heard of, take her? Thus she was led to the feet of Jesus, and to find that her sins were many and all forgiven. "She said: 'Things since then have been up and down with me, but I have never lost the peace I found that morning.'"

Come, Sinner, Come

Words by W.E. Witter   Music by H.R. Palmer

> While Jesus whispers to you,
> Come, sinner, come.

Mr. Witter has said regarding this hymn: "I may say that the origin of 'While Jesus whispers to you' is forever linked with some of the most sacred experiences of my life. I see the old farmhouse in New York State, overlooking the beautiful Wyoming Valley, and those Western hills, which to my childhood eyes were the rim of the world. "It was in the summer of 1877 and I was home from college to nurse my sainted mother through her last illness, and at the same time I was teaching a term in school. "The biography of P.P. Bliss was in our home, and his sweet songs were running through my mind from morn till evening. I prayed that even I might be inspired to write such hymns as would touch hard hearts and lead them to Christ. "One Saturday afternoon, while bunching the hay which had been mown along the roadside, the words of this little hymn seemed to sing themselves into my soul, and with music almost identical with that to which they were later set by the sweet singer, Palmer. "I hastened to the house and, running upstairs, knelt beside the bed of a brother, for whose salvation my mother was in constant prayer. There, upon my knees, I transcribed the words to paper, with a strange consciousness that they God-given and that God would use them." And God had used them, for this hymn has been found very helpful as an invitation at Revival meetings.

Come, Thou Fount

Words by R. Robinson   Music by John Wyetlo

Come Thou Fount of ev'ry blessing
Tune my heart to sing Thy grace.

The author of this hymn, born in 1735, was of lowly parentage. At the age of fourteen his widowed mother sent him to London to learn the trade of barber and hair-dresser. His master found him more given to reading than to his profession. While in London he attended meetings held by the great evangelist, George Whitefield, became converted, and began to study for the ministry. In the latter part of his life Mr. Robinson often indulged in frivolous habits. But on one occasion, while traveling in a stage-coach, he encountered a lady who soon compelled him to admit his acquaintance with religion. She had just been reading this hymn, and she asked his opinion of it, after having told him of the blessings it had brought to her heart. He avoided the subject and turned her attention to some other topic; but the lady, who did not know to whom she was talking, soon returned to the hymn, expressing her strong admiration for its sentiments. Agitated beyond the power of controlling his emotion, Robinson broke out:

"Madam, I am the poor, unhappy man who composed that hymn many years ago, and I would give a thousand worlds, if I had them, to enjoy the feelings I had then."

Come to the Saviour

Words by George F. Root   Music by George F. Root

> Come to the Saviour, make no delay;
> Here in His word He's shown us the way.

"In 1879 I was assisting in revival meetings in Danville, California," writes the pastor of a Presbyterian Church at Oakland. "The meetings were well attended and good interest was exhibited, but for a long time there were no conversions. In the neighbourhood there was a man who, with his wife and children, attended the church regularly, and he was one of its liberal supporters. They were most excellent people, but could not be induced to profess Christ, and did not call themselves Christians. "One day, while the men were holding services in the church the women were having a prayer meeting in the manse nearby. "In the course of the meeting they sang, 'Come to the Saviour, make no delay.' The singing over, they were about to engage in prayer, when the lady above referred to asked them to sing the last verse of this hymn. They sang:

> Think once again, He's with us today;
> Heed now His blest commands, and obey;
> Hear now His accents tenderly say,
> Will you, my children, come?

"The lady was greatly affected and when the singing ceased she said with deep emotion: 'Yes, I will come; I have been very stubborn, but I will not stay away any longer.' The women were all deeply moved, and prayed and praised God with warm hearts. "When the word reached the men they were greatly encouraged at the good news. A revival followed, and at the close of a touching service a few days later, when a call was made for persons who desired to unite with the church, this lady and her husband were the first to respond. They were followed by some of their own children and many other persons - in all twenty-one. "This hymn seemed to have been the means of reaching the wife's heart, and of opening the way for the blessing which followed."

Come Unto Me

Words by Nathaniel Norton   Music by George C. Stebbills

> 'Come unto Me!' it is the Saviour's voice
> The Lord of life, who bids thy heart rejoice.

A man of culture and of extensive reading had given a good deal of thought to the subject of Christianity, but had never acknowledged himself a Christian until one evening at the close of an after-meeting in services conducted by Dr. George F. Pentecost in his own church in Brooklyn. Then he arose and made a public confession of Christ as his Saviour. That night, on his return home, he sat down and wrote the words of this hymn. The next day they were handed to Mr. Stebbins, who was then assisting Dr. Pentecost. Very soon afterward the hymn was sung in the meetings that were still in progress. It at once met with general favour, and for many years was used as a special song of invitation in our meetings, as well as by other evangelists in theirs.

The following testimony was given by a lady who was visiting a seaside resort on the coast of Essex: —

"I came down from London a great sinner, with no thought of eternity. I had been living — as so many do — utterly indifferent to the claims of the gospel, and ignoring the appeals of God's servants, from whom I have often heard the story of Jesus' love. But the Lord met with me as I was walking along the sea front one evening. I heard the sweet strains of children's voices, and I stood and listened to their song. Nothing I had ever heard charmed me so much. Clearly and distinctly came the words upon my ear, and to my heart:

> Jesus is waiting; oh, come to Him now —
> Waiting Today, waiting Today!

"I was riveted to the spot. The Spirit of God was striving with me. I thought of my past ungodly life; I realized that I was a sinner in the sight of God. I knew that Christ had died for sinners; but never in all my life had the truth been brought home to my mind that He had indeed died for me. The devil tempted me to pay no heed to the song which had stirred my very soul, but for the life of me I could not move until it was finished. And I shall never forget the awful solemnity which stole over me as I listened to the words:

Jesus is pleading; oh, list to His voice —
Hear Him today; hear Him today!
They who believe on His name shall rejoice;
Quickly arise and away.

"That night I gave my heart to God. I could resist no longer! This song had been the means of my salvation. I found that the little singers were a party of seven or eight helpless cripples who had come from the east-end of London, and were singing these words as their evening hymn before retiring to rest."

Come Unto Me, and Rest

Words by D. W. Whittle ("El Nathan")   Music by James McGranahan

Brother, art thou worn and weary,
Tempted, tried, and sore oppress'd?

"On a cold night in the fall of 1885, a scantily clad man wandered into Bleecker Street," writes a New York evangelist, under whose personal observation the incident came. "He was foot-sore and weary with much wandering, worn out for want of sleep, and faint from lack of food. The long, cold night was before him, and he knew he must walk the street till morning. "He stepped into a doorway for a little rest. As he sat there he fell to pondering. He was solitary and sad-hearted. Drink had wrought fearful havoc with him, and had left him a homeless, friendless man. Home and loved ones, friends, money and position had all been sacrificed to this appetite. He felt that he was lost, and that no effort could save him. As he thus mused his reverie was broken by the sound of song. "Surprised, he looked up in the direction from which the sound came, and saw across the way an illuminated sign on which were the words, 'Florence Mission.' Glad to get away from the chill and gloom of the street, he went into the mission. As he entered a lady was singing:

Brother, art thou worn and weary,
Tempted, tried, and sore oppress'd?
Listen to the word of Jesus,
Come unto Me, and rest!

"If there was one thing on earth that the man needed it was rest. Rest for the tired, famished body; rest for the tortured heart. 'These things are not for me,' he thought; I am too far gone.' "He wandered the cold streets till morning, but never once did the words of this hymn leave him. The refrain constantly rang in his ears, 'Come unto Me and rest.' He visited the mission many nights, and finally gave his heart to God."

The evangelist adds that this man has been his assistant for many years, and has won hundreds to Christ.

Come, Ye Disconsolate

Words by Thomas Moore   Music by Samuel Webbe

> Come ye disconsolate! where'er ye languish,
> Come to the mercy-seat, fervently kneel.

Thomas Moore, of Dublin, the friend of Lord Byron, wrote some thirty-two songs, published in 1848, which have been united to popular airs of various nations."Come, Ye Disconsolate" has ministered to the soothing of many a troubled heart, and often guided the weary soul to the mercy seat, where alone the accusing conscience may lay its guilty burden down and realize, "Earth has no sorrow that heaven cannot heal."

Consecration

Words by Frances R. Havergal   Music by W. A. Mozart.
                                            Arr. by H. P. Main

> Take my life, and let it be
> Consecrated, Lord, to Thee.

One of the finest consecration hymns in the world, this is a great favourite of the Christian Endeavor Society. Miss Havergal told me of its origin, while we were seated in her home in South Wales. She had gone to London for a visit of five days. There were ten persons in the family she visited, most of them unconverted. She prayed to God to give her all in the house, and before leaving everyone had received a blessing. The last night of her visit, after she had retired, the governess told her that the two daughters wished to see her. They were much troubled over their spiritual condition and were weeping, but Miss Havergal was able to show them the way of life, and they were both joyfully converted that night. She was too happy to sleep, she said, but spent most of the night in praise and renewal of her own consecration; and that night the words of this hymn formed themselves in her mind. In 1879, shortly before her death, I gave a number of Bible-readings in Miss Havergal's home, when she told me the very interesting story of her life.

A few years later I met Miss Havergal's sister again under somewhat amusing conditions. I was traveling in Switzerland. While looking through a large music establishment I found quite a number of music boxes, which played several of the "Moody and Sankey" hymns. I asked the proprietor if these boxes had much of a sale. He said they had, though he did not think much of the tunes they played. Beside me was standing a lady, also looking at the music boxes. She proved to be Miss Havergal's sister. As she turned around and saw me, she threw up her hands and said in a clear voice, "Oh, Mr. Sankey, is that you?" The proprietor proceeded to make profound apologies and, selecting one of his best boxes, he presented it to me.

Dare to be a Daniel

Music by P. P. Bliss   Words by P. P. Bliss

> Standing by a purpose true,
> Heeding God's command.

Mr. Bliss wrote this song especially for his Sunday-school class in the First Congregational Church of Chicago. It has been much admired and was often used by me in connection with Mr. Moody's lecture on Daniel. This hymn and "Hold the Fort" were prohibited by the Sultan from use in Turkey.

Dark is the Night

Words by Fanny J. Crosby   Music by T. E. Perkins

> Dark is the night, and cold the wind is blowing,
> Nearer and nearer comes the breakers' roar;

When I was chorister in Mr. Moody's Sunday-school, on the north side of Chicago, we frequently used this hymn. On the memorable Sunday night when the city was destroyed by fire, and I had made my escape in a small boat out into Lake Michigan, this song came to my mind, and as I sat there watching the city burn I sang:

> Dark is the night, and cold the wind is blowing,
> Nearer and nearer comes the breakers' roar;
> Where shall I go, or whither fly for refuge?
> Hide me, my Father, till the storm is o'er.

Depth of Mercy

Words by Charles Wesley   Music arr. from J. Stevenson

> Depth of mercy! can there be
> Mercy still reserved for me?

An actress in a town in England, while passing along the street, heard singing in a house. Out of curiosity she looked in through the open door and saw a number of people sitting together singing this hymn. She listened to the song, and afterwards to a simple but earnest prayer. When she went away the hymn had so impressed her that she procured a copy of a book containing it. Reading and re-reading the hymn led her to give her heart to God and to resolve to leave the stage. The manager of the theatre pleaded with her to continue to take the leading part in a play which she had made famous in other cities, and finally he persuaded her to appear at the theatre. As the curtain rose the orchestra began to play the accompaniment to the song which she was expected to sing. She stood like one lost in thought, and the band, supposing her embarrassed, played the prelude over a second and a third time. Then with clasped hands she stepped forward and sang with deep emotion:

> Depth of mercy, can there be
> Mercy still reserved for me?

This put a sudden stop to the performance; not a few were impressed, though many scoffed. The change in her life was as permanent as it was singular. Soon after she became the wife of a minister of the Gospel.

Doxology

Words by Thomas Ken, 1695   Music by Wilhelm Frank

> Praise God, from whom all blessings flow.
> Praise Him, all creatures here below.

This doxology has been almost universally adopted as a praise hymn by all churches. Wilhelm Frank, the composer of the tune, "Old Hundred," was a German.

The first Moody and Sankey meeting held in the Agricultural Hall, London, as opened by the singing of "Praise God, from whom all blessings flow."

On the night of October 15, 1884, a great crowd was gathered on the street outside a Republican headquarters in New York City, awaiting the returns of an important election. It was two o'clock in the morning before the last bulletin was posted. Previous to this announcement a thousand voices had been singing uproariously, "We won't go home till morning;" but the moment the message was displayed the stereopticon flashed out the line, "Praise God, from whom all blessings flow. Good night." The Tribune, in reporting the incident, said: "A deep-voiced man in the throng pitched the doxology, and a mighty volume of song swelled upward. Then the lights went out and the happy watchers departed to their homes."

A child on the top of Mount Washington was with her father above the clouds, while a thunderstorm flashed and rumbled below. Where they stood all was perfect calm and sunshine, though the eye found nothing but the blue of heaven and a few rocks to rest on. "Well, Lucy," said her father, "there is nothing to be seen here, is there?" But the child exclaimed: "Oh, papa, I see the doxology! All around seems to say,

> Praise God, from whom all blessings flow;
> Praise Him, all creatures here below;
> Praise Him above, ye heavenly host;
> Praise Father, Son, and Holy Ghost.

The doxology was a great solace to the starving "boys in blue" in Libby prison. Day after day they saw some of their comrades passing away, while fresh, living recruits for the grave arrived. Late one night they heard through the stillness and the darkness the tramp of new arrivals who were stopped outside the prison door until arrangement could be made for them within. In the company was a young Baptist minister, whose heart almost fainted as he looked on those cold walls and thought of the suffering inside. Tired and weary, he sat down, put his face in his hands and wept. Just then a lone voice of deep, sweet pathos, sang from an upper window:

> Praise God, from whom all blessings flow;

A dozen more voices joined in the second line; and so on till the prison was all alive and seemed to quiver with the sacred song. As the song died away in the stillness of the night, the young man arose and said:

> Prisons would palaces prove,
> If Jesus would dwell with me there.

Eternity

Words by Ellen M. H. Gates   Music by P. P. Bliss

> Oh, the clanging bells of Time!
> Night and day they never cease.

Having carried in my pocket for several months the words of the hymn "Eternity," which the author, Ellen M. H. Gates, had sent me, I handed them, one day in Chicago in 1876, to my friend P. P. Bliss, asking him to write music for them. Three days later he bad composed the tune.

The hymn was much used at our meetings both in Great Britain and the United States. Before singing it, I used to tell the story of Robert Annan, of Dundee, Scotland. He was one of the worst men who ever lived in that town, but after having been converted became one of the most useful missionaries of the place. On leaving his little cottage home one morning to go to his mission work, he took a piece of chalk from his pocket and wrote on the flagstone of the walk which led to his house the single word "Eternity." A few minutes later he saw a child fall from one of the vessels in the harbour. Being a bold, strong swimmer, he threw off his coat and shoes, and plunged into the bay. He saved the child, but at the cost of his own life. His body was carried home over the word "Eternity," which he had written a few hours before. On my last visit to Scotland, about five years ago, I went to see his widow, and found that the writing had been cut in the stone by direction of the Honourable James Gordon, the Earl of Aberdeen. Thousands go to see it every year. "Mr. Annan's minister took me to the beautiful cemetery of the place, where a fine monument, ten feet high, marks the last resting-place of the hero.

The Rev. John Macpherson wrote after visiting the deathbed of Robert Annan's youngest daughter:

"As I left the house near midnight, a gleam of light from the window fell upon the pavement and revealed the word 'Eternity!' I started back, and felt I was treading on holy ground. On the morning of the day on which Robert Annan fell a sacrifice to his heroic endeavour to save the life of the drowning boy, he had chalked the word upon the pavement.

"I could not help calling to mind another young man, who moved in a different sphere, the late lamented Hon. James Gordon, son of the Earl of Aberdeen. That young nobleman was deeply impressed by reading that portion of the sketch of Annan's life in which the incident just referred to is related. 'Eternity!' 'Eternity!' kept ringing in his ears. Thus he was stirred up and blessed. So deeply moved was he by the story that, on leaving home for Cambridge, he requested that the word ETERNITY should be carved at his expense on the stone on which Robert Annan had chalked it, so that it might preach for ever afterwards to all who passed that way. Just two days after I had received a letter from his mother conveying her son's request, the young nobleman was accidentally shot dead. When afterwards the awful word was being carved on the pavement-stone, we seemed to hear the united voices of Robert Annan and James Gordon, gathered by Divine grace from the two extremes of social life, calling aloud from on high, 'Cut it deep, very deep; for eternity is long, very long.'"

The following touching narrative is related by a worker at the Evangelistic Services held in Glasgow by Messrs. Whittle and McGranahan, following up my visit there with Mr. Moody in 1881.

"I observed in Bethany Hall, one Sabbath evening, an old fellow-workman of mine. Knowing that he had been a very irreligious man, I thought I would go to my old employer's shop and speak to him, and also to the rest of the workmen. On the following Wednesday I went up, and soon found that something was working in his mind altogether different from the old things.

"'Look here,' said he, 'I didna think that there was muckle truth in religion, but I'm a wee bit staggered aboot it jist noo!'

"'I was glad to see you in the Hall,' said I; 'but tell me what has staggered you.'

"'Weel, ye see, I've a sister, ye ken, an' a wee while ago she was hearin' aboot the meetin's in Bethany Hall. So somehow she an' her companion — jist like hersel', but gey fond of singin' — gaed to the meetin.' Awecl, when she cam' hame, she jist put past her things, an' sat doon by the fire, nae speakin' a word. Syne, the wife noticed her een was fu' o' tears. "Fat's the maitter, Aggy?" Nae answer. "Gang to bed, there's a guid lass; ye'll hae to be up sune the mom." The tears cam' faister. "Oh, Mary! I canna, I canna gang to my bed. I've been hearin' a hymn the nicht I'll niver forget. Oh, I seem to hear the soun' o' bells frae somewhere, callin' 'Eternity! Eternity!' Oh, I'm gaun into Eternity; and oh, hoo dark it is jist noo! Gang to my bed! Na; I'll gang to my knees." An' so she did.'

"'The wife tauld me this, an' I gaed ben awhile. "but I only glowered at her. Weel, the neist nicht she gaed again, an' she sune cam' hame wi' her companion, an' they baith seemed sae glaid, sae happy thegither, an' talked aboot "I am the Door. By Me if any man enter in, he shall be saved," They declared they had entered in. Anyhoo, they were happy. Neist nicht the wife gaed tae, and noo the hale hoose is like a kirk! I've been gaun, an' I want to ken mair aboot these things: so I and Wullie here are comin' on Sabbath nicht, an' Aggy an' some mair o' her companions; an' mither and me would Hke tae hear that sang Aggy heard.'"

A worker in the English Village Mission writes: "I had been engaged during the previous week with a lot of indifferent people in a midland village without the smallest token of blessing, and on that memorable Sunday night of the Tay Bridge disaster I went to the service with a sad heart. The service was a solemn one, and at the close we sang:

> Oh, the clanging bells of Time!
> Night and day they never cease.

"The song touched the hearts of the people. About this time, as we afterwards learned, a number of conversions occurred, and a blessing has rested on that place for many years. One of the converts has been a very successful missionary in a large northern city. I can scarcely remember any place where some one or more of your songs and solos was not used of God in blessing souls. In one church alone I received one hundred and fifty into fellowship, and I think not less than one-third of that number, when making application for membership, mentioned some particular hymn that had led them to decision."

Evening Prayer

Words by J. Edmeston   Music by George C. Stebbings

> Saviour, breathe an evening blessing,
> Ere repose our spirits seal.

Edmeston, a voluminous hymn-writer, was an architect by profession, and a member of the Established Church at Homerton, England, where he resided. The theme of this hymn was suggested to him by a sentence in a volume of Abyssinian travels: "At night their short evening hymn, 'Jesus Forgive Us,' stole through the camp." Though first appearing in the author's "Sacred Lyrics" in 1820, and to be found in the older church hymnals, it had no special prominence until Mr. Stebbins' setting became known. Since then it has come into general use, and has been adopted by many of the church hymnals. The music was written in 1876, for the choir of Tremont Temple, Boston, of which Mr. Stebbins was then the director. Published two years later in "Gospel Hymns Number 3," it became a favourite at once with the great choirs of our meetings and with other evangelistic choirs, and has since then been used wherever the "Gospel Hymns" are sung, even in the remote places of the earth.

It rarely falls to the lot of any hymn to be sung under such trying circumstances as was this, during the Boxer outbreak in China, by a company of beleaguered missionaries who had gathered together one night in great fear lest they should have to suffer the fate of so many who were giving up their lives rather than deny their Lord. The following account of the singing is furnished by Miss Helen Knox Strain, one of the missionaries present that night.

"The Woman's Union Missionary Society has a magnificent work just outside of the city of Shanghai. No harm had come to us up to this time, but serious threats and unpleasant rumours were rife; we dared not so much as put our heads out at night, though forty little soldier-men played at keeping us safe. "Our missionaries have two centres at that place, and they meet often for prayer and consultation. At this particular time the rumours were so frightful, and the threats to burn our homes that very night so distressing, that we had a memorable meeting. Separated from home and friends, facing death in a far-off land, and full of tenderest feelings, we lifted our hearts in song.

> Though destruction walk around us,
> Though the arrows past us fly;
> Angel guards from Thee surround us:
> We are safe if Thou art nigh.

"Out of the storm each soul, renewing its strength, mounted up with wings as eagles and found peace in the secret of His presence. "Our Saviour breathed, in very deed, an 'evening blessing' upon us, the fragrance of which remains even unto this day. The last verse of the hymn, 'should swift death this night o'ertake us,' was omitted. It seemed too probable that it might. We wanted only to think of the safekeeping, and such, thank God, it proved to be."

Even Me

Words by Mrs. Elizabeth Codner   Music by William B. Bradbury

> Lord, I hear of showers of blessing,
> Thou art scattering full and free.

This hymn was suggested to the writer by the news of the great spiritual Revival in Ireland, in 1860-61. It was largely used at our meetings in Great Britain, and is specially popular at evangelistic services. It has been introduced into most of the modem hymnals for congregational use.

A gentleman in England sends this incident: "A poor woman, in a dark village, attended a High Church mission, where the good Gospel hymn, 'Even Me' was sung from a printed leaflet. A few days afterward the old woman became seriously ill, and soon she died. But she seemed to have taken in all the Gospel through this hymn, and to the last repeated with reverence and joy 'Even me, even me,' not remembering one word of the sermon that she heard at the mission. This was in 1877. Soon after we had an evangelistic meeting in the same village, in a barn three hundred years old, where this hymn was sung with great effect.

The following narrative is from the pen of Rev. W. Hay Aitken, Canon of Norwich: —

"During a mission in the West End, a young lady of fashion, who had led a very worldly and thoughtless life, was induced to attend one of my services. As far as I know the sermon did not move her at all; at any rate, it was not anything that I said that led her to a decision. She rose to go as soon as the sermon was over, but on her way down the crowded aisle she got interested in Mrs. Codner's touching hymn, 'Even me,' which was being sung, and which, strange to say, was quite new to her. Just as she was reaching the door they were singing the last verse, which she followed in her own book:

> Pass me not! Thy lost one bringing,
> Bind my heart, O Lord, to Thee!
> While the streams of life are springing,
> Blessing others, oh!, bless me! Even me!

"As she listened, it suddenly flashed into her mind, 'You are that lost one,' and all the way home the words kept recurring over and over again, 'Pass me not! Thy lost one bringing!' She soon found herself alone in her chamber sobbing out the prayer from the very depths of her soul, 'Pass me not! Thy lost one bringing! and, as she lay there, it came to her mind that the Son of Man had come to seek and to save that which was lost. Ere she laid her head on her pillow that night she had learned to rest her soul on a Saviour's love, and was filled with a new strange joy that did indeed seem 'unspeakable and full of glory.' "

Follow On

Words by W. O. Cushing   Music by Robert Lowry

Down in the valley with my Saviour I would go,
Where the flowers are blooming and the sweet waters flow.

"I wrote this hymn in 1878," W. O. Cushing tells me, "longing to give up all for Christ who had given His life for me, I wanted to be willing to lay everything at his feet, with no wish but to do his will, to live henceforth only for his glory. Out of this feeling came the hymn, 'Follow On.'" It was written with the prayer and the hope that some heart might by it be led to give up all for Christ. Much of the power and usefulness of the hymn, however, are due to Mr. Lowry, who put it into song.

Free From the Law

Words by P. P. Bliss   Music by P. P. Bliss

Free from the law, oh, happy condition,
Jesus hath bled, and there is remission.

"What shall I give my husband for a Christmas present?" asked Mrs. Bliss of a friend, just before Christmas, 1871, and at the suggestion of this friend, she purchased and presented Mr. Bliss with a bound volume of a monthly English periodical called "Things New and Old." From reading in this book something in connection with Romans 8, and Hebrews 10, this glorious gospel song was suggested to him.

Gentle Jesus, Meek and Mild

Words by Charles Wesley   Music by Mrs. Jos. F. Knapp

> Gentle Jesus, meek and mild,
> Look upon a little child.

Mr. John B. Gough used to tell the following pathetic story regarding this hymn:

"A friend of mine, seeking for objects of charity, got into the upper room of a tenement house. It was vacant. He saw a ladder pushed through the ceilng. Thinking that perhaps some poor creature had crept up there, he climbed the ladder, drew himself through the hole, and found himself under the rafters. There was no light but that which came through a bull's-eye in the place of a tile. Soon he saw a heap of chips and shavings, and on them a boy about ten years old.

"'Boy, what are you doing here?'

"'Hush! don't tell anybody, please, sir.'

"'What are you doing here?'

"'Hush! pleaseMon't tell anybody, sir. I'm a hiding.'

"'What are you hiding from?"

"'Don't tell anybody, please, sir.'

"'* Where's your mother?'

"'Please, sir, mother's dead.'

"'Where's your father?'

"'Hush! don't tell him! Don't tell him! But look here!'

"He turned himself on his face, and through the rags of his jacket and shirt, my friend saw that the boy's flesh was bruised and his skin was broken. "'Why, my boy, — who beat you like that?'

"'Father did, sir.'

"'What did he beat you like that for?'

"'Father got drunk, sir, and beat me 'cos I wouldn't steal.'

"'Did you ever steal? '

"'Yes, sir; I was a street thief once.'

"'And why won't you steal any more? '

"'Please, sir, I went to the Mission School; and they told me there of God, and of heaven, and of Jesus; and they taught me 'Thou shalt not steal' — and I'll never steal again, if my father kills me for it. But, please, don't tell him! '

"'My boy, you mustn't stay here. You'll die. Now you wait patiently here for a little time. I'm going away to see a lady. We will get a better place for you than this.'

"'Thank you, sir; but, please, sir, would you like to hear me sing a little hymn?'

"Bruised, battered, forlorn, friendless, motherless, hiding away from an infuriated father, he had a little hymn to sing.

"'Yes, I will hear you sing your little hymn.' He raised himself on his elbow, and then sang:

> Gentle Jesus, meek and mild,
> Look upon a little child,
> Pity my simplicity,
> Suffer me to come to Thee.
>
> Fain I would to Thee be brought,
> Gracious Lord, forbid it not:
> In the kingdom of Thy grace,
> Give a little child a place.

"'That's the little hymn, sir. Good-bye.'

The gentleman went away, came back again in less than two hours, and climbed the ladder. There were the chips; and there were the shavings; and there was the boy, with one hand by his side, and the other tucked in his bosom underneath the little ragged shirt — dead.

"Oh, I thank God that He who said, 'Suffer little children to come unto Me,' did not say 'respectable children,' or 'well-educated children.' No! He sends His angels into the homes of poverty and sin, and crime, where you do not like to go, and brings out His redeemed ones; and they are as stars in the crown of rejoicing to those who have been instrumental in enhghtening their darkness in the Mission School, in the Ragged School, or in the Bands of Hope."

Go Bury Thy Sorrow

Words by Mary A. Bachelor   Music by P. P. Bliss

> Go bury thy sorrow,
> The world hath its share.

The author of the hymn was the daughter of a minister. When she wrote these lines she was living with her brother, whom she greatly loved. He also was a minister, and had the usual cares and burdens to carry that are incident to a pastor's life. To him she confided all her joys and sorrows. One day, after having disclosed to him some peculiar trial which she was enduring, she was reproached by her conscience for having needlessly added to his already numerous cares. She stood by the open window, and saw the long, heavy shadows cast by the tall poplar trees across the lawn, and the thought came to her:

"That is just what I have done to my brother! Why did I do it? Why did I not rather bury my own sorrow, and allow only words of cheer and brightness to reach his ears?"

With such thoughts in her mind, and with tears of regret filling her eyes, she retired to her little attic bedroom, and there wrote the hymn that has been so blessed.

For many years this hymn was one of my favourite solos. In its original form it read, "Bury thy sorrow, hide it with care;" but when Mr. Bliss found it in a newspaper he arranged it to read, "Go bury thy sorrow, the world hath its share," and set it to music. It has been blessed to thousands of people, and will remain as one of his best productions when many of his other songs are forgotten.

A lady who had suffered much, and had passed through many great trials, set much store by this hymn. One day as she sang it her little daughter, who was playing in the room, looked up into her mother's face and saw tears rolling down her cheeks.

The child called out: "Mamma, are you digging the sorrows all up again?"

God Be With You

Words by E. Rankin, D.D.   Music by W. G. Tomer

God be with you till we meet again;
By His counsels guide, uphold you.

The late Dr. Rankin, president of Howard University, Washington, D. C., said regarding this oft used parting hymn: "Written in 1882 as a Christian good-bye, it was called forth by no person or occasion, but was deliberately composed as a Christian hymn on the basis of the etymology of 'good-bye,' which is, 'God be with you.' The first stanza was written and sent to two composers - one of unusual note, the other wholly unknown and not thoroughly educated in music. I selected the composition of the latter, submitted it to J. W. Bischoff - the musical director of a little book we were preparing - who approved of it, but made some criticisms, which were adopted. It was sung for the first time one evening in the First Congregational Church in Washington, of which I was then the pastor and Mr. Bischoff the organist. I attributed its popularity in no little part to the music to which it was set. It was a wedding of words and music, at which it was my function to preside; but Mr. Tomer should have his full share of the family honour." William Gould Tomer, the author of the music, is of German ancestry. He has been a school teacher, a soldier in the civil war, and a clerk in the Treasury department. He was teaching school in 1882 when he wrote the music of "God be with you."

Mr. S. E. Burrow, Secretary of the Soldiers' Christian Association, writes:

"The Christian soldier is an inveterate singer, and he loves bright and lively tunes; hence the great popularity of 'Sacred Songs and Solos" among the men of the Soldiers' Christian Association.

"As I move up and down the country visiting the various military stations, I am often amazed at the way in which a group of Christian soldiers will gather around a piano in a Soldiers' Home and sing Sankey's Hymns in succession for a couple of hours without a pause beyond some expression of delight or shout of 'Hallelujah!'

"The ladies in charge of the Home may point suggestively to the clock, only to be answered by three or four together — 'Just one more, miss!" When that one is sung, and the chorus repeated several times, some one asks, as a special favour, that his 'favourite" may be sung, which of course opens the way for the 'favourites' of all the others, until the clock points to the hour for closing.

"But no company of Christian soldiers would dream of separating without singing '494,' and the room rings again with the music of that prime favourite — 'God be with you till we meet again.'

"'494,' however, is not only sung — it has become part and parcel of the Christian Tommy's life. It has entered into his vocabulary and forms a sort of 'password.' Members of the S.C.A. have almost forgotten how to say 'Goodbye 'since '494' answers the purpose more to their liking. Whether it be at the close of a meeting or the parting of a couple of Christian comrades after a brief chat, it is always '494 'that accompanies the handshake. And the response — 'Six further on!' has become equally familiar. That, of course, means hymn 500, 'Blessed Assurance.' So our Christian soldiers part — the one with his '494' praying God to be with his comrade — the other replying with the note of assurance — 'Jesus is mine.'

"Of late, a third hymn has been called into use to serve the purpose of a greeting, and it is now no uncommon thing to hear a Christian lad, in reply to the question — 'How're you getting on, mate?' answer, 'oh. Two ten! 'which, being interpreted, means hymn 210 — 'It is well with my soul!'"

Guide Me, O Thou Great Jehovah

Words by W. Williams   Music by Wm. L. Viner

Guide me, O Thou great Jehovah,
Pilgrim through this barren land.

Written by William Williams; the sweet singer, who was known as the "Watts of Wales." It was first published in Welsh in 1745. Later it appeared in English under the title, "A favourite hymn of Lady Huntingdon's young collegians." This hymn was one of the most popular in our collection, when Mr. Moody and I were holding meetings in Wales.

Hallelujah Tis Done

Words by P. P. Bliss   Music by P. P. Bliss

'Tis the promise of God full salvation to give,
Unto him who on Jesus, his Son, will believe.

In compiling his book, "Gospel Songs," in 1874, Mr. Bliss desired to publish in it the well known hymn, "Hallelujah! Thine the Glory," then much used in religious services. The owners of the copyright refused, and he wrote "Hallelujah, 'tis done," both words and music, to supply the want. Hundreds of souls have been led to decide for Christ by this hymn, and the church has reason to rejoice at that refusal.

A minister from England, in telling of a certain meeting, says: "Among the converts was a man somewhat advanced in years, who was very anxious about the salvation of his wife, and expressed a wish that I should visit her. I did so repeatedly, and explained to her in very simple words the plan of salvation, but she could not comprehend the meaning of my message. Every time I left, however, she would express a strong desire that I return. One day I went in just before dinner, and talked to her about Jesus, but no light seemed to dawn upon her mind. Then the thought struck me to sing something to her, and so I commenced, "'Tis the promise of God, full salvation to give.' When I was through the chorus, she exclaimed, 'Sing it over again.' I did so, time after time, and when I asked her to assist me, she joined in very heartily. The light dawned on her dark mind while we were singing, the big burden of sin was removed from her heart, and her face was lighted up with holy joy as she exclaimed, 'Hallelujah, 'tis done! I do believe in the Son; I am saved.' Just then her husband walked in for his dinner, and she shouted out to him, 'Ah, lad! I've got it! Hallelujah! 'tis done!' Their hearts were full of joy over the wonderful discovery she had made, and I was grateful to God for a sinner brought to Christ by the ministry of holy song."

Hallelujah! What A Saviour!

Words by P. P. Bliss   Music by P. P. Bliss

"Man of Sorrows,' what a name
For the Son of God, who came.

Written in 1876, shortly before his death, this was the last hymn I heard Mr. Bliss sing. It was at a meeting in Farwell Hall in Chicago, conducted by Henry Moorehouse. A few weeks before his death Mr. Bliss visited the State prison at Jackson, Michigan, where, after a very touching address on "The Man of Sorrows," he sang this hymn with great effect. Many of the prisoners dated their conversion from that day.

When Mr. Moody and I were in Paris, holding meetings in the old church which Napoleon had granted to the Evangelicals, I frequently sang this hymn as a solo, asking the congregation to join in the single phrase, "Hallelujah, what a Saviour," which they did with splendid effect. It is said that the word "Hallelujah" is the same in all languages. It seems as though God had prepared it for the great jubilee of heaven, when all his children shall have been gathered home to sing "Hallelujah to the Lamb!"

A pastor, who had always sought to walk with God, came to some of our meetings desiring a richer blessing, and to be more fruitful in his ministry. He was completely "broken to pieces," to use his own expression, and "reconstructed;" and now he declared, his experience was expressed only in this phrase, "Hallelujah! What a Saviour!"

He Knows

Words by Mary G. Braluard   Music by P. P. Bliss

I know not what awaits me,
God kindly veils mine eyes.

When Mr. Bliss lost his life in the terrible railroad wreck at Ashtabula, Ohio, his trunk reached Chicago safely, as it had gone before by another train. In his trunk was discovered this hymn. Mr. Bliss had rearranged the words of the poem to some extent, and had composed the tune. Sentence by sentence, the words are full of pathetic interest in connection with the author's sudden death so soon afterward.

He Leadeth Me

Words by Joseph H. Gilmore   Music by William B. Bradbury

He leadeth me! O, blessed thought!
O, words with heavenly comfort fraught.

"I had been talking," said Mr. Gilmore, "at the Wednesday evening lecture of the First Baptist Church of Philadelphia, in 1862. The Twenty-third Psalm was my theme, and I had been especially impressed with the blessedness of being led by God - of the mere fact of his leadership, altogether apart from the way in which he leads us and what he is leading us to. At the close of the service we adjourned to Deacon Watson's home, at which I was stopping. We still held before our minds and hearts the thought which I had just emphasized. During the conversation, in which several participated, the blessedness of God's leadership so grew upon me that I took out my pencil, wrote the hymn just as it stands today, handed it to my wife - and thought no more about it. She sent it without my knowledge to 'The Watchman and Reflector,' and there it first appeared in print. Three years later I went to Rochester to preach for the Second Baptist Church. On entering the chapel I took up a hymn-book, thinking, 'I wonder what they sing.' The book opened at 'He leadeth me,' and that was the first time I knew my hymn had found a place among the songs of the church. I shall never forget the impression made upon me by coming then and there in contact with my own assertion of God's leadership."

Mr. Bradbury, finding the hymn in a Christian periodical, composed for it the very appropriate tune with which it has ever since been associated.

Hear the Call

Words by W. F. Sherwin   Music by W. F. Sherwin

> Lo! the day of God is breaking;
> See the gleaming from afar!

Mr. Sherwin was of great assistance in our meetings in Boston in 1876. Early in his life Mr. Sherwin manifested decided musical abilities, but being a poor boy, he had to struggle hard to obtain the instruction he so much desired. However, at the age of fifteen he was the leader of a large chorus choir. At twenty-five he was well-known at New England musical conventions. He was brought up a Congregationalist, but while having charge of the music in a Baptist church in Albany, he adopted that denomination. He was an ardent Sunday-school worker, and had part in the preparation of many hymn and song books for use in Sunday-schools and in the temperance work. He was born in Buckland, Mass., March 14, 1826, and died at his home in Dorchester, Mass., April 14, 1888.

Here I Am, Send Me

Words by Daniel March   Music by S. M. Grannis

> Hark! the voice of Jesus crying,
> 'Who will go and work today?'

I found this poem in a newspaper and set the words to a tune by S. M. Grannis entitled "Your Mission" - a hymn which was sung in the Senate Chamber in Washington by Philip Phillips on one occasion when Abraham Lincoln was present. The President was so charmed with the song that he requested that it be repeated.

Hiding In Thee

Words by William O. Cushing   Music by Ira D. Sankey

> O safe to the Rock that is higher than I,
> My soul in its conflicts and sorrows would fly.

"'Hiding in Thee' was written in Moravia, New York, in 1876," writes Mr. Cushing. "It must be said of this hymn that it was the outgrowth of many tears. many heart-conflicts and soulyearnings, of which the world can know nothing. The history of many battles is behind it. But the occasion which gave it being was the call of Mr. Sankey. He said: 'Send me something new to help me in my Gospel work.' "A call from such a source, and for such a purpose, seemed a call from God. I so regarded it, and prayed: 'Lord, give me something that may glorify Thee.' "It was while thus waiting that 'Hiding in Thee' pressed to make itself known. Mr. Sankey called forth the tune, and by his genius gave the hymn wings, making it useful in the Master's work."

Ho! Reapers of Life's Harvest

Words by I. B. Woodbury   Music by I. B. Woodbury

> Ho! reapers of life's harvest,
> Why stand with rusted blade?

President Garfield was fond of this hymn, and it was sung at his funeral. In addressing an audience of young people on one occasion, Garfield said, in substance, regarding his own conversion:

"Make the most of the present moment. No occasion is unworthy of our best efforts. God often uses humble occasions and little things to shape the course of a man's life. I might say that the wearing of a certain pair of stockings led to a complete change in my life. "I had made a trip as a boy on a canal boat and was expecting to leave home for another trip; but I accidentally injured my foot in chopping wood. The blue dye in my home-made socks poisoned the wound and I was kept at home. A revival broke out meanwhile in the neighbourhood, and I was thus kept within its influence and was converted. New desires and new purposes then took possession of me, and I was determined to seek an education in order that I might live more usefully for Christ."

It is said that this hymn has been the means of the conversion of thousands of souls in Australia and Great Britain.

Hold the Fort

Words by P. P. Bliss   Music by P. P. Bliss

Ho! my comrades, see the signal
Waving in the sky

Just before Sherman began his famous march to the sea in 1864, and while his army lay camped in the neighbourhood of Atlanta on the 5th of October, the army of Hood, in a carefully prepared movement, passed the right flank of Sherman's army, gained his rear, and commenced the destruction of the railroad leading north, burning blockhouses and capturing the small garrisons along the line. Sherman's army was put in rapid motion pursuing Hood, to save the supplies and larger posts, the principal one of which was located at Altoona Pass. General Corse, of Illinois, was stationed here with about fifteen hundred men, Colonel Tourtelotte being second in command. A million and a half of rations were stored here and it was highly important that the earthworks commanding the pass and protecting the supplies should be held. Six thousand men under command of General French were detailed by Hood to take the position. The works were completely surrounded and summoned to surrender. Corse refused and a sharp fight commenced. The defenders were slowly driven into a small fort on the crest of the hill. Many had fallen, and the result seemed to render a prolongation of the fight hopeless. At this moment an officer caught sight of a white signal flag far away across the valley, twenty miles distant, upon the top of Kenesaw Mountain. The signal was answered, and soon the message was waved across from mountain to mountain:

Hold the fort; I am coming. W. T. Sherman.

Cheers went up; every man was nerved to a full appreciation of the position; and under a murderous fire, which killed or wounded more than half the men in the fort – Corse himself being shot three times through the head, and Tourtelotte taking command, though himself badly wounded - they held the fort for three hours until the advance guard of Sherman's army came up. French was obliged to retreat.

This historical incident was related by Major Whittle at a Sunday-school meeting in Rockford, Illinois, in May, 1870. Mr. Bliss was present, and the song "Hold the Fort" was at once born in his mind. The next day Whittle and Bliss held a meeting in the Young Men's Christian Association rooms in Chicago. Bliss went on the platform and wrote the chorus of this hymn on the blackboard. He there sang the verses for the first time in public, and the audience joined in the chorus. Soon after he had it published in sheet form.

Mr. Bliss said to me once, not long before his death, that he hoped that he would not be known to posterity only as the author of "Hold the Fort," for he believed that he had written many better songs. However, when I attended the dedication of the Bliss monument, at Rome, Pennsylvania, I found these words inscribed:

> P. P. Bliss,
> Author of "Hold the Fort."

The pine tree from which Sherman's signal was flown was cut down a few years after the war, and was made into souvenirs, I receiving a baton with which to lead my choirs.

"Hold the Fort" was used frequently in our meetings in Great Britain during 1873-74. Lord Shaftesbury said at our farewell meeting in London: "If Mr. Sankey has done no more than teach the people to sing 'Hold the Fort,' he has conferred an inestimable blessing on the British empire."

On a trip to Switzerland, in 1879, I stopped over Sunday in London with the family of William Higgs, and attended morning services at the Metropolitan Tabernacle. While seated in a pew with Mrs. Higgs and three of her daughters, I was discovered by Mr. Spurgeon. At the conclusion of his address he sent one of his deacons down to the pew, inviting me to his private room at the rear of the pulpit. There I was warmly greeted by the great preacher. In the course of our conversation he said: "A few days ago I received a copy of a bill pending in Parliament in relation to the army, with a letter from a Christian gentleman, a member of the parliament, asking if I couldn't preach a sermon on this bill. I have decided to preach that sermon tonight, and I want you to come and sing, 'Hold the Fort.' I replied that he was not a man to be denied; and although I had not expected to sing in public in London on this trip, I would gladly comply with his wish if I could have a small organ to accompany myself upon. This I supposed that he would not have, as he did not approve of organs at public worship and never used one in his church; but he replied that when I arrived at the meeting there would be an instrument on the platform for me. In the evening, at the close of his address he announced that I was present and would sing 'Hold the Fort;' and he asked them all to join heartily in the chorus. An organ had been secured from the Students' College. When the chorus was sung it was heard blocks away. At the conclusion of the service Mr. Spurgeon exclaimed: "There now, I think our roof will stay on after that!"

On reaching Switzerland I sang in many cities. Sailing across Lake Lucerne, and ascending the Rigi, there I again sang 'Hold the Fort,' much to the interest of the Swiss peasants.

An indication of the impression this and other American songs made upon the people may be seen in the case of the two actors who came on the stage in one of the largest theaters in England and attempted to caricature Mr. Moody and myself. The galleries struck up "Hold the Fort," and kept on singing the piece until the actors had to withdraw from the stage. On their reappearing, with the purpose of continuing the performance, the song was again started, and continued until that part of the entertainment was given up. I have been informed that the cabling of this incident to this country at the time it took place turned the attention of our countrymen more thoroughly to our work across the sea than all the reports previously sent in relation to the movement over there.

Shortly after the evangelistic work of Henry Varley in Yorkville and Toronto, about 1875, when the songs in the first edition of "Gospel Hymns" were heard all over the land, a carpenter and his apprentice were working on a building in Yorkville. The man was a Christian and had consecrated his fine tenor voice to the Master's use. The boy had just given himself to Jesus and was also a singer for the Lord. One morning, as they met at the usual hour for work, the following dialogue took place between them:

"Do you know who is coming here to work today?"

"No, I did not hear of anybody coming here."

"Well, there is; and it is Tommy Dodd."

"And who might Tommy Dodd be?"

"He is a painter, and the greatest drunkard and wife-beater in Yorkville."

"Well, Joe, we must give him a warm reception."

"Yes, we will sing like everything, so that he can't get a bad word in."

So, when Tommy Dodd came, they struck up "Hold the Fort." And they kept on singing till he left his work and came closer to listen. He asked them to sing it over and over again, joining heartily in it himself, for Tommy was very fond of singing. This was followed by an invitation to the young men's prayer-meeting, where the Spirit led him to surrender to Christ. Afterward he was found at the church instead of the saloon, singing the sweet songs of Zion.

Dr. R. A. Torrey, on his return from England recently, called on me and told me that while he and Mr. Alexander were holding meetings in Belfast, one of the most enthusiastic helpers was a typical Irishman, well-known as an active worker all over the city. "He was constantly bringing drunkards to the front and dealing with them," said Dr. Torrey, "and holding meetings in the open air all over the city. The story of his conversion was exceedingly interesting. At that time he was a prisoner in a cell in Belfast. The window of his cell was open. Mr. Sankey was singing 'Hold the Fort' in another building. The words floated across through the open window into his cell and went home to his heart. There in his cell he accepted Christ under the influence of this hymn. I think he never saw Mr. Sankey in his life."

Hold Thou My Hand

Words by Grace J. Frances   Music by Hubert P. Main

> Hold Thou my hand: so weak I am and helpless,
> I dare not take one step without Thy aid.

Written by Grace J. Frances, which is a nom de plume of Fanny Crosby. Hubert P. Main wrote the music. It became a great favourite of Mrs. C. H. Spurgeon, who asked permission to republish it in her collection of hymns.

Holy, Holy, Holy Lord God Almighty

Words by Reginald Heber, D.D.   Music by John B. Dykes

> Holy, holy, holy! Lord God Almighty!
> Early in the morning our song shall rise to Thee;

This majestic hymn was written by Bishop Heber, who was born in Cheshire, England, 1783, and educated at Oxford. He served in the church at Hodnet for about twenty years, when he was appointed

Bishop of Calcutta, East India. He wrote fifty-seven hymns, which were published by his widow in 1842. Heber died 1826 in the prime of his life.

The tune "Nicea" was composed by Dr. John Bacchus Dykes for this hymn, and is one of the best of his compositions. Nicea was the place in Asia Minor where the first Ecumenical Council was held in the year 325, and it was there that the doctrine of the Holy Trinity was promulgated, declaring the eternal sonship of Christ, and his equality with the father. Dr. Dykes was born at Kingston-upon-Hull, in 1823; and was a graduate of Cambridge. He wrote many excellent tunes, and did much to elevate the congregational psalmody of England. He died 1876.

Home of the Soul

Words by Mr. Ellen H. Gates   Music by Philip Phillips

I will sing you a song of that beautiful land,
The far away home of the soul.

"Now I saw in my dream that these two men [Christian and Hopeful] went in at the gate; and lo, as they entered, they were transfigured; and they had raiment put on them that shone like gold. "There were also those that met them with harps and crowns and gave them to them; the harps to praise withal, and the crowns in token of honour. Then I heard in my dream that all the bells in the city rang again for joy, and that it was said unto them: 'Enter ye into the joy of your Lord!'... Now, just as the gates were opened to let in the men, I looked in after them, and behold, the city shone like the sun; the streets also were paved with gold; and in them walked many men, with crowns on their heads and palms in their hands, and golden harps to sing praises withal... After that, they shut up the gates which, when I had seen, I wished myself among them."
– Bunyan's "Pilgrim's Progress."

"The above extract," wrote Philip Phillips, "I sent to Mrs. Ellen H. Gates, asking her to write a suitable hymn. "When the verses were forwarded to me, in 1865, I seated myself in my home with my little boy on my knee, and with Bunyan's immortal dream book in my hand, and began to read the closing scenes where Christian and Hopeful entered into the city; wondering at Bunyan's rare genius, and like the dreamer of old wishing myself among them. At this moment of inspiration I turned to my organ, with pencil in hand, and wrote the tune. This hymn seems to have had

God's special blessing upon it from the very beginning. One man writes me that he has led in the singing of it at a hundred and twenty funerals. "It was sung at the funeral of my own dear boy, who had sat on my knee when I wrote the tune."

And I sang this hymn over the remains of my beloved friend, Philip Phillips, at Fredonia, New York.

How Firm a Foundation

Words by G. Keith   Music by M. Portogallo

> How firm a foundation, ye saints of the Lord,
> Is laid for your faith in His excellent word.

"Once at evening devotion in the old Oratory of Princeton Seminary," Dr. C. S. Robinson relates, "the elder Hodge, then venerable with years and piety, paused as he read this hymn, preparatory to the singing. In the depth of his emotion he was obliged to close his delivery of the final lines with a gesture of pathetic and adoring wonder at the matchless grace of God in Christ; and his hand silently beat time to the rhythm instead: 'I'll never, no, never, no, never forsake.'"

Giving an account of a visit to General Jackson at the Hermitage, in 1843, James Gallager says in the Western Sketch Book: "The old hero was then very frail and had the appearance of extreme old age; but he was reposing with calmness and confidence on the promise and covenant of God. He had now been a member of the church for several years." During the conversation which took place, the General turned to Mr. Gallager, and remarked:

"There is a beautiful hymn on the subject of the exceeding great and precious promise of God to His people. It was the favourite hymn of my dear wife, till the day of her death. It commences in this way: 'How firm a foundation, ye saints of the Lord.' I wish you would sing it now."

So the little company sang the entire hymn.

I Am Praying for You

Words by S. O'Maley Cluff   Music by Ira D. Sankey

> I have a Saviour, He's pleading in glory;
> A dear, loving Saviour, tho' earth friends be few.

On our first visit to Ireland, in 1874, we came across these words in a printed leaflet. It was the second hymn to which I wrote music, and it was much used in our meetings in London. It has long been a favourite prayer-meeting hymn in many churches.

At the close of a gospel service in Evanston, Illinois, the minister was requested to visit a man who was not likely to live many days, and who was a spiritualist. Though pressed by other engagements, the minister said, "I will take time." He called, but thought it not best to introduce the subject of religion because of the patient's known hostility to evangelical views. Seeing a little organ in the room, the minister asked if he might sing a song. Consent being given, he sang "I have a Saviour, He's pleading in glory."

The sick man seemed pleased, and asked the minister to sing it again. This he did, and then gave other songs. Thus he sang the truths which he had not the courage to mention in conversation. The songs evidently accomplished their work; for when the minister called again the sick man's heart had been opened, and the truth had been savingly received through their instrumentality.

A gospel worker, of Hunter, New York, tells of this experience in connection with the hymn: "While I was holding revival meetings at Hensonville, New York, a man and his wife were converted through the hymn 'I Am Praying for You.'

The song went directly to the heart of the wife. All the way to her home the first line of the hymn, 'I have a Saviour, He's pleading in glory,' kept ringing in her ears, and next morning as she awoke she heard my voice singing, 'I have a Saviour.' "That night she came to Jesus. Her husband followed immediately after her. They had sent out invitations for a large dancing party at that time, which no doubt would have injured the meetings very much had it taken place; but the dance was turned into a prayer-meeting. I shall never forget the night she stood up in a crowded church, and said, 'Oh, Brother L-, your singing "I have a Saviour" brought us to Jesus.'"

A young man who came from Sweden writes: "'I Am Praying for You' was the first Moody and Sankey hymn I ever heard. It was on a cold winter night up in the land of the midnight sun, more than a quarter of a century ago. Two evangelists had come to the neighbourhood, but had found it difficult to get a place in which to hold their meetings. "At last a poor woman opened for them her log house, consisting of two rooms. From house to house the meetings were announced. I was a small boy, and out of curiosity I attended the first meeting. About twenty people were present, seated on chairs borrowed from the neighbours. At one end of the low, dark room the evangelists were seated, by a small table on which two homemade candles were burning. After one of the evangelists had led in prayer, he said to the other, 'Sing one of Sankey's hymns.' Upon which he sang this now well-known hymn, 'I Am Praying for You,' accompanying himself on a guitar. Since then I have heard these sweet hymns sung in many European countries, and in the small meeting-houses and primitive homes of the settlers on the Western plains, as well as by choirs of hundreds and congregations of thousands in the larger cities of this broad land."

I Am Thine, O Lord

Words by Fanny J. Crosby   Music by W. H. Doane

I am Thine, O Lord,
I have heard Thy voice.

This popular and useful consecration hymn was written by Fanny Crosby and set to music by W. H. Doane, and has been largely adopted by Christian Endeavor societies throughout this country and Great Britain.

Fanny Crosby was visiting Mr. W. H. Doane, in his home in Cincinnati, Ohio. They were talking together about the nearness of God, as the sun was setting and the evening shadows were gathering around them. The subject so impressed the well-known hymn-writer, that before retiring she had written the words to this hymn, which has become one of the most useful she has ever written. The music by Mr. Doane so well fitted the words that the hymn has become a special favourite wherever the Gospel Hymns are known.

I Gave My Life for Thee

Words by Frances R. Havergal   Music by P. P. Bliss

I gave My life for thee,
My precious blood I shed.

Fifteen years after this hymn was written. Miss Havergal said about it: "Yes, 'I gave My life for thee,' is mine, and perhaps it will interest you to hear how nearly it went into the fire instead of nearly all over the world. It was, I think, the very first thing I wrote which could be called a hymn–written when I was a young girl, in 1859. I did not half realize what I was writing about. I was following very far off, always doubting and fearing. I think I had come to Jesus with a trembling faith, but it was a 'coming in the press' and behind, never seeing his face or feeling sure that he loved me; I scribbled these words in a few minutes on the back of a circular, and then read them over and thought, 'Well, this is not poetry, anyhow; I won't trouble to write this out.' "I reached out my hand to put it in the fire, when a sudden impulse made me draw it back, and I put it, crumpled and singed, in my pocket. Soon after this I went to see a dear old woman in the almshouse. She began talking to me, as she always did, about her dear Saviour, and I thought I would see if she, a simple old woman would care for these verses, which I felt sure nobody else would even care to read. I read them to her, and she was so delighted with them that I copied them out and kept them. And now the Master has sent them out in all directions, and I have heard of their being a real blessing to many."

Miss Havergal showed the hymn some time afterward to her father, and he wrote a melody especially for it, called "Baca," to which the words are usually sung in Great Britain. But it is the tune which Mr. Bliss composed for it that became popular in America and which in Britain is set to Dr. Pierson's hymn, "Once I was Dead in Sin."

I Hear Thy Welcome Voice

Words by Lewis Hartsough   Music by Lewis Hartsough

I hear Thy welcome voice
That calls me, Lord, to Thee.

The words and music of this beautiful hymn were first published in a monthly entitled "Guide to Holiness," a copy of which was sent to me in England in 1873. I immediately adopted it and had it published in "Sacred Songs and Solos." It proved to be one of the most helpful of the revival hymns, and was often used as an invitation hymn in England and America.

Shortly after this hymn was written, while it was being sung by a large congregation in Washington, a passing merchant stopped to listen. It had been twenty years since he had crossed the threshold of a church. The congregation was on their feet and sinners were passing to the altar for prayer. Stanza after stanza of this hymn was sung, with increasing interest. The Holy Spirit so pressed the Lord's claims that the merchant yielded and joined the penitents. He was converted and this hymn became his favourite. He sang it in his home, on the street, and in his store. It seemed a special inspiration to him. One morning, about two weeks after his conversion, as he started for his store, his wife, having accompanied him to the door to say good-bye, heard him joyfully begin to sing

> I am coming, Lord,
> Coming now to Thee,

as he reached the street. She listened a little while, looking after him, and then turned to her room. A few moments later the door-bell rang. She answered it in person, only to find that men were bearing home her husband's dead body. He had slipped on the icy pavement and was instantly killed. The memory of those last words of song that fell upon her ears, as he triumphantly sang

> I am coming, Lord,
> Coming now to Thee,

was to her a lasting comfort.

"While holding meetings at Eastbourn," says an English evangelist, "a man by the name of David was converted. His very wicked workmate, whose name was Stephen, noticed the change in him the next day, and asked David what had caused it. David boldly confessed that he had found the Saviour at the Mission, and expressed a wish that Stephen would accompany him there next Sunday to which he finally agreed. "As we began the service on Sunday evening, I gave out the hymn, 'I hear Thy welcome Voice.' During the singing I noticed that the Spirit had touched a man who was sitting on the first form under the platform. After a short comment on the verses, I said: 'We will have the prayer meeting at once,' and in another minute I was down by the side of Stephen–for it was he–and with my arm around his neck I said to him: 'The Lord is speaking to you, is he not?' "After the meeting Stephen testified that he had been able to knock down two men in a fight, but that he never was so knocked down in all his life as when he felt my arm around his neck. Stephen became a brave and true follower of Christ. He brought his wife to church, and though at first she had ridiculed her husband, she, too, soon gave heed to the 'welcome voice.'"

"I was in great darkness and trouble for some days," said a poor woman, rejoicing and yet weeping; "and just a little time ago, when Mr. Sankey was singing these words" (pointing to them with her finger), "'Tis Jesus calls me on,' my bonds were broken in a moment, and now I am safe in His arms."

I'll Go Where Thou Would'st I Should Go

Words by Mary Brown   Music by Carrie E. Rounsefell

> It may not be on the mountain's height,
> Or over the stormy sea.

This well-known missionary and consecration hymn was adopted by a class of over a hundred missionary nurses at the Battle Creek (Michigan) Sanitarium as their class hymn. Every Sunday afternoon they would gather for a social meeting and always sing, "I'll go where Thou would'st I should go, dear Lord," which they called "their hymn." In this class were students from nearly every State of the Union, from Australia, South Africa, South America. Bulgaria, Armenia, and nearly all the European countries. At the close of the course they agreed that after they had parted and gone to their different fields, they would sing this hymn every Sunday afternoon as they had done during their happy class days.

I Love To Tell the Story

Words by Miss Kate Haukey   Music by W. G. Fischer

> I love to tell the story
> Of unseen things above.

Last winter a young man appeared here from British Columbia," says

111

a letter from Surrey, England, "He was in the Royal Marines. He was a total abstainer and was doing all he could to promote temperance among his comrades. While here he went to church, and the curate, who had a conversation with him, was much pleased with his manly behaviour and resolute desire to do right. He wore a medal and had good-conduct marks on his clothes. "This man was the little boy whom Miss T. had picked up in Battersea Park many years before, and who had learned of the gospel of salvation entirely by listening to the maidservants singing sacred songs while scrubbing doorsteps and cleaning windows. The hymn that, as a child, he seemed to make entirely his own was, 'I love to tell the story,' though he knew several others when he was picked up in the park. As he had never been to church or chapel, the hymns were the only channel through which divine truth had been conveyed to him, and by which the first seed was sown in his heart that made him a man of character and usefulness."

I Need Thee Every Hour

Words by Annie S. Hawk.   Music by Robert Lowry

> I need Thee every hour,
> Most gracious Lord.

This hymn was first sung at a Sunday-school convention in Cincinnati, in November of 1872. Two years later I sang it for the first time at Mr. Moody's meetings in the East End of London. After that we often used it in our prayer-meetings.

A chaplain of the State prison at Concord, Massachusetts, tells how an ex-prisoner, who had never had a home in his life, prepared one, humble but tasteful home and then asked the chaplain to help him dedicate it. Together they entered the home – the man's wife had not yet come – and the service began." Mr. B., with evident brokenness of spirit, for he was naturally a proud man and not unacquainted with larger surroundings, could not refrain from some criticism upon his poor things; but his heart was so full that his embarrassment was only temporary, and he immediately went on with a firm purpose. He started the hymn, 'I need Thee every hour' for the first number of the service."

The singing of this hymn at a meeting in Chicago, at the time of the World's Fair, led to the writing, by Major D.W. Whittle, of the now famous song,

> Moment by moment I'm kept in His love
> Moment by moment I've life from above.

I Stood Outside the Gate

Words by Miss J. Pollard   Music by Hubert P. Main

> I stood outside the gate,
> A poor wayfaring child.

A friend in London sends the following narrative of conversion which came under his personal observation. It is the testimony of a woman who was first aroused through an open-air meeting within a stone's throw of her little general shop. She says:

"I am sixty-eight years of age. I have lived here for the last fifteen years, during which time my shop has been opened as regularly as clockwork every Lord's Day. One Sunday in January I closed my shop in the evening, and went to the service at the Mission Hall. That night the Lord plainly told me that I was a sinner, and that, unless I repented, I must perish. On the following Sunday I stopped at home, my sins still staring me in the face, and I striving against my own conscience. In the evening, hoping to drive away my thoughts, I went to see some friends, but the Lord followed me, for, to my disgust, they commenced singing some of Sankey's hymns. Everybody in that little company seemed happy — except me. An offended God; a guilty conscience; a tempting devil. I was afraid to tell my troubles. Oh, what a state to be in! Oh, the wretchedness of the weeks I thus spent! Shortly afterwards I again visited the Mission Hall in the evening. I listened to an address on 'Zaccheus, make haste and come down.' I thought to myself, Zaccheus obeyed the call of Jesus, but I refused. An arrow pierced my heart. I vowed there and then that if I lived until another Sabbath I would not open my shop.

"One of the friends from the Hall called upon me during the week, and I told him my condition. 'Praise the Lord!' he exclaimed; 'you are on the right track.' What, I thought, no faith, a hard heart, and sixty-eight years of sin weighing me down, and I on the right track? Oh, could I but think so! I went to the Prayer Meeting the following Lord's Day, and the prayers seemed to be all for me. There appeared to be something I wanted to grasp, but had not the faith to reach it. I went home to dinner, but not a morsel passed my lips. My appetite had left me; but in its place there was the hungering and the tliirsting for the Living Bread, which only the Spirit of God could have created. I opened my Bible with the hope of finding some relief, then I took up 'Songs and Solos' exclaiming, 'Lord, I can get no further; on Thee I cast all my care.' The Hymn Book opened at No. 225, and I read:

> I stood outside the gate,
> A poor wayfaring child;
> Within my heart there beat
> A tempest loud and wild;
>
> A fear oppressed my soul,
> That I might be too late!
> And oh, I trembled sore,
> And prayed outside the gate.
>
> 'Oh, Mercy!' loud I cried,
> Now give me rest from sin!
> 'I will!' a voice replied,
> And Mercy let me in.

"In a moment I felt the burden removed, and a heavenly peace, that my tongue cannot describe, came over me as I realized that Jesus had passed me through the gate. I could not help exclaiming, 'Bless the Lord, O my soul; and all that is within me, bless His holy name.'"

I Will

Words by D. W. Whiittle ("El Nathan")   Music by James McGranahan

> Once more, my soul, thy Saviour, through the Word,
> Is offered full and free.

This hymn was suggested by the responses of the young men of Limerick to Mr. Moody's question: "Will you trust Christ?"at our first meeting in that city in 1883. The following is a record of that memorable occasion:

"Speaking from a considerable experience of the labours of Messrs. Moody and Sankey I can confidently say that nowhere, under the most favouring conditions, had their message seemed to secure from the very outset a readier entrance into the hearts and sympathies of the people. In the theatre, pit and stage, boxes and galleries, were packed with an audience that appeared to represent every social stratum of the community, and that listened to speech and song as for dear life. It seemed that a power greater than any mere human attraction had chained the people to their seats. Mr. Sankey sang again, and Mr. Moody rang the Gospel changes on the words 'receive,' 'believe,' 'take,' and 'trust.' And when he applied the old question: 'Who will trust and not be afraid?' the responses were neither few nor faint." "I will!" rang out from all parts of the vast audience, and thus large numbers accepted Christ that night.

A boy, after telling how he had been saved at one of our meetings, added to his companions, "You're not too young; make up your mind; say 'I will take Christ.' That's the way."

I Will Sing of My Redeemer

Words by P. P. Bliss   Music by James McGranahan

> I will sing of my Redeemer,
> And His wondrous love to me.

This beautiful hymn was written by P. P. Bliss and set to music by James McGranahan, and is one of his most famous compositions. When Mr. Bliss so sadly met his death in the railroad disaster at Ashtabula, Ohio, December 29, 1876, Mr. McGranahan was selected to take his place as evangelistic singer in connection with Major Whittle, and much good was accomplished through their united efforts. He wrote much of the music in the Gospel Hymns, of which he was one of the joint compilers.

I Will Sing the Wondrous Story

Words by F. W. Rawley   Music by Peter P. Bilborn

> I will sing the wondrous story,
> Of the Christ who died for me.

The words of this hymn were written by F. H. Rawley, and the music by Peter Bilhorn, from whom I secured it in 1887 for use in Gospel Hymns and Sacred Songs and Solos. The hymn commenced in its original form, "Can't you sing the wondrous story," from which I changed it to "I will sing." It was greatly blessed in our meetings in Aberdeen, Glasgow, and other places in Great Britain, many persons testifying to having been benefited by its use.

In the Cross of Christ I Glory

Words by Sir John Bowring   Music by Ithamar Conkey

> In the cross of Christ I glory,
> Towering o'er the wrecks of time.

Sir John Bowring, a native of Exeter, England, is the author of this strengthening hymn. He was nominally a Unitarian, but in fact he was a man who lived and died possessed of a clear, strong evangelical faith in the virtue of the blood of the atonement. Before he was sixteen he had mastered five languages without the aid of a teacher. He was engaged in the woolen trade with his father, but early took to literary pursuits, and distinguished himself therein. He was twice elected to Parliament. In 1828 the University of Groningen conferred upon him the degree of LL. D. In 1845 he was appointed English consul at Canton, China, and he finally became Commander-in-Chief and Vice Admiral of Hong Kong. He was knighted by the Queen in 1854. He died in 1872, with peace in his heart and in the hope of the resurrection of the just. On his tombstone is inscribed, "In the Cross of Christ I Glory."

Sir John Bowring was one of the most remarkable men of his day. He was born 1792, his father being a manufacturer of woolen goods for China and other distant countries. When only six years of age Sir John had mastered six languages, and before long he knew no less than thirteen. At the age of forty-three he was elected to the Parliament, and after filling many positions of honour, both home and abroad, he was knighted in 1854. He wrote many excellent hymns, besides volumes of political, economic and religious essays, which caused him to become a member of nearly every learned society in Europe. He lived to be over eighty years of age, and died in peace and joyful hope of the resurrection. On his tombstone may be found the first line of this, his immortal hymn, "In the cross of Christ I glory."

The tune "Rathbun," by Ithamar Conkey, of New York City, fits the words splendidly. Mr. Conkey was born 1815. He was a noted bass singer, and for a long time connected with the Calvary Church, New York. He died 1867.

In the Secret of His Presence

Words by Ellen Lakshmi Goreh   Music by George C. Stebbins

In the secret of His presence how my soul delights to hide!
Oh, how precious are the lessons which I learn at Jesus' side!

The author of the words of this beautiful hymn was a high-caste native of India. After her conversion to Christianity, it is said, she spent some years in the home of an English clergyman, and wrote the poem "In the Secret of His Presence" while there. It made its appearance in a book of poems of which she was the author. In 1883 the attention of Mr. Stebbins was called to it, and he wrote the music at that time. The hymn was first sung by him as an offertory in one of the churches in Brooklyn, New York. It was often repeated as an offertory, and on occasions was sung in evangelistic services. But it had its larger introduction to the public during the All-Winter Mission conducted by Mr. Moody and myself in London in the winter of 1883-84, when I sang it frequently, as did Mr. Stebbins, who spent several months assisting in the mission. It was also often sung by Miss Beaucham, daughter of the late Lady Beaucham and since the wife of Colonel Drury-Lowe, one of the heroes of the Indian Mutiny, and uncle of Lord Curzon, Viceroy and Governor-General of India. The hymn at once came into general favour, and the deeply spiritual tone of the words brought blessing to many. The song was afterwards published in "Gospel Hymns," and in "Sacred Songs and Solos." Very soon it found its way into all parts of the world. Dr. Hudson Taylor, head of the great China Inland Mission, stated at Northfield that it was the favourite hymn of his missionaries.

The winter of 1890-91 Mr. and Mrs. Stebbins spent in India. While visiting the city of Allahabad, the home of Miss Goreh, Mr. Stebbins sought her out and made her acquaintance. He found her engaged in mission work among the women of India, a modest, devoted Christian, held in high esteem by missionaries of all denominations and by all who knew her. Thus the two singers whose names had become associated in Christian song met each other, one from the far East, and one from beyond far Western seas – both inspired by the same Lord, in the secret of whose presence they long since came to abide.

It is Finished

Words by James Proctor   Music by Ira D. Sankey

> Nothing, either great or small
> Nothing, sinner, no.

The Scotch people are especially fond of this hymn. The author prefaced it with these lines: "Since I first discovered Jesus to be 'the end of the law for righteousness to everyone that believeth,' I have more than once met with a poor sinner seeking peace at the foot of Sinai instead of Calvary, and I have heard him again and again in bitter disappointment and fear groaning out, 'What must I do?' I have said to him, 'Do, do? What can you do? What do you need to do?'"

It is Well with My Soul

Words by H. G. Spafford   Music by P. P. Bliss

> When peace, like a river, attendeth my way,
> When sorrows like sea-billows roll.

When Mr. Moody and I were holding meetings in Edinburgh, in 1874, we heard the sad news of the loss the French steamer, "Ville de Havre," on her return from America to France, with a large number of members of the Ecumenical Council, whose meetings had been held in Philadelphia. On board the steamer was a Mrs. Spafford with her four children. In mid-ocean a collision took place with a large sailing vessel, causing the steamer to sink in half an hour. Nearly all on board were lost. Mrs. Spafford got her children out of their berths and up on deck. On being told that the vessel would soon sink, she knelt down with her children in prayer, asking God that they might be saved if possible; or be made willing to die, if that was His will. In a few minutes the vessel sank to the bottom of the sea, and the children were lost. One of the sailors of the vessel, named Lockurn – whom I afterward met in Scotland – while rowing over the spot where the vessel disappeared, discovered Mrs. Spafford floating in the water. Ten days later she was landed at Cardiff, Wales. From there she cabled to her husband, a lawyer in Chicago, the message, "Saved alone." Mr. Spafford, who was a Christian, had the message framed and hung up in his office. He started immediately for England to bring his wife to Chicago. Mr. Moody left his meetings in Edinburgh and went to

Liverpool to try to comfort the bereaved parents, and was greatly pleased to find that they were able to say: "It is well; the will of God be done."

In 1876, when we returned to Chicago to work, I was entertained at the home of Mr. and Mrs. Spafford for a number of weeks. During that time Mr. Spafford wrote the hymn, "It is well with my soul," in commemoration of the death of his children. P. P. Bliss composed the music and sang it for the first time at a meeting in Farwell Hall. The comforting fact in connection with this incident was that in one of our small meetings in North Chicago, a short time prior to their sailing for Europe, the children had been converted.

While still living in Chicago Mr. and Mrs. Spafford became much interested in the Second Coming of Christ. So zealous did Mr. Spafford become that be decided to go to Jerusalem with his wife and the one remaining daughter, and there await the coming of the Lord. Mr. Spafford died there not long afterward. Mrs. Spafford is the head of a society whose headquarters are in a building outside of Jerusalem, where a large number of people live, having all things in common. When I visited Jerusalem some years ago I met Mrs. Spafford on the Street of David. The next day I received a call from Miss Spafford, who is very popular among the natives and has become the teacher for a large body of children, instructing them in English literature and in American ways. This hymn was heard by a gentleman who had suffered great financial reverses in the panic of 1899, and who was in deepest despondency. When he learned the story of the hymn he exclaimed: "If Spafford could write such a beautiful resignation hymn I will never complain again."

I've Found a Friend

Words by J. G. Small   Music by George C. Stebbins

> I've found a Friend, oh, such a Friend!
> He loved me ere I knew Him.

The author of this hymn, J. G. Small, who was born in Edinburgh in 1817, and died in 1888, wrote many hymns and poems and published several collections of sacred song.

On one occasion when Mr. Moorehouse and I were holding meetings at Scarboro, in the north of England, the services were attended by a number of Quaker ladies, among them a cousin of John Bright, the great English statesman. Wishing to have this hymn sung at one of the meetings, this lady wrote out the following request: "Will Mr. Sankey please repeat the hymn, 'I've found a Friend,' in his usual way?" In thus wording her note she avoided asking me to sing, which is against the custom of the Society of Friends.

"We were holding a cottage prayer-meeting in a lodging house," says a minister of Nottinghamshire, England, "when a young man lodging there came in to the meeting in a funseeking manner. We sang, prayed and read a chapter out of God's Word, and then the young man asked if we would sing a hymn for him. He chose

> I've found a Friend, oh, such a Friend!
> He loved me ere I knew Him.

"When we had sung one verse he began to shed tears, and I am glad to say that he gave his heart to God through the singing of that beautiful hymn. The next morning he left the place, but before leaving he wrote me a letter, of which I give these extracts: 'I asked you to sing that hymn because it was a favourite of my darling sister, who is waiting for me at the gates in heaven. I have now promised to meet her there. By God's help, if we do not meet again on earth, I promise to meet you in heaven. You will always think of me when you sing, "I've Found a Friend." Show this letter to my two other friends.'"

Jesus, and Shall it Ever Be?

Words by Joseph Grigg   Music by H. Baker, Mus. Bac.

> Jesus, and shall it ever be
> A mortal man ashamed of Thee!

This well known hymn, which is found in nearly every hymn book, is said to have been written by Joseph Grigg when but a child. It had for its heading, when first published, "Shame of Jesus conquered by love, by a youth of ten years."

The author was the son of poor parents, and was brought up to mechanical pursuits; but he forsook his trade and became a minister, and preached in Silver Street, London, where he was very useful.

At a later period he wrote,

> Behold, a Stranger at the door,
> He gently knocks, has knocked before;

Has waited long, is waiting still:
You use no other friend so ill.

Jesus is Mine!

Words by Mrs. C. J. Bonar (Alt.)   Music by T. E. Perkias

Fade, fade, each earthly joy,
Jesus is mine!

This hymn, which has been largely used in Revival meetings and evangelistic services, was penned by the wife of Dr. Horatius Bonar. Originally it commenced:

Pass away, earthly joy,
Jesus is mine!

It has undergone many alterations, and the words as they stand in the popular hymn books of the day are those by which the hymn is best known.

Rev. E. P. Hammond relates the following striking story regarding this hymn:

When Mr. J. Denham Smith was holding a series of meetings in the Metropolitan Hall in Dublin, his own little boy about four years of age was very much interested, and deeply convicted of his sinfulness. He was very fond of singing, as were all the members of his father's family. One evening after they returned from the children's meeting, his mother and sisters gathered around the piano and began to sing some of their familiar hymns, when his voice mingled with the rest. Though so young, he had caught many of the refrains and could join in them most heartily. Finally, they came to the hymn which he had often heard the congregation sing, commencing,

Now I have found a Friend, Jesus is mine;
His love shall never end, Jesus is mine.

Though all the rest of the family present united in singing these words, his little lips were closed; at length he said, "Please, mamma, don't sing that hymn; Jesus is not mine yet." When his father returned they told him of it, but he replied, "Willie is too young to understand these things. After tea we will sing some more hymns, and bring in the one he objected to." They did so, and Willie again remonstrated, exclaiming, "Mamma, didn't I ask you not to sing that hymn? Jesus is not mine yet. I cannot sing it." The father was surprised, but still said nothing. Next morning, Willie did not come down to breakfast. After waiting for him some time, his father went upstairs, and there found him kneeling down by his bed, engaged in prayer. When the door opened he arose, and in the most earnest manner asked, "Papa, when is the next children's meeting? "Being told that it would be on Friday, he said, "Won't you ask them to pray for me, that the Holy Spirit may go up and down in my heart, so that I can with the rest sing, 'Now I have found a Friend, Jesus is mine?'"

At the next children's meeting Willie was present drinking in every word. At the close he pressed his way to his father's side, and putting his hand in his, he said, "Now, dear papa, I can sing with the rest, 'Now I have found a Friend, Jesus is mine! '"

From that time this little boy lived a consistent Christian life. Nine years after, when I was holding meetings in that same hall, that boy, then thirteen years of age, was present. Though I knew well his early history, I asked him if he was a Christian. He said he had reason to believe that he was. I then asked him when it was that he first began to love the Saviour. His quick, decisive answer was, "It seems to me that I always loved Him. I cannot remember the time when I first felt His love in my heart." And yet there was no doubt of the hour when he was so enabled to view the loving Jesus bleeding on Calvary's cross for him, when his heart went out in love and consecration, and the Spirit of God said to him, "Believe on the Lord Jesus Christ, and thou shalt be saved."

Jesus I Will Trust Thee

Words by Mary J. Walker   Music by Ira D. Sankey

> Jesus, I will trust Thee,
> Trust Thee with my soul.

Major Whittle gives an example of this hymn's usefulness, out of many instances: "I was holding meetings in Belfast. At one of the after-meetings I noticed a man remaining behind when almost all the others had gone. I spoke to him and found that he was a merchant in the city. He was in much distress about his sins. "I showed him Christ the Saviour, who died for sinners, and tried to get him to appropriate that Saviour to himself. "I saw there was a great struggle going on in his soul, the powers for good and evil evidently striving for the mastery. We went down on our knees and prayed. Then after a while he straightened himself up and gave vent to his feelings in this hymn, for he was a capital singer:

> Jesus, I will trust Thee,
> Trust Thee with my soul;
> Guilty, lost, and helpless,
> Thou canst make me whole.

"It was a song of victory over Satan, and a song of praise to Christ, through whom he had conquered. From that hour he has done splendid work for Christ among the worst of men."

Jesus Lover of My Soul

Words by Charles Wesley   Music by Simeon B. Marsh

> Jesus, Lover of my soul,
> Let me to Thy bosom fly.

Several incidents have been narrated as having suggested to Charles Wesley this hymn. One, that a narrow escape from death in a storm on the Atlantic inspired him to portray the thoughts of a Christian in deadly peril. Another, that as he stood at an open window on a summer day a little bird, pursued by a hawk, sought refuge in his bosom, giving him the idea of pointing out the soul's one sure place of refuge in time of need.

Mrs. Mary Hoover, of Bellefonte, Pennsylvania, whose grandmother was the heroine of the story, has related to her pastor this family tradition: Charles Wesley was preaching in the fields of the parish of Killyleagh, County Down, Ireland, when he was attacked by men who did not approve of his doctrines. He sought refuge in a house located on what was known as the Island Band Farm. The farmer's wife, Jane Lowrie Moore, told him to hide in the milk house, down in the garden. Soon the mob came and demanded the fugitive. She tried to quiet them by offering them refreshments. Going down to the milk house, she directed Mr. Wesley to get through the rear window and hide under the hedge, by which ran a little brook. In that hiding-place, with the cries of his pursuers all about him, he wrote this immortal hymn. Descendants of Mrs. Moore still live in the house, which is much the same as it was in Wesley's time.

The great evangelist and president of Oberlin College, Charles G.

Finney, was walking about his grounds shortly before his death. In the church where he had preached for forty years the evening service was going on. Presently he heard this hymn floating to him from the distance. He joined with the invisible congregation in singing the hymn to the end. Before the next morning he had joined the choir about the throne.

"An ungodly stranger," said Mr. Spurgeon, "stepping into one of our services at Exeter Hall, was brought to Christ by the singing of 'Jesus, Lover of my soul.' 'Does Jesus love me?' said he; 'then why should I live in enmity with Him?'"

Tom was a drummer boy in the army, and the men called him "the young deacon" because of his sobriety and religious example. One day the chaplain found him sitting under a tree alone, with tears in his eyes.

"Well, Tom, my boy, what is it?"

"I had a dream last night, which I can't get out of my mind."

"What was it?"

"My mother was a widow, poor but good. She never was like herself after my sister Mary died. A year ago she died, too; and I, having no home and no mother, came to the war. But last night I dreamed the war was over and I went back home, and just before I got to the house my sister and mother came out to meet me. I didn't seem to remember that they were dead. How glad they were "Oh, sir, it was just as real as you are real now."

"Thank God, Tom," said the chaplain, "that you have such a mother, not really dead, but in heaven."

The boy wiped his eyes and was comforted. The next day Tom's drum was heard all day long in a terrible battle. At night it was known that "the young deacon" was lying wounded on the field. In the evening, when all was still, they heard a voice singing away off on the field, and they felt sure that it was Tom's voice. Softly the words of "Jesus, Lover of my soul" floated on the wings of the night. After the second verse the voice grew weak and stopped. In the morning the soldiers found Tom sitting on the ground, leaning against a stump, dead.

A vessel had gone on the rocks in the English Channel. The crew, along with their captain; took to the boats and were lost. They might have been safe, had they remained on the vessel, as a huge wave carried her high up on the rocks. On the table in the captain's cabin was found a hymnbook, opened at this hymn, and in it lay the pencil which had marked the favourite words of the captain. While the hurricane was howling outside and the vessel sinking, he had drawn his pencil beneath these words of cheer:

> Jesus, Lover of my soul,
> Let me to Thy bosom fly,
> While the nearer waters roll,
> While the tempest still is high.

"I would rather have written that hymn of Wesley's, 'Jesus, Lover of my soul,'" Henry Ward Beecher once said, "than to have the fame of all the kings that ever sat on earth. It is more glorious; it has more power in it. I would rather be the author of that hymn than to hold the wealth of the richest man in New York. It will go on singing until the trump brings forth the angel band; and then I think it will mount up on some lip to the very presence of God."

A party of tourists formed a part of a large company gathered on the deck of an excursion steamer that was moving slowly down the Potomac one beautiful evening in the summer of 1881. A gentleman who has since gained a national reputation as an evangelist of song, had been delighting the party with the happy rendering of many familiar hymns, the last being the sweet petition so dear to every Christian, beginning, "Jesus, Lover of my soul." The singer gave the first two verses with much feeling, and a peculiar emphasis upon the concluding lines that thrilled every heart. A hush had fallen upon the listeners that was not broken for some seconds after the musical notes had died away. Then a gentleman made his way from the outskirts of the crowd to the side of the singer, and accosted him with:

"Beg your pardon, stranger, but were you actively engaged in the late war?"

"Yes, sir," the man of song answered courteously.

"I fought under General Grant."

"Well," said the first speaker, "I did my fighting on the other side, and think, indeed am quite sure, I was very near you one bright night, eighteen years ago this very month. It was much such a night as this. If I am not very much mistaken you were on guard duty. We, of the South, had sharp business on hand, and you were one of the enemy. I crept near your post of duty, my murderous weapon in my hand; the shadows hid me. As you paced back and forth you were humming the tune of the hymn you have just sung. I raised my gun and aimed at your heart, and I had been selected by my commander for the work because I was a sure shot. Then out upon the night rang the words:

> Cover my defenceless head
> With the shadow of Thy wing.

Your prayer was answered. I couldn't fire after that. And there was no attack made upon your camp that night. You were the man whose life I was spared from taking."

The singer grasped the hand of the southerner, and said with much emotion:

"I remember that night very well, and also the feeling of depression and loneliness with which I went forth to my duty. I knew my post was one of great danger, and I was more dejected than I remember to have been at any other time during the service. I paced my lonely beat, thinking of home and friends, and all that life holds dear. Then the thought of God's care for all that He has created came to me with peculiar force. If He so cared for the sparrows, how much more for man, created in His own image; and I sang the prayer of my heart, and ceased to be alone. How the prayer was answered I never knew till this evening."

Dr. George Duffield-himself the author of so fine a hymn as "Stand up, stand up for Jesus" – in his old age paid this tribute out of a lifelong experience: 'One of the most blessed days of my life was when I found, after my harp had long hung on the willows, that I could sing again; that a new song was put in my mouth; and when, ere ever I was aware, I was singing, 'Jesus, Lover of my soul.' If there is anything in Christian experience of joy and sorrow, of affliction and prosperity, of life and death-that hymn is the hymn of the ages!"

This was the last hymn we sang as the body of Mr. Moody was being lowered into the grave.

Jesus Loves Even Me

Words by P. P. Bliss   Music by P. P. Bliss

> I am so glad that our Father in heaven
> Tells of His love in the Book He has given.

"I think it was in June, 1870, that 'Jesus Loves Even Me' was written," writes Major Whittle. "Mr. and Mrs. Bliss were at that time members of my family in Chicago. One morning Mrs. Bliss came down to breakfast and said, as she entered the room: 'Last night Mr. Bliss had a tune given to him that I think is going to live and be one of the most useful that he has written. I have been singing it all the morning, and I cannot get it out of my mind.' She then sang the notes over to us. The idea of Bliss, in writing the hymn, was to bring out the truth that the peace and comfort of a Christian are not founded so much upon his love to Christ as upon Christ's love to him, and that to occupy the mind with Christ's love would produce love and consecration – as taught in Romans 5:5, 'The love of God [to us] is shed abroad in our hearts by the Holy Ghost, which is given unto us.' How much God has used this little song to lead sinners and doubting Christians to look away to Jesus, eternity alone can tell."

Mr. Bliss said that this song was suggested to him by hearing the chorus of the hymn, "Oh, how I love Jesus," repeated very frequently in a meeting which he attended. After joining in the chorus a number of times the thought came to him, "Have I not been singing enough about my poor love for Jesus, and shall I not rather sing of His great love for me?" Under the impulse of this thought he went home and composed this, one of his most popular children's hymns.

A young woman went to a meeting in Dundee, where she heard Mr. Sankey singing the children's hymn:

> I am so glad that our Father in heaven
> Tells of His love in the book He has given:
> Wonderful things in the Bible I see;
> This is the dearest that Jesus loves me.
> I am so glad that Jesus loves me,
> Jesus loves me, Jesus loves even me.

While the hymn was being sung she began to feel for the first time in her life that she was a sinner. All her sins came up in an array before her; and so numerous and aggravated did they appear that she imagined she could never be saved. She said in her heart, 'Jesus cannot love me. He could not love such a sinner as I.' She went home in a state of extreme mental anguish, and did not sleep that night. Every opportunity to obtain more light was eagerly seized. She took her place in the inquiry-room; and there she found, to her astonishment and joy that Jesus could, did, and does love sinners. She saw in God's open word that it was for sinners that He died, and for none others. When she realized this she began to sing:

> I am so glad that Jesus loves me,
> Jesus loves me, Jesus loves even me.

Quiet, thoughtful, modest, and in every respect a consistent disciple of Jesus, she is now a member of a church here, and is much esteemed by her fellow-Christians.

The following letter was sent to me by a worker during my first visit with Mr. Moody to Dundee in 1874:

"Dear Sir, — The Lord is using in many ways your service of praise. Some of these come to your knowledge; many do not. A Christian mother who has been attending some of these meetings, taught her little girl, a child scarcely three years of age, to say, 'Jesus loves me, even me!' Her father, who would not be prevailed on by his wife to go to any of the meetings, on returning from his work the other evening, was met by the little one at the door, saying 'Pa, Jesus loves me, Jesus loves even oo' (you).' Her father's heart was touched, tears filled his eyes. The little one accomplished what exhortation had failed to do. Will you pray that God would bless his attendance at the meetings?"

A commercial traveller in relating the story of his conversion while Mr. Moody and I were holding meetings at the City Hall, Glasgow, tells how disappointed he was in not being able to converse with Mr. Moody at the conclusion of a meeting. He goes on to say:

"I went down the stairs, and in going down I said, 'Well, if they won't speak to me, surely God will.' I went home, thinking and praying in my heart that God would show me the way home to Himself. I was saying, 'Well, I'll begin and try to love Jesus for what He has done for me.' I was passing down Stockwell Street in this frame of mind, when some persons passed me, singing the refrain of that beautiful hymn,

> I am so glad that Jesus loves me, Jesus loves even me.

"The words struck me. I felt as if a load were passing from my heart. 'If He loves me,' I said, 'all I have to do is to believe in that love of His.' Here I had been trying to love Jesus, when all the while Jesus had been loving me. I put faith in that love, and found peace. 'Yes,' I said, and I stamped my foot on the ground as I said it; 'yes, though all the devils in hell try to move me from it, I will trust in the love that Jesus has had for me.'"

A minister was holding meetings in Indiana. A few miles distant lived an old Englishman who had not been inside a church for seven years. He was persuaded to take his children to the meeting one Sunday night. He declared afterward that nothing of what was said or done interested him until the close of the service, when 'Jesus loves me' was sung. On his way home, and until he went to sleep, he could think of nothing but the hymn. When he awoke in the morning the first thing he thought of was, 'Jesus loves me.' He could not get it out of his mind, and when he was out in the field afterward he could think of nothing else. Was it possible that God could love a sinner like him? His eyes were so blinded with tears that he could not see to go on with his work. Out on that lonely field the old man found his Saviour. The next evening he visited the meeting, and as he told his experience tears were in the eyes of all the people.

During the winter after the great fire in Chicago, when the place was being built up with small frame houses for the poor, a mother sent for me one day to visit her little sick girl, who was one of our Sunday-school scholars. I remembered her quite well, and was glad to go. Finding that she was beyond hope of recovery, I asked how it was with her.

"It is all well with me," she replied; "but I wish you would speak to father and mother."

It was plain that she loved Jesus, and I asked her when she became a Christian. "Don't you remember last Thursday in the Tabernacle," she said, "when we had the children's meeting, and you sang 'Jesus loves me,' and don't you remember how you told us that if we would give our hearts to Him He would love us? It was that day that I gave myself to Jesus. And now I am going to be with Him, for the doctors say that I will die today."

The testimony of that little girl, in that neglected quarter of the city, did more to encourage me to sing on than anything else, for she was my first convert.

This song was much used in the meetings conducted by Mr. Moody in Great Britain in 1873-4, and was given out to the congregation as an opening hymn more often than any other. As written by Mr. Bliss it consisted of three verses and a chorus. Someone unknown to the writer has written three additional verses beginning, 'Jesus loves me, and I know I love Him.'"

Jesus Love Me

Words by Anna B. Warner   Music by William B. Bradbury

Jesus loves me! This I know
For the Bible tells me so.

Dr. Jacob Chamberlain, who for many years has been working among the Hindus, writes as follows regarding this hymn, long one of the most popular children's songs in the world: "Many years ago I translated into Telugu the children's hymn, 'Jesus loves me' and taught it to the children of our day-school. "Scarcely a week later, as I was going through the narrow streets of the native town on horseback, I heard singing that sounded natural, down a side street. I stopped to listen, cautiously drawing up to the corner, where unobserved I could look down the street and see and hear. "And there was a little heathen boy, with heathen men and women standing around him, singing away at the top of his voice:

Jesus loves me! This I know,
For the Bible tells me so...
Yes, Jesus loves me!
The Bible tells me so!

"As he completed the verse someone asked the question: 'Sonny, where did you learn that song?' "'Over at the Missionary School,' was the answer. 'Who is that Jesus, and what is the Bible?' 'Oh! the Bible is the book from God, they say, to teach us how to get to heaven, and Jesus is the name of the divine Redeemer that came into the world to save us from our sins; that is what the missionaries say.' "'Well, the song is a nice one. Come, sing us some more.' And so the little boy went on – a heathen himself, and singing to the heathen – about Jesus and His love. That is preaching the Gospel by proxy,' I said to myself, as I turned my pony and rode away, well satisfied to leave my little proxy to tell his interested audience all he himself knew, and sing to them over and over that sweet song of salvation."

Jesus of Nazareth Passeth By

Words by Emma Campbell   Music by T. E. Perkins

What means this eager, anxious throng,
Which moves with busy haste along?
The hymn was written during a religious revival in Newark, New Jersey,

in 1863-'64, where hundreds were converted. One afternoon Mr. R. G. Pardee made a very earnest address from Luke 18:37: "They told him that Jesus of Nazareth passeth by." Miss Emma Campbell was present, heard the address and saw how the community was stirred, and soon afterward she wrote these stanzas. E. P. Hammond, who had conducted the revival meetings, tried the verses to the tune of 'Sweet hour of prayer.'"

Later Mr. T. E. Perkins wrote the tune to which this hymn is now sung. It was one of the first favourites at our meetings in England. The printed records of the meetings of these days bear testimony that hundreds confessed to have accepted Christ during the singing of this hymn as a solo.

Andrew A. Bonar – brother of Dr. Horatius Bonar, the great hymn-writer – speaking of this hymn in his "Life of James Scott," says, "Some of us in listening to these two messengers, the one singing, the other preaching, used to think of what is told in Second Kings 3:15. Elisha, before beginning to prophesy, called for a minstrel, and when the camp of soldiers had been calmed and melted by harp and song, the hand of the Lord came upon the speaker. Had you been in Edinburgh during the four months when these brethren were there in 1873, you would have seen multitudes of all ages and stations hastening to the place of meeting, at whatever hour, any day of the week. The scene was exactly that described in the hymn, so often sung, and so much blessed,

> What means this eager, anxious throng,
> Which moves with busy haste along,
> These wondrous gatherings day by day?
> What means this strange commotion, pray?'

An officer of the English army sends me the following incident: "A soldier was stationed at Edinburgh Castle, and one evening left his post on a pass until midnight. He had a week's pay in one pocket and the washing money earned by his wife in the other, and was on his way to the public house to have a night in gambling. His eye caught the poster outside the Tolbooth Church, announcing your meetings. The officer liked the singing, and went in just to hear one song. As he entered Mr. Moody was preaching on 'The Blood.' That had no interest for him. After the address you sang, 'Jesus of Nazareth passeth by.' He listened with deep interest to the hymn. 'Too late, too late,' was God's arrow to his soul. An officer of his regiment and I went into the inquiry-room, and among a great crowd we saw this comrade's red coat. He was in great distress. We spoke to him, holding to John 3:16.

"That night the man went home instead of to the public house, and his wife was astonished to see him so early, and sober. He laid down all the money on the table, which astonished her still more. Then he went to bed, but was in too great distress to be able to sleep. The words 'Too late, too late' rang in his ears. About two o'clock in the morning John 3:16 gleamed into his soul. He leaped from the bed, pleaded that grand promise, and Jesus received him. "This was told the following morning by himself at the Castle. He held to his faith, and when the regiment left he was known throughout the camp as a man of God. The glorious Gospel with him began in song and goes on in song."

A similar experience is related by another convert: "It was on the 28th of December that I like (I dare say) a great many others, went up to the Assembly Hall, out of sheer curiosity, an unconverted sinner. I heard Mr. Moody preach, and I am sorry to say I was very little affected by it. After Mr. Moody had finished his discourse, Mr. Sankey sang, 'Jesus of Nazareth passeth by.' I was deeply moved by it, and when he came to the lines,

> Too late! Too late! Will be the cry;
> Jesus of Nazareth has passed by;

I thought to myself, will that not be my cry? Will God not then say to me, 'Depart from me, I never knew you?' I felt a great anguish of soul, but I went home without remaining to the inquiry-meeting. All the way home those two lines still rang in my ears. It was a long time before I could go to sleep. My brain seemed all afire; my past sins came up one by one before my mind. At last I fell asleep, but only to wake with a start under the impression that a bright light had suddenly been extinguished in my room, and had left me in utter darkness. Immediately those lines sounded in my ears. I was able to be the interpreter of my own dream. The bright light was Jesus, and the darkness was that of my own soul; for He had passed by and I had not been saved. I had very little sleep that night. On the Monday night I came to the inquiry meeting and Mr. – spoke to me, showing me plainly that I had nothing to do – Christ had done it all. I was only to believe in him. And before I left the hall that evening, by the blessing of God I was able to accept Christ as my Saviour. Upon going home I opened a Bible, and the first words that met my eye were John 3:16: 'God so loved the world that He gave His only begotten Son, that whosoever believeth in Him should not perish, but have everlasting life.' I knew the whosoever included myself, and I rejoiced in it. I am doing so now; and, by the help of God, I hope to do so till I find myself in my Saviour's arms."

At one of our early meetings in Edinburgh an old gentleman, more than seventy years of age, threw himself down on his knees and, sobbing like a child, said: "I was utterly careless about my soul until last night, but I have been so unhappy since I could not sleep. I seemed to hear ringing in my ears, 'Jesus of Nazareth passeth by,' and I feel that if I am not saved now, I never shall be."

A lady traveling in the East tells of a visit she made to the Girls' Orphanage in Nazareth, an institution established many years ago in the town where Jesus spent so many years of His early life. The Orphanage was established by a society of Christians in London. Here the lady heard the children sweetly singing: "Jesus of Nazareth passeth by," and she says that the children were sure the words were all meant for them.

"It was a few evenings ago," said a youth in the Young Men's Meeting in Roby Chapel, "when Mr. Sankey was singing in the Free Trade Hall, Manchester, 'Jesus of Nazareth passeth by,' that I was made to feel the need of my Saviour; and when he came to these words. 'Too late, too late,' I said to myself it must not be too late for me, and I took Him to my heart there and then."

A young naval officer attended one of our meetings in London. On being asked how he liked the address he replied: "I did not hear it, but I did like that song, 'What means this eager, anxious throng?' He was invited to attend again, and he responded: "Well, I enjoyed that solo, and I will go to hear the singing." He did so; the same song was sung again, and so moved him that he remained for the inquiry meeting. There he was saved through the mercy of God. A week later, in an accident, he was instantly killed, and so suddenly passed into the company of the redeemed.

Jesus Saves

Words by Priscilla J. Owens   Music by Wm. J. Kirkpatrick

> We have heard the joyful sound;
> Jesus saves! Jesus saves!

Mr. Kirkpatrick is a resident of Philadelphia, and was associated with John R. Sweeney in the publication of several hymn-books. He is the author of many popular hymns, "Jesus saves," and "Meekly wait and murmur not," perhaps being the best known of his compositions. Both of these hymns were extensively used in our meetings, and greatly blessed to many souls.

Jesus, Saviour, Pilot Me

Words by Edward Hopper   Music by J. E. Gould

> Jesus, Saviour, pilot me,
> Over life's tempestuous sea.

The author of this hymn was born in New York in 1818, and for many years was the pastor of the Church of Sea and Land, in that city. The hymn was first published in 1871, in "The Sailors' Magazine."

Major D. W. Whittle told me the following incident in connection with this hymn: "I went with General O. O. Howard to hold meetings for the soldiers at Tampa, Florida, and one day while going through the camp I found a young man dying of fever. I knelt by his side and asked him if he was a Christian. He replied that he was not, but said that his father and mother were Christians; and he asked me to pray for him. I did so, but no deep impression was made upon his heart. I went away with a sorrowing heart and promised to return another day. Two days later I visited him again and, praying with him, the Lord put into my mind to sing, 'Jesus, Saviour, pilot me.' "The dying soldier said: 'Oh, that sounds good; it puts me in mind of my beloved sister in Michigan, who used to sing this hymn for me before I entered the army.' "He wanted me to repeat it over and over again for him, and finally he asked: 'Will Jesus be my pilot into the haven of rest?' I told the young man that Jesus would. "'Then,' he said, 'I will trust Him with all my heart.' "The next day I called to see him again, but his comrade said: 'He passed away during the night.'"

Jewels

Words by W. O. Cushing   Music by G. F. Root

> When He cometh, when He cometh,
> To make up His jewels.

This hymn was written by W. O. Cushing and set to music by G. F. Root, and is one of the most popular children's hymns in the world. He wrote many hymns for me, among the most popular of which may be mentioned, "Hiding in Thee" and "There'll be no Dark Valley." William Orcott Cushing was born in Hingham, Mass., 1823, and was converted while yet a child. He entered the ministry, and continued therein for many years, until he partly lost the power of speech. This caused him to give up preaching, but the prayer which he made, "Lord still give me something to do for Thee!" was wonderfully answered, and he was permitted to write hymns for children, many of which have been blessed to tens of thousands throughout the world, whom his voice as a preacher could never have reached. "Jewels" takes rank with "Come to the Saviour" and "I am so glad that Jesus loves me," two of the most popular children's hymns in the world. Mr. Cushing died 1902.

A minister returning from Europe on an English steamer visited the steerage, and after some friendly talk, proposed a singing service – if something could be started that "everybody" knew – for there were hundreds of emigrants there from nearly every part of Europe. "It'll have to be an American tune, then," said the steerage-master; "try 'His Jewels.'" The minister struck out at once with the melody and words

> When He cometh, when He cometh,

And scores of the poor, half-fed multitude joined voices with him. Many probably recognized the music of the old glee, and some had heard the sweet air played in the church steeples at home. Other voices chimed in, male and female, catching the air and sometimes the words – they were so easy and so many times repeated – and the volume of song increased, till the singing minister stood in the midst of an international concert, the most novel that he ever led. (Theron Brown's Story of the Hymns and Tunes).

George Frederick Root, Doctor of Music, the author of the tune, was born in Sheffield, Mass., 1820, and died 1895.

Just as I Am

Words by Charlotte Elliott   Music by William B. Bradbury

Just as I am, without one plea,
But that Thy blood was shed for me.

Miss Charlotte Elliott was visiting some friends in the West End of London, and there met the eminent minister, Cesar Malan. While seated at supper, the minister said he hoped that she was a Christian. She took offense at this, and replied that she would rather not discuss that question. Dr. Malan said that he was sorry if he had offended her, that he always liked to speak a word for his Master, and that he hoped that the young lady would someday become a worker for Christ. When they met again at the home of a mutual friend, three weeks later, Miss Elliott told the minister that ever since he had spoken to her she had been trying to find her Saviour, and that she now wished him to tell her how to come to Christ. "Just come to Him as you are," Dr. Malan said. This she did, and went away rejoicing. Shortly afterward she wrote this hymn, "Just as I am, without one plea." It was first published in "The Invalid's Hymn Book," in 1836.

"In all my preaching," said her brother, H. V. Elliott, "I have not done so much good as my sister has been permitted to accomplish by writing her one hymn, 'Just as I am.'"

A little street waif in New York City came to a missionary with a torn and dirty piece of paper, on which this hymn was printed.

"Please, sir," he said, "father sent me to get a clean copy like that."

The missionary learned that the child's sister had loved to sing it, and that this copy had been found in her pocket after her death. The father wanted to obtain a clean copy of the verses in order to frame them.

During a service of song in a Christian church, John B. Gough was asked by a man in the pew with him what was to be sung, as the announcement had not been heard. The questioner was most repulsive in appearance, because of a nervous disease that disfigured his face and form. When the singing began, Gough was driven almost to frenzy by the harsh and discordant tones of the singer by his side. But when they came to "Just as I am, poor, wretched, blind," the wretched creature lifted his sightless eyes to heaven and sang with his whole soul. The great orator, in his impassioned and inimitable way, said:

"I have heard the finest strains of orchestra, choir, and soloist this world can produce, but I never heard music until I heard that blind man sing, 'O, Lamb of God, I come, I come.'"

Knocking, Knocking

Words by Mrs. Harriet Beecher   Stowe Music by George F. Root

> Knocking, knocking, who is there?
> Waiting, waiting, oh, how fair.

This hymn was written by Mrs. H. B. Stowe, the well-known author of "Uncle Tom's Cabin." Mrs. Stowe wrote several hymns, but this is perhaps the most popular. The tune was written by George F. Root.

The Rev. W. Hay Aitken, Canon of Norwich, relates the following incident regarding this hymn:

"A little girl, only eight years old, coming home with her mother from an evangelistic meeting remarked, 'Mother, I don't think that hymn ends right, because you see it leaves the Saviour outside at the close:

> Yes, the pierced hand still knocketh,
> And beneath the crowned hair,
> Beam the patient eyes, so tender.
> Of thy Saviour waiting there.

I don't think it ought to end like that.' So with her mind and heart filled with this thought the little maiden remained for a season closeted in her room. When at last she reappeared she slipped a little bit of paper into her mother's hand. 'There, mother,' she exclaimed, 'I think it ought to have something at the end like that.'

"Her mother, greatly astonished, unfolded the paper and read as follows:

> Enter! enter! Heavenly Guest!
> Welcome! welcome! to my breast.
> I have long withstood Thy knocking,
> For my heart was full of sin,
> But Thy love hath overcome me,
> Blessed Jesus! — oh, come in!

"The mother was so struck with the child's verse, as well indeed she might be, that she forwarded it with an explanatory note to a religious newspaper, and thus it met my eye, and I incorporated it into the version of the hymn in our mission book.

"In a mission I was holding in a country town in the Midlands I came into contact with a young fellow who seemed much in earnest, but found great difficulty in accepting and applying to his heart the simple Gospel message. The choir were singing the third and what was originally the last verse of this particular hymn, while the verse added by the little maiden still remained to be sung. An inspiration seemed to seize me, and bending over the young man's shoulder I pointed to this verse and whispered, 'Run your eye over those words while they are finishing the verse that they are now singing, and then join in with all your heart in singing that last verse.' He glanced obediently at the verse, his face shadowed with the dull and bewildered expression of religious despondency, feeling, no doubt, as if there was and could be no blessing for him.

"'Now,' I whispered, 'sing it with all your heart!' and the next moment, to my great satisfaction, he was joining with heart and voice. It was really like a transformation scene in a dissolving view. I closely watched his face as he sang, and saw it gradually light up, until I may say it was all ablaze with a new brightness, for the prayer 'Enter, enter! Heavenly Guest; Welcome! welcome! to my breast!' was being answered, and as the hymn closed I grasped his hand and whispered, 'It's all right now, isn't it?' Back came the joyous response, 'Yes, thank God, it is all right now! 'And he went on his way rejoicing. His joining with heart and voice in the words of the little maiden's verse had done more for him than all the explanations of the Gospel offered by my friend and myself during our mission."

Lead Kindly Light

Words by John H. Newman   Music by John B. Dykes

Lead, kindly Light, amid the encircling gloom,
Lead Thou me on.

Dr. Newman wrote this hymn in 1833, just before he entered upon the tractarian movement in the Established Church. He had been at Rome, and stopping at Sicily on his homeward way, he there became dangerously ill of fever. Upon recovery, he took passage on an orange boat for Marseilles, being under the impression that he must return to England and begin a movement for the reformation of the Church in accord with his peculiar views. The sailing vessel was becalmed for a week in the Straits of Bonifacio, between Corsica and Sardinia. It was on this vessel and under such circumstances, his body sweltering in the heat and his mind racked with conflicting views as to his duty in the contemplated mission to the Established Church, that he penned the lines of this now cherished hymn. Its original title was "The Pillar of the Cloud," the hymn appearing first in "The British Magazine."

Let the Lower Lights be Burning

Words by P. P. Bliss   Music by P. P. Bliss

> Brightly beams our Father's mercy
> From His lighthouse evermore.

The words of this hymn were suggested to Mr. Bliss on hearing Mr. Moody tell the following incident: "On a dark, stormy night, when the waves rolled like mountains and not a star was to be seen, a boat, rocking and plunging, neared the Cleveland harbour. 'Are you sure this is Cleveland?' asked the captain, seeing only one light from the lighthouse. "'Quite sure, sir,' replied the pilot. "'Where are the lower lights?' "'Gone out, sir.' "'Can you make the harbour?' "'We must, or perish, sir!' "With a strong hand and a brave heart the old pilot turned the wheel. But alas, in the darkness he missed the channel, and with a crash upon the rocks the boat was shivered, and many a life lost in a watery grave. Brethren, the Master will take care of the great lighthouse; let us keep the lower lights burning!"

Let the Saviour In

Words by J. B. Atchinson   Music by E. O. Excell

> There's a Stranger at the door;
> Let Him in!

In Great Britain this favourite hymn brought blessing to a retired colonel of the English army, at one of Mr. Moody's meetings on the banks of the Thames. The colonel had become anxious about his spiritual condition, and decided to go to London to attend our meetings there. At the conclusion of one of the evening services, as he was about to leave the great building, his attention was arrested by a sweet voice singing,

"Let the Saviour in."

On taking the train at Paddington station for Bournemouth, the song remained in his heart and the wheels of the train seemed to repeat in his ears the refrain, "Let him in! Let the Saviour in!" He went again to London and sought out the singer whose voice had so impressed him. She was a lady of high rank, and in the course of a few months became the wife of the gallant colonel. A year later they moved to Florida, where I had the pleasure of visiting them in their home. On my invitation, they accompanied me to a near-by town where I was holding meetings. At the conclusion of my lecture the lady sang this hymn again, and so sweetly that it moved the audience to tears.

Missionary Hymn

Words by R. Heber   Music by Dr. Lowell

From Greenland's icy mountains.
From India's coral strand.

The author of this hymn was Dean of Hodnet and afterward Bishop of Calcutta. He was visiting his father-in-law, the Vicar of Wrexham, they being together in the Vicar's study on the Saturday before Whitsunday, 1819. Each was preparing a missionary sermon to be delivered the following day, when the Vicar spoke up:

"Heber, write something appropriate to sing at our services tomorrow."

Immediately retiring to the other end of the room, Heber sat down by the window and composed the four stanzas which now constitute this hymn. He wanted to add a fifth, but the Vicar said: "Nay; you will only destroy the beauty and symmetry of the composition; let it stand." The song was sung for the first time on that Whit-sunday. Bishop Heber laid down his life, seven years later, on the mission field of India. Of the many hymns which he wrote, nearly all are in common use.

Moment by Moment

Words by D. W. Whittle   Music by May Whittle Moody

Dying with Jesus, by death reckoned mine;
Living with Jesus a new life divine.

While I was attending the World's Fair, in Chicago, Henry Varley, a lay preacher from London, said to Major Whittle: "I do not like the hymn 'I need Thee every hour' very well, because I need Him every moment of the day."

Soon after Major Whittle wrote this sweet hymn, having the chorus:

> Moment by moment I'm kept in His love;
> Moment by moment I've life from above;
> Looking to Jesus till glory doth shine;
> Moment by moment, O Lord. I am Thine.

Mr. Whittle brought the hymn to me in manuscript a little later, saying that he would give me the copyright of both the words and music if I would print for him five hundred copies on fine paper, for distributing among his friends. His daughter, May Whittle, who later became the wife of Will R. Moody, composed the music. I did as Mr. Whittle wished; and I sent the hymn to England, where it was copyrighted on the same day as at Washington.

In England the hymn became very popular. Falling into the hands of the well-known Andrew Murray, of South Africa, then visiting London, he adopted it as his favourite hymn. A year later Mr. Murray visited Northfield, and while holding a meeting for men in the church he remarked: "If Sankey only knew a hymn which I found in London, and would sing it, he would find that it embraces my entire creed."

I was very anxious to know what hymn it was, and when he had recited it I said to him: "Doctor, that hymn was written within five hundred yards of where we are standing."

For years Dr. Murray had his wife sing this hymn in nearly all his meetings. It also became a great favourite in South Africa during the war.

More Love to Thee, O Christ

Words by Mrs. Elizabeth Prentiss   Music by W. H. Doane

> More love to Thee, O Christ!
> More love to Thee.

This favourite hymn was written by Mrs. Elizabeth Payson Prentiss, who was born in Portland, Me., 1818, and in 1845 became the wife of George L. Prentiss, D. D., who afterward became Professor of Theology at the Union Seminary, New York City. The hymn was written in 1869, and first printed on a fly-sheet. It became a useful revival hymn in the years that followed. Mrs. Prentiss, who wrote many well-known poems, was an invalid the greater part of her life, and died in 1878. The music was composed by W. H. Doane.

More to Follow

Words by P. P. Bliss   Music by P. P. Bliss

> Have you on the Lord believed?
> Still there's more to follow.

The suggestion for this hymn came to Mr. Bliss through hearing Mr. Moody tell the story of a vast fortune which was left in the hands of a minister for one of his poor parishioners. Fearing that it might be squandered if suddenly bestowed upon the beneficiary, the wise minister sent him a little at the time with a note, saying:

"This is thine; use it wisely; there is more to follow."

Must I Go, and Empty-Handed?

Words by C. C. Luther   Music by George C. Stebbins

> Must I go, and empty-handed?
> Thus my dear Redeemer meet?

During a series of evangelistic meetings A. G. Upham referred in his sermon to a young man who, dying after only a month of Christian service, said to a friend, "No, I am not afraid; Jesus saves me now. But oh! Must I go, and empty-handed?" The incident made a strong impression upon C. C. Luther for whom Mr. Upham was preaching – and in a few minutes the words of this hymn had arranged themselves in Mr. Luther's mind. A few days later he handed them to Mr. Stebbins, who composed the popular tune with which they are associated.

About fifteen years ago a man who was living a reckless, godless life, went to a Sunday morning service in a mission hall in Essex, England. This hymn was used in the service, and as the third verse was rendered,

> Oh, the years of sinning wasted,
> Could I but recall them now,
> I would give them to my Saviour,
> To His will I'd gladly bow.

The man was so forcibly impressed that he could not take part in the singing. He went home miserable, and was unable to eat any dinner. In the afternoon he went to a Bible-class for workingmen, conducted at the other end of the village. As he entered the same hymn was being sung that had made him so miserable in the morning, "Must I go, and empty-handed?" The man was so moved by the words of the hymn, and so impressed by the coincidence of its being sung at both places where he had attended, that it resulted in his conversion. He lived a consistent life thereafter, showing a real change of heart and a strong desire to no longer waste his years in sinning.

My Ain Countrie

Words by Mary Lee Demarest   Music by Mrs. Ione T. Hanns
                                              (arr. by H. P. M.)

> I am far frae my hame,
> an' I'm weary aften-whiles,
> For the longed-for hame-bringin',
> an my Faither's welcome smiles.

Many years ago John Macduff and his young bride left Scotland on a sailing vessel for America, there to seek their fortune. After tarrying a few weeks in New York they went west, where they were successful in accumulating a good competence. By-and-by the wife's health began to fail. The anxious husband said that he feared she was homesick.

"John," she replied, "I am wearying for my ain countrie; will ye not taik me to the sea, that I may see the ships sailing to the homeland once more?"

Her husband's heart was moved with compassion. In a few weeks he sold their Western home and took his wife east to a pleasant little cottage by the sea, whose further shore broke on the rocks that line the coast of Scotland. She would often sit and gaze wistfully at the ships sailing from the bay, one after another disappearing below the horizon on their way to her ain countrie. Although she uttered no complaint, it was evident that she was silently pining away. John was afraid that she would die in a foreign land; and as an effort to save her he sold his New England home, and took her back across the ocean. She was speedily recovered by the keen mountain air, the sight of purple heather, nodding bluebells, and hedge-rows white with fragrant hawthorn blossoms in bonnie Scotland, her own dear native land. To her it was home. And there is no sweeter word in any language than home!

A few years prior to this time, in 1838, Mary Lee was born at Croton Falls, New York. At an early age she lost her mother and was left in charge of a Scotch nurse, from whom she learned something of the Scottish dialect. And her grandfather, a native of Scotland, had often sung little Mary to sleep with Scottish lullabies. As a young woman she was refined and highly educated, and she exhibited unusual literary talent. Most of all she was esteemed for her noble Christian character, manifested in daily life. At the age of twenty-three, Mary Lee wrote this immortal poem after hearing the story of John Macduff and his wife, and published it first in "The New York Observer." Later it appeared in a volume of her poems. After her marriage to Mr. Demarest they resided in Pasadena, California, where she died in 1887. While visiting that town a number of years later, I went to the cemetery to see if I could find the grave of the beloved hymn-writer, but was unable to do so. Afterward I learned that her body was brought east and buried in a small town not far from Albany, New York.

This hymn was one of my favourite solos, and was much loved by Mr. Moody.

My Country, 'Tis of Thee

Words by S. F. Smith, D. D.   Music by Henry Care,

My country, 'tis of thee,
Sweet land of liberty.

The words of this popular hymn, now known as the national hymn of America, were written in 1832. Dr. Smith says: "I found the tune in a German music book, brought to this country by the late William C. Woodbridge, and put into my hands by Lowell Mason, because I could read German books and he could not." The real origin of the tune is much disputed, but the credit is usually given to Henry Carey. The hymn was first sung at a children's Fourth of July celebration, in the Park Street Church, Boston. Dr. Samuel Francis Smith was born in Boston, October 21, 1808. He died in the same city, November 16, 1895, at the "New York and New England" depot, while on his way to fulfil an engagement to preach at Readville. While traveling in Egypt I met the author's son, who is a missionary in that country, and said to him that if I ever got home I would sing his father's song with new interest; for I was now more than ever convinced that my beloved America, the land of liberty, was the dearest of all lands to me.

Dr. Smith visited the Board of Trade in Chicago in May of 1887. While sitting in the gallery he was pointed out to some of the members. Soon he became the center of considerable notice. All at once the trading on the floor ceased, and from the wheat-pit came the familiar words, "My country, 'tis of thee." After two stanzas had been sung, Dr. Smith arose and bowed. A rousing cheer was given by the men on the floor, to which Dr. Smith was now escorted by the secretary of the Board. The members flocked around Dr. Smith and grasped his hand. Then they opened a passage through the crowd and led him to the wheat-pit, where they took off their hats and sang the rest of the hymn.

My Faith Looks Up to Thee

Words by Ray Palmer   Music by Dr. Lowell Mason

> My faith looks up to Thee,
> Thou Lamb of Calvary.

"I gave form to what I felt," says Dr. Palmer, "by writing, with little effort, the stanzas. I recollect I wrote them with tender emotion and ended the last line with tears." He placed the manuscript in a pocketbook, and carried it there for some time. One day, in Boston, he met Dr. Lowell Mason, who inquired if Mr. Palmer had not some hymn to contribute to his new book. The pocket-book was produced and the hymn was brought to light. Dr. Mason took a copy of the song, and after reaching home was so much impressed with it that he wrote for it the famous tune "Olivet," to which it is usually sung. A short time after he met the author on the street and exclaimed:

"Mr. Palmer, you may live many years and do many good things, but I think you will be best known to posterity as the author of 'My faith looks up to Thee.'"

The hymn was published in 1832, but did not at first receive much notice. Andrew Reed, D.D., of Scotland – who wrote "Why not tonight?" for which I composed the music-found a copy of the hymn in a religious newspaper while traveling in this country, took it home, and published it anonymously in his hymn-book.

Dr. Palmer wrote me the following incident: "During the Civil War, and on the evening preceding a terrible battle, six or eight Christian young men, who were looking forward to deadly strife, met together in one of their tents for prayer. After spending some time in committing themselves to God, and in Christian conversation, and freely speaking together of the probability that they would not all survive the morrow, it was suggested by one of the number that they should draw up a paper expressive of the feelings with which they went to stand face to face with death, and all sign it; and that this should be left as a testimony to the friends of such of them as might fall. This was unanimously agreed to. After consultation, it was decided that a copy of 'My faith looks up to Thee' should be written out, and that each man should subscribe his name to it, so that father, mother, sister or brother might know in what spirit they laid down their lives. Of course, they did not all meet again. The incident was related afterward by one who survived the battle."

My Jesus, I Love Thee

Anonymous   Music by A. J. Gordon

My Jesus, I love Thee, I know Thou art mine,
For Thee all the follies of sin I resign.

The author of this beautiful hymn, which has become so familiar to us, was a Canadian. William Ralph Featherston was born and reared in or near Montreal, Canada. In 1858, when only about sixteen years of age, he composed the words of the hymn which has outlived him. He sent the lines to his aunt, Mrs. E. Featherston Wilson, for criticism. Mrs. Wilson, herself a poetess, commended it highly and wrote her nephew to have it published. In 1862 the hymn first appeared in the "London Hymn Book "— without the author's name. The music was composed by Rev. A. J. Gordon, D.D. Mr. Featherston died in Montreal in 1870, aged twenty-eight. Mr. Featherston's name has never appeared in connection with the hymn. Mrs. Featherston Wilson, now of Los Angeles, California, still cherishes among her treasures the original copy of the hymn in Mr. Featherston's handwriting.

A Protestant Episcopal Bishop of Michigan once related the following incident to a large audience in one of E. P. Hammond's meetings in St.

Louis. "A young, talented and tender-hearted actress was passing along the street of a large city. Seeing a pale, sick girl lying upon a couch just within the half-open door of a beautiful dwelling, she entered, with the thought that by her vivacity and pleasant conversation she might cheer the young invalid.

"The sick girl was a devoted Christian, and her words, her patience, her submission and heavenlit countenance, so demonstrated the spirit of her religion that the actress was led to give some earnest thought to the claims of Christianity, and was thoroughly converted, and became a true follower of Christ. "She told her father, the leader of the theater troupe, of her conversion, and of her desire to abandon the stage, stating that she could not live a consistent Christian life and follow the life of an actress. "Her father was astonished beyond measure, and told his daughter that their living would be lost to them and their business ruined, if she persisted in her resolution. Loving her father dearly, she was shaken somewhat in her purpose, and partially consented to fill the published engagement to be met in a few days. She was the star of the troupe, and a general favourite. Every preparation was made for the play in which she was to appear. "The evening came and the father rejoiced that he had won back his daughter, and that their living was not to be lost. The hour arrived; a large audience had assembled. The curtain rose, and the young actress stepped forward firmly amid the applause of the multitude. But an unwonted light beamed from her beautiful face. Amid the breathless silence of the audience she repeated:

'My Jesus, I love Thee, I know Thou art mine;
For thee all the follies of sin I resign;
My gracious Redeemer, my Saviour art Thou;
If ever I loved Thee, my Jesus, 'tis now.

"This was all. Through Christ she had conquered, and, leaving her audience in tears, she retired from the stage, never to appear upon it again. Through her influence her father was converted, and through their united evangelistic labours many were led to God."

This selection was sung by a thousand voices at the funeral of the Scotch missionary hero, Robert Annan, who was drowned in the bay of Dundee while attempting to rescue a drowning child, in 1867. Under the hymn "Eternity," previously mentioned in this book, more will be found concerning Robert Annan.

My Mother's Prayer

Words by T. C. O'Kane   Music by T. C. O'Kane

As I wandered round the homestead,
Many a dear familiar spot.

"My Mother's Prayer" was sung at nearly all our temperance meetings, both in England and America, and many souls were led to Christ by the tender memories awakened by this hymn. It was first published by Philip Phillips, in his book, "Dew Drops." A minister writes the following: "What our mothers sang to us when they put us to sleep is singing yet. We may have forgotten the words; but they went into the fibre of our soul, and will forever be a part of it. It is not so much what you formally teach your children as what you sing to them.

A hymn has wings and can fly every whither. One hundred and fifty years after you are dead, and "Old Mortality' has worn out his chisel in re-cutting your name on the tombstone, your great-grandchildren will be singing the song which this afternoon you sing to your little ones gathered about your knee.

There is a place in Switzerland where, if you distinctly utter your voice, there come back ten or fifteen echoes, and every Christian song sung by a mother in the ear of her child shall have ten thousand echoes coming back from all the gates of heaven. Oh, if mothers only knew the power of this sacred spell, how much oftener the little ones would be gathered, and all our homes would chime with the songs of Jesus!"

My Prayer

Music by P. P. Bliss   Words by P. P. Bliss

More holiness give me.
More strivings within.

Two years before the tragic death of Mr. Bliss, Mr. Moody, who was then in Scotland, had written him urging him to give up business and use his gifts exclusively in setting forth the Gospel. Mr. and Mrs. Bliss were ready to do this if they could see it as the call of God. Mrs, Bliss's characteristic remark was: 'I am willing that Mr. Bliss should do anything that we can be sure is the Lord's will, and I can trust the Lord to provide for us; but I do not want him to take such a step simply on Mr. Moody's will."

At the same period Mr. Bliss had received the offer of a lucrative appointment as a conductor of the Handel and Haydn Society of San Francisco. There was much prayer and much hesitation on Mr. Bliss's part in approaching a decision upon the matter. He doubted his ability to be useful in Gospel work; doubted whether the drawing he felt toward an evangelistic career was of the Lord or of his own inclination.

Just at this time the Rev. C. M. Saunders invited Mr. Bliss and Major Whittle to go to Waukegan, Illinois, to conduct meetings for three or four evenings.

The following remarkable record is well worth introducing here as being the occasion which led to the writing of this familiar consecration hymn: "The first evening there was no marked result. Although it rained hard, the meeting on the second evening was twice as large. As Mr. Bliss sang his own 'Almost Persuaded,' with a heart yearning to bring wavering ones to decision for Christ, the impression was so irresistible that many arose while he sang, unable to withhold their craving for the help of prayer. That night there was the joy in Waukegan of those who had come to Christ with full purpose of heart, and had found the new bliss of accepting His love. The hearts of the three men of God who had entered on the work were deeply awed. 'The next afternoon,' says one of them, 'we all three met in the vestry of the church where our meetings were held, and spent some hours in prayer. Mr. Bliss made a formal surrender of everything to the Lord; gave up his Musical Conventions; his writing of secular music; gave up everything, and in a simple, child-like trusting prayer, he placed himself, with any talent, any power, God had given him, at the disposal of the Lord. It was a wonderful afternoon. As I think back upon the scene in that little vestry, and recall Bliss's prayer, and the emotions that filled us all in the sense of God's presence, the room seems lit up in my memory with a halo of glory.

"This Consecration Meeting was followed by a wonderful gathering in the evening. Some twenty or more accepted Christ, and a spirit of deep conviction was upon many souls. We returned to Chicago in the morning, praising God — Bliss to find substitutes for his Conventions, and I to resign my business position. From that Wednesday, March 25, 1874, up to December 15, 1876, when I parted from him no more to meet on earth, I never heard Mr. Bliss express a regret that he made this surrender, that he gave himself to God for His work.' "

This hymn, perhaps one of the most beautiful of all his compositions, was written by Mr. Bliss, 1873, after he had given up his musical convention work entirely and entered fully upon his lifework for the Master. It seems that it was only after he had given up everything and committed himself and all his gifts to the Lord's service, that he was enabled to write such a hymn as this. Bliss called the hymn "My Prayer," but thousands in every Christian land have made it their prayer as well, and it will continue to voice a heartfelt want of millions in years to come.

The hymn was a special favourite with Mr. Moody, and was often quoted by him as a hymn that would live in the church of God, while the children of God continue to call upon his name in prayer.

Mr. Bliss was at the time of his death a member of the First Congregational Church of Chicago. The pastor, Dr. E. P. Goodwin, in an address on the death of Mr. and Mrs. Bliss, referred to the singing of this hymn as follows:

"On one of the last occasions when he was with us, on a flying visit to our city, made during his work as an evangelist, he came in late one evening and sat at the rear of the church. Espying him, I called him forward to sing the hymn, 'My Prayer.' He struck the keys on the piano, stooped forward, and, reading the words in the latter part of the first verse, 'More joy in His service,' said, I do not think I can sing that as a prayer any more; it seems to me that I have as much joy in serving the blessed Master as it is possible for me to bear.'"

Nearer, My God to Thee

Words by Sarah F. Adams   Music by Dr. Lowell Mason

> Nearer, my God, to Thee,
> Nearer to Thee.

One of my last lectures on "Sacred Song and Story" was delivered before a large audience in the Church of the Covenant, in Washington, D. C., at which the late Secretary of State, John Hay, members of Congress, and Judges of the Supreme Court were present. The favourite hymn, "Nearer, my God, to Thee," was sung very heartily by the congregation. I requested the pastor, Dr. Hamlin, to make an appointment for an interview with President McKinley. Two days later we visited the White House. The

President greeted me warmly, saying he was very glad to meet me, as he had often heard me sing in Ohio.

"I understand that you are quite a fine singer yourself," I replied. He smiled and said:

"I don't know as to that, but I try to sing with the spirit and with the understanding."

He seemed very bright and happy, and he gave me his autograph. The next day the President went to New York and attended service at the Fifth Avenue Presbyterian Church, during which "Nearer, my God, to Thee" was sung. The President's voice was heard, as he joined heartily in his favourite hymn. A reporter took a photograph of the President as he was singing, which appeared the next day in one of the New York papers. In 1902, in Buffalo, as he lay dying by the hand of an assassin, the martyred President was heard singing faintly,

> Nearer, my God, to Thee,
> Nearer to Thee;
> E' en though it be a cross
> That raiseth me!
> Still all my song shall be
> Nearer, my God, to Thee,
> Nearer to Thee!

And thus passed away one of the noblest men of our age. On the day of his funeral, at Canton, Ohio, all trains, trolley cars and nearly all machinery in the United States were stopped for five minutes, and "Nearer, my God, to Thee" was sung in nearly every church in the land.

Bishop Marvin, of the Methodist Episcopal Church, was traveling during the Civil War in the wilds of Arkansas. He was feeling much depressed, for the Union troops had driven him from his home. As he approached a dilapidated old log cabin he heard some one singing, "Nearer, my God, to Thee." He alighted and entered the house. There he found a poor woman, widowed and old, who was singing in the midst of such poverty as he had never seen before. His despondency vanished and he went on his way happy and trustful, because of the faith which he had seen and the hymn which he had heard.

A little drummer boy was found, after the battle of Fort Donelson, by one who visited the field. The poor lad had lost an arm, which had been carried away by a cannon ball, but even as he lay there dying he was singing, "Nearer, my God, to Thee."

Near the Cross

Words by Fanny J. Crosby   Music by W. H. Doane

> Jesus, keep me near the Cross,
> There a precious fountain.

Like many other hymns by this author, the words were written to a tune already composed by Mr. Doane, and at his request. The words and tune are remarkably well adapted to each other, and the hymn will continue to be used long after many more pretentious ones have been forgotten.

No Hope in Jesus

Words by W. O. Cushing   Music by Robert Lowry

> Oh, to have no Christ, no Saviour!
> No Rock, no Refuge nigh!

From the "Rescue Mission," of Syracuse, New York, comes this incident. "One of the workers at the Rescue Mission sat at the window sewing. She is not a grand singer, in fact, scarcely ever sings in the meeting; but alone by herself she sings the Gospel songs. She was singing:

> Oh, to have no Christ, no Saviour...
> How dark this world must be!

"When she had finished she heard some one calling, and saw two girls looking over a neighbouring fence. "One said: 'Won't you please sing that again?'

"I am afraid some of us would have begun to make excuse, and say we were not singers. But this soul sang it over again, praying God to bless the song, and then went to talk with them. She recognized them as inmates of a house of evil resort, and asked permission to call on them. They would not grant this, but the next day one came to the mission and threw herself weeping, into the arms of the singer, saying: "'I have been so unhappy since I heard you sing! You remind me of my mother and the days when I was innocent and good. I had a good home, but quarreled with my mother, ran away and got into a life of sin; I am tired of it, won't you pray for me?' They had prayer, and the poor wandering one was led to the Saviour. She said: 'I'll never go back to that place again. I'm going to the poor-master and ask him to send me home.'

"The worker furnished the money to pay her fare to her home in a neighbouring city, and she went away rejoicing. This was some time ago. One evening the girl, accompanied by her father, paid a visit to the mission. She was happy in Christ, and had led eleven souls to Him, her father and mother being among the number. Her father was full of praise and thanksgiving to God for what He had done for his erring child, and tears ran down his cheeks as he thanked the singer for the song, and for the help she had been to his daughter. Her desire is to work among the fallen ones from among whom she was rescued."

None of Self and All of Thee

Words by Theo. Monad   Music by James McGranahan

> Oh, the bitter pain and sorrow
> That a time could ever be.

The words of this excellent hymn were written by Theodore Monod, of Paris, in whose church we held meetings. Mr. Monod acted as interpreter for Mr. Moody. These meetings were well attended, and many professed conversion. As we left Paris Mr. Moody remarked that if he was a young man again he would give his life to France.

Not Half has ever been Told

Words by J. B. Atchinson   Music by O. F. Presbrey

> I have read of a beautiful city,
> Far away in the kingdom of God.

"A young skeptic in Ohio," writes Dr. O. F. Presbrey, "was wasting away with consumption. His family was greatly distressed, for nothing seemed to awaken in him an interest regarding his soul. One day, as he lay on the sofa, his sister, sitting at the organ, sang, 'Not half has ever been told.' "He seemed much affected and said, 'Oh, sister, sing that hymn again, I never had anything touch my heart like that before.' "The hymn was sung again, and day by day he listened to it. Within two months his spirit took its singing as it went,

> Not half of that city's bright glory,

To mortals has ever been told.

A clergyman had a son who was sent up into the north woods of Canada in search of health. After a few weeks his father was summoned, and found him in a dying condition. On the evening before his death they sang together "Not half has ever been told." The father says that he can never forget the joy and peace which filled the soul of his dying boy as they sang of that beautiful city of which he was so soon to be an inhabitant.

Nothing but the Blood of Jesus

Words by Robert Lowry   Music by Robert Lowry

What can wash away my stain?
Nothing but the blood of Jesus.

This very simple hymn was first introduced at a camp meeting in Ocean Grove, N. J., where it immediately took possession of the people. It has been found very useful in inquiry and prayer meetings.

Not Now, My Child

Words by Mrs. Pennefather   Music by Ira D. Sankey

Not now, my child, – a little more rough tossing,
A little longer on the billows' foam.

Mrs. Pennefather, the author of this hymn, was the wife of one of the ministers who invited Mr. Moody and I to England in 1873. She was one of the founders of the Mildmay Conference, in the north of London, and also organized the famous Deaconess Society, composed of many ladies of distinction who therein seek a field for religious effort. I arranged her hymn to music, and often used to sing it as a solo.

A young lady of a titled family, walking one day along the Strand, saw crowds pushing into the large building where we were holding meetings. Following the crowd, she soon found herself seated and listening to a stirring sermon by Mr. Moody. I also sang this hymn as a solo. The whole service much impressed the young lady. At the conclusion of the meeting, when Mr. Moody invited all who desired to become Christians to rise, she stood up with hundreds of others, and later went into the inquiry-room and there gave her heart to God. When she went home she announced to her family that she had become a Christian, and they laughed her to scorn. After a few weeks she decided to leave her home and cast in her lot with those who were living for Christ. She went to Mrs. Pennefather, and put on the dress of a deaconess. There she continued for over a year. One day, more than a year later, she received a letter from her father, a Lord of the realm, asking her to accompany him on his yachting trip to the north of Scotland. While on the trip she was successful in leading her father to the Saviour.

Landing in Scotland, they found some friends from London in a little fishing village. On Sunday the question arose as to where they would attend service. They finally agreed to go to a neighbouring village where a visiting clergyman was to give an address. The young lady and her father were greatly impressed with the sermon. The next day when they returned to the yacht, his Lordship remarked that he would like to have that clergyman preach his funeral sermon. On the return trip the old gentleman caught a severe cold, and died soon afterward. The young lady communicated her father's wish to the clergyman, and he conducted the funeral services. The clergyman became interested in the young lady, and sought her hand in marriage. After their wedding they moved to Scotland, residing on a large estate to which the clergyman had fallen heir. When Mr. Moody and I were carrying on the campaign in Scotland we were invited to visit their castle. During our visit there we held meetings in the neighbourhood for the miners. At the suggestion of our host we used to go into the forest and cut down trees for exercise. Before leaving the estate each of us planted a tree near the castle gate, and the clergyman named one of them "Moody," and the other "Sankey."

Nothing but Leaves

Words by L. E. Akerman   Music by Silas J. Vau

Nothing but leaves!
The Spirit grieves o'er years of wasted life.

Mrs. Lucy Evelina Akerman, the author of this hymn, died in Providence, Rhode Island, 1874, at the age of twenty-four.

The hymn was a special favourite at the early Moody and Sankey meetings. I often sang it as a solo for Mr. Moody's lecture on "The Holy Spirit." While singing it in Birmingham a lady was convinced, as she wrote me afterwards, that her life had been nothing but leaves; and she then decided to devote the rest of her life to rescuing her lost sisters. She secured a building, which she called "The Rescue Home," and for years she gathered in poor, wretched girls from the streets of the city, gave them employment, and taught them the way of life. Through her efforts hundreds of girls were saved. After her death the city officials took up her work, employing other women, who are still engaged in seeking the lost ones. On my last visit to England I had the pleasure of visiting this rescue home and singing for the inmates.

"During the mission in 1884," writes M. C. Boardman, of Stratford, East London, "the hymn 'Nothing but leaves' was often sung. "It brought conviction to one of the stewards. He said that this song disturbed him. For years he had been a professor of religion, but with personal interest in view. He said he trusted that henceforth there would be fruit as well as leaves in his life. From that time he has been an ardent Christian worker."

O Child of God

Words by Fanny J. Crosby   Music by Ira D. Sankey

O child of God, wait patiently
When dark thy path may be.

During the summer of 1886, Fanny Crosby was my guest at Northfield. One day I composed this tune, and said to her:

"Why not write a poem for this tune to-night?" The spirit of poetry did not seem to be upon her, and she answered:

"No, I cannot do it at present."

The following day we went for a drive, and expected her to go with us, but to our astonishment, she asked to be excused, saying that she had something she wished to do. After we had gone, a number of students came in and had a pleasant chat with Fanny Crosby, and after they had gone she sat down at the piano and played my tune over, and the words of the hymn came to her as they now stand.

Upon our return she hastened to meet us, and recited the verses to me.

Fanny Crosby spent eight summers with us at Northfield, and on a recent visit here she told me that some of her happiest days were those at Northfield, and, referring to this hymn, she said she knew that she had been permitted to do a little good there. She also told me that she knew that many a poor soul had been comforted by this simple hymn.

O For a Thousand Tongues to Sing

Words by Charles Wesley   Music by Oliver Holden

> O for a thousand tongues to sing
> My great Redeemer's praise.

When Charles Wesley consulted Peter Bohler as to the propriety of praising God, he replied, "Had I a thousand tongues, I would praise him with all" – an expression that is believed to have inspired the opening line of this hymn which Wesley wrote in 1739, to commemorate the first anniversary of his new birthday, the day of his conversion. When John Wesley made his collection of hymns for the use of the Methodists, he selected this one to stand as the first hymn in the book. To this day it remains in that place of honour, and as S. W. Duffield says, it "well deserves the prominence."

O God, Our Help

Words by Isaac Watts   Music by H. W. Greatorex

> O God, our help in ages past,
> Our hope for years to come.

This is Watts' version of the 90th Psalm. Its use has been universal, and is one of his best compositions. It has been translated into many languages. As written by Watts it began, "Our God." This was changed by John Wesley to "O God, our help," etc.

Oh, To Be Nothing

Words by Georgiana M. Taylor   Music by R. G. Halls.
(arr. by P. P. Bliss)

> Oh, to be nothing, nothing,
> Only to lie at His feet.

Miss Taylor wrote me as follows concerning the origin of this hymn: "The idea for the hymn came into my mind through reading the expression, 'Oh, to be nothing,' in a volume of an old magazine. I think it occurred in an anecdote about an aged Christian worker. At all events the words haunted me; I mused on their meaning, and the hymn was the outcome."

Some one has misinterpreted the true meaning of the hymn, and has written another entitled, "Oh, to be something." But it is not in accordance with the Master, who made Himself nothing; nor is it in the spirit of the text which says that he that abaseth himself shall in due time be exalted.

This hymn was much used as a solo in our meetings in Great Britain, and became popular on both sides of the Atlantic.

Oh, What are you Going to Do?

Words by Fanny J. Crosby   Music by Philip Phillips

> Oh, what are you going to do, brother?
> Say, what are you going to do?

Away back in 1867 this hymn was written and dedicated to the Young Men's Christian Associations of America. For many years I used it both in Great Britain and America. Many testimonies have been given of the blessing it has brought to young men who have heard it sung.

"I have a young men's Bible-class," writes a Christian worker in Rotherham, England." Some years ago one of my scholars brought a stranger to the class, who had just come to our town on business. He continued to attend very regularly for about a year. "Having obtained a better business appointment in a distant town, he told me before leaving the class that when he first arrived he had fully made up his mind to shake himself free from all religious influence; as he had come to a strange town where no one knew him, he would enjoy himself any way he chose. But he consented to attend the class just once. The first hymn sung was,

> Oh, what are you going to do, brother?
> Say, what are you going to do?

"He could not get it out of his head all the week, and it was the means of entirely setting aside his intentions. On arriving at his new home he immediately united with a Christian church. "His steady, consistent life won for him further promotion in business, and he now fills a position of usefulness and responsibility in an important town. All the good he had received he attributed to that hymn on the first Sunday of his residence here."

On Jordan's Stormy Banks

Words by the Samuel Stennett   Music by T. C. O'Kane

> On Jordan's stormy banks I stand,
> And cast a wishful eye.

Of the many hymns written by Dr. Stennett, this is one of the most famous. The author was born at Exeter, England. His father was the pastor of the Baptist Church, in Little Wild Street, London. With this church young Sennett united. He became his father's assistant, and later his successor, continuing in that pastorate until his death, in 1795, at the age of sixty-eight. He was noted as the friend of King George III. The hymn was first published in Rippon's "Selections," in 1787.

While visiting the Holy Land I sang this hymn on the banks of the Jordan, opposite Mount Horeb, where God showed Moses the promised land of Canaan. As the banks of the Jordan are not stormy, the word "rugged" has by many been substituted for "stormy" in the first line.

One More Day's Work for Jesus

Words by Miss Anna Warner   Music by Robert Lowry

> One more day's work for Jesus;
> One less of life for me.

One day, while the children in a Mission Chapel were singing "One more day's work for Jesus," a woman passing by stopped outside to listen. She went home with these words fixed in her mind. The next day, as she was bending over the washtub, the words of the hymn came to her again and aroused the question, "Have I ever done one day's work for Jesus in all my life?" That marked the turning point. There and then she began to work for Christ. She washed the clothes for Jesus, cleaned the house for Jesus, administered the needs of her family for Jesus. A new light came into her life; and at the close of that day she could sing with a different feeling and a new enthusiasm:

> One more day's work for Jesus;
> How sweet the work has been.

One Sweetly Solemn Thought

Words by Phoebe Cary   Music by Phillip Phillips

> One sweetly solemn thought
> Comes to me o'er and o'er.

This hymn was composed in a little third-story bedroom one Sunday morning in 1852, after the author had come from church. Miss Carey was then twenty-eight. She died in Newport, Rhode Island, nineteen years later.

A gentleman traveling in China found at Macao a company of gamblers in a back room on the upper floor of a hotel. At the table nearest him was an American, about twenty years old, playing with an old man. While the gray-haired man was shuffling the cards, the young man, in a careless way, sang a verse of "One sweetly solemn thought," to a very pathetic tune. Several gamblers looked up in surprise on hearing the singing. The old man, who was dealing the cards, gazed steadfastly at his partner in the game, and then threw the pack of cards under the table.

"Where did you learn that song?" he asked.

The young man pretended that he did not know that he had been singing. "Well, no matter," said the old man, "I have played my last game, and that's the end of it. The cards may lie there till doomsday, and I'll never pick them up." Having won a hundred dollars from the young man, he took the money from his pocket and, handing it over to the latter, said: "Here, Harry, is your money; take it and do good with it; I shall with mine."

The traveler followed them downstairs, and at the door heard the old man still talking about the song which the young man had sung. Long afterward a gentleman in Boston received a letter from the old man, in which he declared that he had become a "hardworking Christian," and that his young friend also had renounced gambling and kindred vices.

Only a Beam of Sunshine

Words by Fanny J. Crosby   Music by John R. Sweney

> Only a beam of sunshine, but oh, it was warm and bright;
> The heart of a weary trav'ler was cheered by its welcome sight

Fanny Crosby says: "It was a cold, rainy day, and everything had gone wrong with me during the morning. I realized that the fault was mine; but that did not help the matter. About noon the sky began to clear; and a friend, standing near me said, 'There is only a beam of sunshine, but oh, it is warm and bright;' and on the impulse of the moment I wrote the hymn."

Only a Step to Jesus

Words by Fanny J. Crosby   Music by W. H. Doane

Only a step to Jesus!
Then why not take it now?

The editor of a religious periodical in the South sends me the following incident, which occurred while he was holding meetings in a small town: "One night a prominent man of the county, not a Christian, was in town. Having heard of the fine singing, he went to the meeting for a few minutes to listen to a song or two. He heard only one song and then went away; but that song went with him. "It was,

Only a step to Jesus!
Then why not take it now?

"The words stayed with him, and were repeated over and over. They came back to him the next day, and awakened inquiry regarding himself which at last led him into repentance and a happy conversion. Many people wept as he related his experience before the church."

Only Remembered By What We Have Done

Words by Horatius Bonar   Music by Ira D. Sankey

Fading away like the stars of the morning,
Losing their light in the glorious sun.

Dr. Horatius Bonar, of Edinburgh, wrote the words of this hymn, which I set to music in 1891. I sang it as a solo in the Tabernacle in London at the funeral of my friend, C. H. Spurgeon, the great London preacher.

Only Trust Him

Words by J. H. S.   Music by J. H. Stockton

> Come, every soul by sin oppressed
> There's mercy with the Lord.

While on the way to England with Mr. Moody in 1873, one day in mid-ocean, as I was looking over a list of hymns in my scrapbook, I noticed one commencing, "Come every soul by sin oppressed," written by John Stockton, with the familiar chorus,

> Come to Jesus,
> Come to Jesus,
> Come to Jesus just now.

Believing that these words had been so often sung that they were hackneyed, I decided to change them and tell how to come to Jesus by substituting the words, "Only trust him." In this form it was first published in "Sacred Songs and Solos" in London. While holding meetings in Her Majesty's Theater in Pall Mall, London, and singing this hymn, I thought I would change the chorus again, and asked the people to sing,

> I will trust Him,
> I will trust Him,
> I will trust Him just now.

Then as we sang I decided to change it once more, and asked them to sing, "I do trust him." God blessed this rendering of the hymn to eight persons present, who testified afterward that by the change they were led to accept salvation.

"I am much interested in sacred songs," writes a missionary in England, "because it was the first verse of 'Only trust Him' that opened the door of my heart to let the Master into my soul in all his fullness. I was in the army, and found my way to the Woolwich Soldiers' Home, where I heard the Gospel; and for a fortnight I was groping in the dark for peace, when one evening I heard the singing of 'Only trust Him,' which brought light into my soul. I have ever since been happy, serving Him with my whole heart. I am now a missionary to my comrades."

Onward, Christian Soldiers

Words by S. Baring-Gould   Music by A. S. Sullivan

Onward, Christian soldiers!
Marching as to war.

Written for a special occasion, the author was totally unprepared for the subsequent popularity of this hymn. In 1895 he said regarding its composition: "Whit-Monday is a great day for school festivals in Yorkshire. One Whit-Monday, thirty years ago, it was arranged that our school should join forces with that of a neighbouring village. I wanted the children to sing when marching from one village to another, but couldn't think of anything quite suitable; so I sat up at night, resolved that I would write something myself. 'Onward, Christian soldiers' was the result. "It was written in great haste, and I am afraid some of the rhymes are faulty. Certainly nothing has surprised me more than its popularity. I don't remember how it got printed first, but I know that very soon it found its way into several collections. I have written a few other hymns since then, but only two or three have become at all well-known." The tune to which it is now sung is the one by which Sir Arthur Sullivan is likely to be known longest to posterity.

Mr. Moody would not give out this hymn in connection with his meetings, as he thought it contained too much vain boasting. He would exclaim: "We are a nice lot of soldiers!"

Out of the Shadow-land

Words by Ira D. Sankey   Music by Ira D. Sankey

Out of the shadow-land, into the sunshine,
Cloudless, eternal, that fades not away.

I wrote this hymn especially for the memorial service held for Mr. Moody in Carnegie Hall, where I also sang it as a solo. It was the last sacred song to which I wrote both the words and music. The idea was suggested by Mr. Moody's last words, "Earth recedes; heaven opens before me... God is calling me and I must go." On account of its peculiar association with my fellow-labourer in the gospel for so many years.

Over the Line

Words by Ellen K. Bradford   Music by E. H. Phelps

> Oh, tender and sweet was the Master's voice
> As He lovingly called to me.

We were holding meetings in Springfield, Massachusetts, in 1878. One day, at the noon meeting in City Hall, a minister rose on the platform and bore testimony to the way the Lord had blessed one of his sons, a Yale student. "My son," he said, "happened be seated beside a gentleman from England in one of Mr. Moody's meetings. Tarrying for the after-meeting, he was spoken to by the gentleman beside him about becoming a Christian. After half an hour spent in talking they went out into the street, and the gentleman said that he would gladly walk home with my son if he had no objection, as he had nothing else to do. They came at last to the gate which led to my home. Before parting, the earnest Christian worker said he would like to offer one more prayer for my boy. Holding the young man's hand, he asked that the Lord would enable him to decide the great question that very night. With this prayer they separated. The gentleman left town the next day, and may never know how God heard and answered his prayer.

"My son was greatly impressed. Approaching the house, he stopped suddenly, made a deep line across the graveled walk with his cane, and said: 'Now, I must decide this question, for or against Christ, tonight. If I cross the line my life shall be for him; but if I go around it, it will be for the world.' "Standing there considering the great question with himself for an half hour, at last he cried: 'O God, help me to decide aright!' "Then he went bounding over the line, and came into my room and said: 'Father, I wish you would pray for me! I have decided to be a Christian.'" The minister said that his heart went out in supplication to God to keep and bless his boy.

This story affected the audience to tears. One of the newspapermen, Mr. E. H. Phelps, proprietor of one of the leading papers of the city, took down the father's story and published it the next morning. And Mrs. Bradford, of Palmer, in the same state, after reading the incident in the paper, sat down and wrote "Over the Line." She sent the hymn to the editor of the paper, Mr. Phelps, and he at once set it to music. Three days later he handed the song to me. I adapted it and had it published in

"Gospel Hymns." It has been blessed to thousands of souls all over the world, leading to the conversion of very many.

"While I was holding a series of revival meetings at Brigham, Utah," relates an Iowa clergyman, "a man was brought to a full surrender of himself to Christ by the singing of the hymn, 'Over the Line.' The first two or three meetings made him very angry, and he determined not to go any more; but as the services increased in interest his anxiety and troubled mind induced him to return, yet only as an observer. He remained in the lecture-room, which opened into the audience-room. Here he was noticed walking the floor, as if in bodily pain. But when at the close of the meeting we sang this hymn, he advanced toward the pulpit, made a long step as though stepping over some object, reached out his hand and said in a loud, determined voice: 'I have stepped over the line.' This dramatic surrender to Christ and public profession had a powerful effect upon the audience, and many more followed his example."

A missionary sends me the following incident: "I was holding a gospel meeting one Sunday in a Woman's Christian Temperance Union mission. We were on our bended knees when the Spirit said to me, sing, 'Over the Line.' "When we arose I turned to the lady at the organ, who had a consecrated voice, and said, sing 'Over the Line.' At the close a man rose and spoke as follows: "'I came away from home and family and work two weeks ago in a drunken spree. Since I came to your city I have often heard of this mission, and was asked to come, but with oaths I refused up to an hour ago, and then I entered this room. The same spirit of unbelief possessed me until this lady began to sing. Those words went to my heart; they were all written for me, and as she sang the last verse I crossed the line, I gave myself, and – with a deep sob – He took me.'"

Pass Me Not

Words by Fanny J. Crosby   Music by W. H. Doane

Pass me not, O gentle Saviour,
Hear my humble cry.

An earnest Christian pastor told of a young man about whom he had long felt much anxiety, as he had seemed so unconcerned about his soul, and was, in reality, a real cause of disturbance and interruption in the classes for other young men.

Meeting him one day, the loving pastor sought once more to influence him, urging, "We want you for Christ and His service." There was a certain change in his manner which did not escape the eye of the prayerful watcher for souls, and – lacking time to do more – he seized the opportunity to secure the presence of his young friend at a Christian Endeavor meeting soon to be held. True to his promise he was there. When an opportunity was given for some of the young men to choose a song, it was seen that he was urging his companion to select some particular hymn. The other, yielding to his request, asked if the hymn, "Pass me not, O gentle Saviour," might be sung; and both young men joined in the singing with evident interest and heartiness. Later in the evening it was requested that all who were definitely on the Lord's side would confess their allegiance by standing. Whereupon the one over whom the heart of the pastor was specially yearning rose at once, and with decision.

"Tell me about your conversion," the thankful Pastor requested at the close of the meeting, when hands were clasped in glad, brotherly welcome and recognition.

"Oh, yes," assented the other. "It was all through that hymn we have just sung. I was working on the canal at G–, and there was a meeting being held at the Mariner's Chapel nearby. The words floated out over the water, and from the tug where I was working I could hear them plainly enough. When they were just going to sing those lines–

> While on others Thou are calling,
> Do not pass me by!

A great fear came over me, and I thought, 'Oh, if the Lord were to pass me by, how terrible it would be!' Then and there, on the tug, I cried out: 'O Lord, do not pass me by.' And with a bright smile – "he didn't pass me by. I am saved."

A young Christian traveller found himself in a commercial room one night where, the party being large and merry, it was proposed that each gentleman present should give a song. Many of the usual character on such occasions were sung. It came to the turn of our young friend, who excused himself on the plea that he knew no songs they would care to hear. In derision, a gentleman present asked if he could not give them one of Sankey's hymns; and several others cried out that they would join in the chorus. He decided to take them at their word; and chose this hymn, being well known, with its simple Gospel teaching — and with a silent prayer that God would use it for His glory, he sang as perhaps he never sang before. All present joined in the chorus. Before its close there were moist eyes and troubled hearts. The spirit of jollity and fun was gone; but the Spirit of God was there. Several gathered around our young friend, thanking him for his song. He retired to rest, grateful for grace given.

He had not been long in his bedroom when he heard a knock at the door. It was opened by a young traveller who requested permission to come in. He was in deep trouble. The song had brought back to his memory the strains he had heard a deceased mother sing. He knew his life had not been right; and the inquiry had been upon his lips, "What must I do to be saved?" He was pointed to Christ, and retired with a brighter hope. Scarcely had his inquirer left than another knock was heard at the bedroom door. This time it was an elderly traveller. The song had reminded him of lost peace and joy. He was a backslider; and the singer had the joy of pointing another sinner back to a loving Saviour. It was nearly two o'clock before he could lie down; but it was with heartfelt joy and gratitude to Him who had thus honoured his personal testimony to Christ.

No hymn in our collection was more popular than this at our meetings in London in 1874. It was sung almost every day in Her Majesty's Theatre, in Pall Mall, and has been translated into several languages.

At one of our noonday prayer-meetings in Glasgow a prominent gentleman was awakened by the singing of this hymn. He had been very much opposed to our meetings, and his opposition was not lessened when he saw his wife converted. That day he had agreed to attend the meeting for the last time, as a sort of concession; and that was the day when the Spirit of God touched him by this hymn.

Paece! Be Still!

Words by Miss M. A. Baker   Music by H. R. Palma

Master, the tempest is raging!
The billows are tossing high!

When a deep and comforting spiritual experience finds expression it will surely bring comfort to others, as this hymn has done many times.

Miss Mary A. Baker has told of its origin:

"Dr. Palmer requested me to prepare several songs on the subject of the current Sunday-school lessons. One of the themes was 'Christ Stilling the Tempest.' It so expressed an experience I had recently passed through, that this hymn was the result.

A very dear and only brother, a young man of rare loveliness and promise of character, had been laid in the grave, a victim of the same disease that had already taken father and mother. His death occurred under peculiarly distressing circumstances. He was more than a thousand miles away from home, seeking in the balmy air of the sunny South the healing that our colder climate could not give. Suddenly he grew worse. The writer was ill and could not go to him. For two weeks the long lines of telegraph wires carried back and forth messages between the dying brother and his waiting sisters, ere the word came which told us that our beloved brother was no longer a dweller on the earth.

Although we mourned not as those without hope, and although I had believed on Christ in early childhood and had always desired to give the Master a consecrated and obedient life, I became wickedly rebellious at this dispensation of divine providence. "I said in my heart that God did not care for me or mine. But the Master's Own voice stilled the tempest in my unsanctified heart, and brought it to the calm of a deeper faith and a more perfect trust. Since then I have given much of my time and strength to active temperance work as a member of the Woman's Christian Temperance Union. Witnessing the unparalleled suffering that comes to sisters, wives and mothers through the legalized curse of our land, the rum traffic, which is yearly slaying its thousands and tens of thousands in their early manhood and hurrying them into dishonoured graves, I have come to feel a keen sense of gratitude for the sweet memories left of my departed brother. God's way is best.

"I supposed that the hymn had done its work and gone to rest. But, during the weeks when our nation kept watch by the bedside of our greatly beloved President Garfield, it was republished as especially appropriate to the time, and was sung at some of the many funeral services held throughout the United States. It is quite a surprise to me that this humble hymn should have crossed the seas and been sung in far distant lands to the honour of the Saviour's name."

Precious Promise God Has Given

Words by Nathaniel Niles   Music by P. P. Bliss

Precious promise God hath given
To the weary passer by.

This well-known hymn was written by Mr. Nathaniel Niles, a resident of Morristown, N. J., and, at that time a lawyer in New York City. He was born at South Kingston, R. I., 1835. The verses were composed on the margin of a newspaper in the railway car one morning while on his way to business. The tune was written by P. P. Bliss, and published in his Gospel Songs in 1874, and later furnished by him for Gospel Hymns. I soon afterward published it in Sacred Songs and Solos, in England, where it became one of the most useful hymns in connection with our meetings. Mr. Moody often requested it to be sung in connection with his lectures on "The Precious Promises."

Pull for the Shore

Words by P. P. Bliss   Music by P. P. Bliss

Light in the darkness, sailor, day is at hand!
See o'er the foaming billows fair Haven's land.

On one occasion the vessel on which Mr. Moody was returning from Europe, accompanied by his oldest son, was disabled by the breaking of a propelling shaft. Mrs. Moody was at my home in Brooklyn, waiting to receive them on their arrival. Day after day passed without word from the steamer, and Mrs. Moody became almost frantic with anxiety. At last I received this cable dispatch from Mr. Moody: "Saved, thank God." I learned afterwards that the people gathered around him and begged him to pray for their deliverance. Several infidels on board, who had been making light of Mr. Moody's work, were found kneeling at his side, and through the earnestness of his prayers and divine help they were led to Christ.

Rescue the Perishing

Words by Fanny J. Crosby   Music by W. H. Doane

Rescue the perishing,
Care for the dying.

Fanny Crosby returned, one day, from a visit to a mission in one of the worst districts in New York City, where she had heard about the needs of the lost and perishing. Her sympathies were aroused to help the lowly and neglected, and the cry of her heart went forth in this hymn, which has become a battle-cry for the great army of Christian workers throughout the world. It has been used very extensively in temperance work, and has been blessed to thousands of souls. Mr. Moody was very fond of it, and has borne testimony to its power to reach the hearts of wanderers. It was also a favourite of the two great temperance workers, Frances E. Willard and Francis Murphy.

On a stormy night a middle-aged man staggered into the Bowery Mission. He was intoxicated, his face unwashed and unshaven, and his clothes soiled and torn. He sank into a seat, and, gazing around, seemed to wonder what kind of a place he had come into. "Rescue the perishing" and other gospel hymns were sung and seemed to interest him, and to recall some memory of his youth long since forgotten. As the leader of the meeting told the simple story of the Gospel, and how the Lord had come to seek and save sinners, the man listened eagerly. The leader in his younger days had been a soldier and had seen hard and active service. In the course of his remarks he mentioned several incidents which had occurred in his experience during the war, and he gave the name of the company in which he served. At the close of the meeting the man eagerly staggered up to the leader and in a broken voice said:

"When were you in that company you spoke of?"

"Why, all through the war," said the leader.

"Do you remember the battle of –?"

"Perfectly."

"Do you remember the name of the captain of your company at that time."

"Yes, his name was –."

"You are right! I am that man. I was your captain. Look at me today, and see what a wreck I am. Can you save your old captain? I have lost everything I had in the world through drink, and I don't know where to go."

He was saved that night, and was soon helped by some of his former friends to get back his old position. He often told the story of how a soldier saved his captain, and how much he loved the words of "Rescue the perishing."

One evening the author was present at a mission meeting when this hymn was sung. A young man arose and told the story of his wanderings: hungry and penniless, he was strolling through the streets one night when he heard the sound of singing. Entering the hall, he caught the words,

> Back to the narrow way
> Patiently win them;
> Tell the poor wanderer a Saviour has died.

His heart broke in penitence. "I was just ready to perish," he said; "but that hymn, by the grace of God, saved me." Fancy the scene, when the author and the speaker stood face to face, their eyes filled with tears, and the audience thrilled with the pathos of the meeting!

A man in Sussex, England, gives this testimony: "I believe I can attribute my conversion, through the grace of God, to one verse of that precious hymn, 'Rescue the perishing.' I was far away from my Saviour, and living without a hope in Jesus. I was very fond of singing hymns, and one day I came across this beautiful piece, and when I had sung the words,

> Touched by a loving heart,
> wakened by kindness,
> Chords that were broken will vibrate once more,

I fell upon my knees and gave my heart to the Lord Jesus Christ. From that hour I have followed him who, through this verse, touched my heart and made it vibrate with his praises ever since."

Fanny Crosby returned, one day, from a visit to a mission in one of the worst districts in New York City, where she had heard about the needs of the lost and perishing. Her sympathies were aroused to help the lowly and neglected, and the cry of her heart went forth in this hymn, which has become a battle-cry for the great army of Christian workers throughout the world. It has been used very extensively in temperance work, and has been blessed to thousands of souls. Mr. Moody was very fond of it, and has borne testimony to its power to reach the hearts of wanderers. It was also a favourite of the two great temperance workers, Frances E. Willard and Francis Murphy.

Rest for the Weary

Words by S. Y. Harmer   Music by William McDonald

> In the Christian's home in glory,
> There remains a land of rest;

A fifteen-year-old girl, of good family, was present at one of our meetings in the Free College Church of Glasgow, in 1874, and at the close of the meeting remained among the inquirers at the College Hall. Here she was spoken to by a lady, and was led to Christ. Going home, she told her mother that she was now happy in the Lord. That very night she was taken sick, symptoms of scarlet fever appearing. Prayer was offered for her at the daily prayer-meetings. Perhaps most of her friends thought that the Lord would answer their supplications by restoring her to health; but he had a purpose of another kind. He meant to take her away to himself, and to teach others by her removal. When it was evident that she was dying she told her father that she was going home to Christ. Near the end, he tried to sing with her "In the Christian's home in glory." She caught up the words,

> There my Saviour's gone before me,
> To fulfil my soul's request.

And faithfully repeated them until her voice died away; those were the last words she was heard to utter. Before this she had sent a message of thanks to Mr. Moody and myself, and to the lady who had led her to Christ.

"Ah," said Mr. Moody, in telling of this, "would not anyone have regretted missing the opportunity of helping this soul, who has sent back her thanks from the very portals of glory?"

Ring the Bells of Heaven

Words by William O. Cushing   Music by George F. Root

> Ring the bells of heaven! there is joy today
> For a soul, returning from the wild.

"'Ring the bells of heaven' was written," says the author, "to fit a beautiful tune sent me by George F. Root, entitled, 'The little Octoroon.' After receiving it, the melody ran in my head all day long, chiming and flowing in its sweet musical cadence. I wished greatly that I might secure the tune for work in the Sunday-school and for other Christian purposes. When I heard the bells of heaven ringing over some sinner that had returned, it seemed like a glad day in heaven. Then the words 'Ring the bells of heaven,' at once flowed down into the waiting melody. It was a beautiful and blessed experience, and the bells seem ringing yet."

A little girl in England, who was much beloved by her parents, was dying. She had been very fond of our hymns and would often speak of how much she loved them. A few days before she died she said to her mother: "When I am gone, mother, will you ask the girls of the school to sing that hymn,

> Ring the bells of heaven! There is joy today,
> For a soul returning from the wild;
> See! The Father meets him out upon the way,
> Welcoming His weary, wandering child!
> Glory! Glory! How the angels sing!
> Glory! Glory! How the loud harps ring!

Half an hour before her departure she exclaimed: "Oh, mother, listen to the bells of heaven! They are ringing so beautifully!"

Rock of Ages

Words by A. M. Toplady   Music by Dr. Thomas Hastings

> Rock of Ages, cleft for me,
> Let me hide myself in Thee.

In the year 1756 a young man of sixteen, while visiting with his mother in Ireland, attended an evangelistic meeting held in a barn at the little village of Codymain. At this meeting the young man was converted. He was none other than Augustus Montague Toplady, who afterwards wrote this famous hymn. Of his conversion the author says: "Strange, that I, who had so long sat under the means in England, should be brought right unto God in an obscure part of Ireland, midst a handful of people met together in a barn, and by the ministry of one who could hardly spell his own name. Surely it was the Lord's doing, and is marvelous."

At the age of twenty-two Toplady received orders in the Church of

England. He was a strong Calvinist, and the author of many popular hymns. He died in 1778. "Rock of Ages" was first published in 1776, in "The Gospel Magazine," of which he was the editor. The hymn has been more or less altered and rearranged several times since then, but the sentiment remains the same.

It was to this hymn that the beloved Prince Consort, Albert of England, turned, repeating it constantly upon his deathbed. "For," said he, "if in this hour I had only my worldly honours and dignities to depend upon, I should be poor indeed."

On board the ill-fated steamer, Seawanhaka, was one of the Fisk University singers. Before leaving the burning ship and committing himself to the merciless waves, he carefully fastened life-preservers upon himself and his wife. Some one cruelly dragged away that of his wife, leaving her without hope, except as she could cling to her husband. This she did, placing her hands firmly upon his shoulders, and resting there until her strength becoming exhausted she said, "I can hold on no longer! ""Try a little longer," was the response of the wearied and agonized husband; "let us sing 'Rock of Ages.' "And as the sweet strains floated over those troubled waters, reaching the ears of the sinking and dying, little did they know whom they comforted.

But lo! as they sang, one after another of the exhausted ones were seen raising their heads above the overwhelming waves, joining with a last effort in this sweet, pleading prayer:

> Rock of Ages, cleft for me,
> Let me hide myself in Thee.

With the song seemed to come strength; another and yet another was encouraged to renewed efforts. Soon in the distance a boat was seen approaching. Could they hold out a little longer? Singing still they tried; and soon, with superhuman strength, laid hold of the lifeboat, upon which they were borne in safety to land.

This is no fiction; it was related by the singer himself, who said he believed Toplady's sweet "Rock of Ages "saved many another besides himself and his wife.

Mrs. L. S. Bainbridge, who, with her husband, visited China for the purpose of studying Christian missions, tells the following incident: "The Chinese women, it seems, are so anxious to 'make merit' for themselves; that they will perform any labour to escape the painful transmigrations of the next life. "They dread to be born again as dogs or cats, and the highest hope possessed by them is to be reborn as men. In order to secure this they do any and every meritorious act. One woman had excavated with her poor, weak hands a well twenty feet deep, and it was only after this achievement that she learned of the free Gospel of salvation. She was now a woman of eighty, and, stretching out her aged and crippled fingers, we sang together,

> Nothing in my hand I bring,
> Simply to Thy cross I cling.

Years ago, when a ship sank in the Bay of Biscay, a man who was saved was asked what the passengers were doing when the ship went down. He said that the last he heard was "Rock of Ages," sung by all who could join in it. Several tunes have been written for this hymn. The most popular one, however, being the tune by Dr. Thomas Hastings who was born at Washington, Connecticut, in 1784 and who died in New York in 1872. He wrote many hymns and published several hymnbooks. I have in my possession a large number of hymns set to music by Mr. Hastings which have never been published.

The Rev. John Macpherson relates the following striking story of conversion through the singing of this immortal hymn. He had been urged by a Christian young man to visit a young woman who was dying. He says:

We spoke to her of Jesus. She listened closely, but said she had heard all that again and again. She knew she was a sinner, and unforgiven. She felt certain that if she died in her present state she would perish. After some conversation, reading and prayer, we gave up in despair, and were about to leave. My hand was on the door, when the moaning voice of the dying girl fell upon my ear. "A dark, dark eternity!" she sobbed out. Turning round, and seeing that imploring look of anguish, and hearing the hasty, half-choked breathing — the beginning of the horrid death-rattle, which, though familiar to one's ear, always inspires a shudder — I found it impossible to take another step. "O God!" I said in my heart, "what wilt Thou have me to do?" Suddenly, and for the first time in my life, it stnick me that I might sing a hymn.

"Shall I sing a hymn?" I asked.

"Oh, yes, you may!" replied the girl, seemingly much pleased that we were to stay a little longer. We sang the well-known hymn, "Rock of

Ages," and had reached the third stanza:

> Nothing in my hand I bring.
> Simply to Thy cross I cling,

when suddenly the girl started from her pillow, and sat up in the bed with folded hands. Physical strength seemed to have returned to the wasted form; her countenance began to beam; and to our astonishment she exclaimed, "Oh, sir. He has come!" Stopping short in the singing, I said, "Who has come?" "Jesus!" was the joyful reply. Had the sun shone out at that hour, my companion and I could scarcely have been more amazed at the sudden change. The burden under which she had groaned for months was, as she told us, entirely gone. She saw Jesus, she said, in a new light; and she could trust Him as the bearer of sin and the Saviour of the lost. The way of salvation was now so plain to her that she was able freely to discourse to us of what she believed and felt; and much did she wonder at her blindness and hardness of heart in holding out against the Saviour so long.

Several tunes have been written for this hymn, one of the most popular, however, being the tune by Dr. Thomas Hastings, who was born at Washington, Connecticut, in 1784, and who died in New York in 1872. He wrote many hymns and published several hymn books. I have in my possession a large number of hymns set to music by Dr. Hastings which have never been published.

Safe in the Arms of Jesus

Words by Fanny J. Crosby   Music by W. H. Doane

> Safe in the arms of Jesus,
> Safe on His gentle breast.

Mr. Doane came into a room in New York, once, where Fanny Crosby was talking with Mr. Bradbury, the father of Sunday-school music, and said to her: "Fanny, I have written a tune and I want you to write words for it."

"Let me hear how the tune goes," she replied. After Mr. Doane had played it over for her on a small organ, she at once exclaimed: "Why, that tune says, 'Safe in the arms of Jesus,' and I will see what I can do about it."

She at once retired to an adjoining room, where she spent half an hour alone. On returning she quoted to Mr. Doane the words of this now immortal hymn. It was first published in the book entitled "Songs of Devotion."

Fanny Crosby is one of the most celebrated of hymn-writers, and has written more than five thousand hymns, many of which have become very widely known. She was born in 1820, and lost her eyesight when six months old, through the ignorant application of a hot poultice to her eyes. In 1835 she entered the New York Institution for the Blind, where she was graduated in 1842. She was a teacher at this institution from 1847 to 1858, when she was married to Mr. Alexander Van Alstyne, who also was blind. Mrs. Van Alstyne has written her hymns under her maiden name.

The Rev Dr.. George Duffield, just before his death, said of her work: "I rather think her talent will stand beside that of Watts and Wesley, especially if we take into consideration the number of hymns she has written." At her present age of eighty-five she is still active, and she is always happy.

A party of steerage passengers were gathered one foggy day below decks on an Allan liner near the entrance of the Belle Isle Straits. They were cold and cheerless and weary of the voyage, though only two days out, and a lady had come down to talk and sing to them. The subject was "Stepping over the line," and the song was "Safe in the arms of Jesus." She told the story of a young sailor, who was summoned to his mother's death-bed.

"Willie," said the mother, looking up at him with tearful eyes, "sing to me once more 'Safe in the arms of Jesus.'"

"Mother," he replied, "I can't sing that song. It would be a lie; I am not safe, and I can't sing a lie."

The speaker said that she thanked God that the young sailor afterward stepped over the line and was safe. After the story was told and a hymn sung, a man suddenly left his place among the listeners. The lady was troubled. Had she offended him or was his conscience stricken? She watched for him day after day, but a storm succeeded the fog, and it was not until the last day of the voyage that she saw him again. Then, while the vessel was moored in Moville Harbour, and all was bustle on deck, the tall Scotchman sought her, saying:

"Oh, I am so glad that I have found you again! I could not leave without thanking you for those words you sang, 'Safe in the arms of Jesus.' I felt that I could not sing that hymn, as I was not safe. I have been to church all my life, and have taken the sacrament; but I was not safe, and I could not sing it. Then came the storm and I was miserable, for I thought we might go to the bottom and I should be lost."

"And what did you do then?" asked the lady.

"Why, I remembered how you said that we might trust the Lord Jesus to save us now – and I did trust Him right there in my berth. I stepped over the line, and now I can praise Him, for I am safe in His arms, and I wish to live to His glory."

Two little girls were playing in a corner of the nursery with their dolls, and singing as they played,

> Safe in the arms of Jesus,
> Safe on His gentle breast.

Their mother was writing, only stopping now and then to listen to the little ones' talk, unobserved by them.

"Sister, how do you know that you are safe?" asked Nellie, the youngest.

"Because I am holding Jesus with both my hands tight!" was the reply.

"Ah, that is not safe," said Nellie. "Suppose Satan came along and cut your two hands off!"

The sister looked much troubled for a few moments, dropped her doll and thought deeply. Suddenly her face shone with joy, and she cried out, "Oh! I forgot! I forgot! Jesus is holding me with His two hands, and Satan can't cut His hands off; so I am safe!"

A party of friends, traveling in the Alps, commenced to sing the first verse of this hymn, when, much to their surprise, they heard the second verse taken up on another mountain peak, as a response; and though the two parties of tourists could not see each other, they sang the alternate verses and passed on their way.

A gentleman of London writes me as follows: "My dear little girl Mary, aged six, greatly loved the hymn, 'Safe in the arms of Jesus,' and, having learned the tune, was continually singing it. One day, having a longing, wistful look in her eyes after singing it, I said to her: 'What are you thinking of, darling?' "She answered: 'I do want to go and be with Jesus.' "I asked her what I should do without her, she being my only little girl. "She sighed and said: 'Very well, then I won't go just yet, though I should like to.' "A few weeks after this, she was seized with scarlet fever of a very malignant type. She was buried in six days. The morning she was taken ill she said to her little brother, who was ill in the same room: "'Look here, Willie, I can find my own hymn myself now, "safe in the arms of Jesus.'" She showed it to Willie, who asked if they should sing it. 'No,' she said, 'I can't sing with my head this way.' She then became delirious and never spoke rationally again. She soon took her flight to the arms of Jesus, where she had so longed to be."

A working man was awakened in the Free Trade Hall at Manchester by the singing of the hymn, "Safe in the arms of Jesus." He tells how he sang the first verse carelessly through, but that when he came to the second, "Safe from corroding care," he was suddenly brought to a standstill. The people all around him were evidently in earnest, they meant what they were singing; it was not so with him. He looked at the verse. He felt he could not sing it with truth; for him to sing it was sheer mockery. So he sat down in great trouble. "That night," he says, "I went home in agony. Next morning I went to my work; but I had not got over the trouble. My shopmates saw there was something up with me. They asked, 'What was the trouble? 'I told them, 'My soul! my soul!' Two nights after I was no better. I went again to the meeting; there I heard I must look to Christ, and Him alone. Just then I was enabled to look; I went home, rejoicing in the Lord, a new and happy man."

At the close of one of our meetings in the Circus in Glasgow a woman came to me when I was seated with an inquirer. After waiting until I was at liberty, she said: "Mr. Sankey, I want to tell you something about my daughter Maggie. She was converted when you were here eight years ago, but has now gone home to heaven, and I want to tell you what she said when she was dying. She asked me to get her little hymn book, and when I brought it she asked me to turn to No. 25, saying, 'I want to sing it.' 'Why, my child,' said I, 'you are not able to sing.' 'Yes,' she said, 'I want to sing one more song before I go; will you please turn to the twenty-fifth hymn, "Safe in the arms of Jesus." I found it for her and she began to sing at these lines,

> Hark! 'tis the voice of angels;
> Borne in a song to me,
> Over the fields of glory,
> Over the jasper sea.

"Her voice then seemed to fail her, and she said: 'Mother, lift me up.'

I put my arms under her and lifted my poor girl up, and then she raised her eyes to heaven and said: 'Jesus, I am coming; Jesus, I am coming.' The doctor, who was standing by her side, said: 'How can you sing when you are so weak?' "She replied: 'Jesus helps me to sing; Jesus helps me to sing.' And with those words upon her lips, she died in my arms." "The mother said that she took the little hymn-book and laid it upon the girl's breast; it was buried with her.

Once when labouring in London I went to Basel, Switzerland, for a few days' rest. The evening I got there I heard under my window the most beautiful volume of song. I looked out and saw about fifty people, who were singing

> Safe in the: arms of Jesus,
> Safe on His gentle breast

in their own language, but I recognized the tune. I spoke to them through an interpreter. The next evening I held a song service in an old French church in that city. The church was packed with people, and many stood outside on the street.

Dr. John Hall, of the Fifth Avenue Presbyterian Church, in New York, said of this hymn, in a great Sunday-school convention in Brooklyn, that it gave more peace and satisfaction to mothers who had lost their children than any other hymn he had ever known. It has become very famous throughout the world, and was one of the first American hymns to be translated into foreign languages.

Saved by Grace

Words by Fanny J. Crosby   Music by George C. Stebbins

> Some day the silver cord will break,
> And I no more as now shall sing.

In 1894 Mr. Moody and I were holding meetings in England. It was decided between us that Mr. Moody should remain in England while I returned to America to assist Dr. A. J. Gordon, of Boston, in conducting the Summer Conference in Northfield. I was entertaining Fanny Crosby in my summer home there. One evening I asked the popular hymn-writer if she would make a short address to her many friends gathered at the convention. She at first declined, but on further persuasion she consented to speak for a few moments. I led her forward to the desk on which lay the Bible and, standing there; she spoke beautifully for a short time. Closing her remarks, she recited a hymn never before heard in public, entitled "Saved by Grace."

I afterward learned that my friend, L. H. Biglow – after attending a prayer-meeting conducted by the late Dr. Howard Crosby, where the subject was "Grace" – had asked Fanny Crosby to write a hymn on that subject. She immediately retired to an adjoining room, and in the course of an hour returned with the words,

> Some day the silver cord will break,
> And I no more as now shall sing.

Mr. Biglow secured the words from her, and put them in the safe among other hymns which she had written; but the song was evidently forgotten until recited by its author at Northfield.

A reporter of a London paper who was present at Northfield took her address, and also the hymn, which he carried back to England and published in his paper, thus sending it around the world. Four or five weeks later I found it in a copy of his paper. Cutting it out, I handed it to George C. Stebbins, asking him to set it to music. During the following years the song became one of Mr. Moody's favourites, and is now sung by hundreds of thousands of people throughout the world.

A newspaper of Allegheny, Pennsylvania, recently gave this incident in startling headlines:

"The congregation of Christ Protestant Episcopal Church, Union Avenue, Allegheny, Robert Meech, rector, was startled yesterday morning, by a sensational supplement to the morning service. "The church was well filled and devout worshipers responded to the service as read by the rector. The reading had been concluded, and the rector was about to make the usual announcements of future services when an incident occurred such as old Christ Church had never dreamed of. Out of the usual line in a church of this denomination, it was nevertheless marked in its effect, and will never be forgotten by those present.

"In the fourth pew from the front aisle of the church sat a neatly-dressed woman of intellectual face, apparently about thirty years of age. Her presence as a stranger had been noticed by many, and her deep, tearful interest in the service had been quietly commented on by those who occupied the adjoining pews. At the point mentioned she rose to her feet and, struggling with emotion, began to speak. The startled congregation was all attention, and she was allowed to proceed. Rapidly and eloquently she told of her going out from the church and of her return to it. In graphic words she painted the hideousness of sin and the joys of a pure life, and as she spoke men and women gave way to their emotions and listened breathlessly to the end of the narration.

"I was christened in this church," she said, "and attended Sunday-school in the basement when good old Dr. Paige was rector. My mother was a devout member here, and taught me the right way. At the age of fifteen I deserted my home and married an actor. For a number of years I followed the profession, leading such a life as naturally accompanies it. In dramatic circles, in variety business, and in the circus, I spent those godless years.

"About two years ago I was in the city of Chicago. One afternoon I was on my way to Ferris Wheel Park to spend the afternoon in revelry, when I happened on the open-air meeting which the Epworth League of Grace Methodist Episcopal Church was conducting on North Park Street. I stopped through curiosity, as I believed, to listen; but I know now that God arrested my footsteps there. They were singing 'Saved by Grace,' and the melody impressed me. Recollections of my childhood days came trooping into my soul, and I remembered that in all the years of my absence my mother, until her death nine years ago, had been praying for me.

"I was converted and, falling on my knees on the curbstone, I asked the Father's pardon. Then and there I received it, and I left the place with a peace which has never forsaken me. I gave up my business at once and have lived for his service ever since. I have been but a few days in this city. Last night I visited the Hope Mission, and the Lord told me I must come here and testify what he had done for me. I have not been in this building for many years, but it seems only yesterday that I left it. I have been sitting in the pew directly opposite the one once occupied by my mother and myself, and I feel her presence today. I could not resist the impulse to give this testimony. The Lord sent me here."

The congregation was profoundly impressed. The rector descended from the chancel and, approaching the speaker, with tears in his eyes, bade her Godspeed. The service went on. At its conclusion many members of the congregation shook hands with the stranger and told of their impressions. A stranger might have imagined himself in a Methodist

Episcopal church, so intense was the feeling. The strange visitor departed with a sense of duty done. All she said was: "I feel that the Lord Jesus and mother have been here."

Saviour Like a Shepherd Lead Us

Words by Dorothy A. Thrupp   Music by Wm. B. Bradbury

> Saviour, like a shepherd lead us,
> Much we need Thy tend'rest care.

This beautiful little hymn is supposed to have been written by Miss Dorothy A. Thrupp, and first published in Miss Thrupp's Hymns for the Young, in 1836. The music by which it is now so well known, both in America and Great Britain, was written by William Bradbury. It was much used in our meetings as a congregational hymn in connection with the subject of the Good Shepherd.

Saviour, More than Life to Me

Words by Fanny J. Crosby   Music by W. H. Doane

> Saviour, more than life to me,
> I am clinging, clinging close to Thee.

Tune preceded words in this instance. It was in 1875 that Mr. Doane sent the tune to Fanny Crosby, and requested her to write a hymn entitled "Every day and hour." Her response in the form of this hymn gave the blind hymn-writer great comfort and filled her heart with joy. She felt sure that God would bless the hymn to many hearts. Her hope has been most fully verified, for millions have been refreshed and strengthened as they have sung it. At the suggestion of Mr. D. W. McWilliams, who was superintendent of Dr. Cuyler's Sunday school for twenty-five years, it was put into "Gospel Hymns."

Saviour, Visit Thy Plantation

Words by John Newton   Music (Rathbun) by Ithamar Conkey

> Saviour! Visit Thy plantation;
> Grant us, Lord, a gracious rain.

In his youth Mr. Newton was employed in planting lime and lemon trees on a plantation in Africa. One day his master sneeringly said to him: "Who knows but by the time these trees grow up and bear, you may go home to England, obtain the command of a ship, and return to reap the fruit of your labours?"

John Newton really did return, in command of a ship, and with some hope of heaven in his heart, and saw the trees he had planted grown up and bearing fruit.

At the age of eleven he went to sea with his father. He drifted away from his pious mother's teachings and grew into an abandoned and Godless sailor. He was flogged as a deserter from the navy, and for fifteen months he lived, half-starved and ill-treated, on the above mentioned plantation, under a slave-dealer.

His Christian belief matured while in command of a slave-ship. He soon became an ardent worker for Christ.

In 1805, when no longer able to read his text, his reply when pressed to discontinue preaching, was: "What, shall the old African blasphemer stop while he can speak?" He was a lifelong friend of the great hymn-writer, William Cowper, and himself wrote a large number of hymns.

"Saviour, Visit Thy Plantation" is usually sung to the tune "Rathbun," written by Ithamar Conkey.

Scatter Seeds of Kindness

Words by Mrs. Albert Smith   Music by S. J. Vail

> Let us gather up the sunbeams,
> Lying all around our path.

For many years this was the favourite hymn of Francis Murphy, the great temperance lecturer, and was the keynote of all his meetings. I had the pleasure of attending many of his services in Chicago, and have seen him move an audience to tears by his pathetic rendering of this hymn. It is believed that thousands of drinking men have been saved through its instrumentality.

I had the pleasure of meeting the author of this hymn in Illinois in 1878, and was surprised to learn that she herself was childless, although very fond of children, as shown in the tender expressions in the latter portion of the hymn:

How those little hands remind us,
As in snowy grace they lie,
Not to scatter thorns – but roses
For our reaping by and by.

Shall We Gather at the River

Words by Robert Lowry   Music by Robert Lowry

Shall we gather at the river
Where bright angel feet have trod?

On a sultry afternoon in July, 1864, Dr. Lowry was sitting at his study table in Elliott Place, Brooklyn, when the words of the hymn, "Shall we gather at the river?" came to him. He recorded them hastily, and then sat down before his parlour organ and composed the tune which is now sung in all the Sunday-schools of the world. In speaking of the song, Dr. Lowry said:

"It is brass-band music, has a march movement, and for that reason has become popular, though, for myself, I do not think much of it. Yet on several occasions I have been deeply moved by the singing of this very hymn. "Going from Harrisburg to Lewisburg once I got into a car filled with half-drunken lumbermen. Suddenly one of them struck up, 'Shall we gather at the river?' and they sang it over and over again, repeating the chorus in a wild, boisterous way. I did not think so much of the music then, as I listened to those singers; but I did think that perhaps the spirit of the hymn, the words so flippantly uttered, might somehow survive and be carried forward into the lives of those careless men, and ultimately lift them upward to the realization of the hope expressed in the hymn.

"A different appreciation of it was evinced during the Robert Raikes centennial. I was in London, and had gone to a meeting in the Old Bailey to see some of the most famous Sunday school workers of the world. They were present from Europe, Asia and America. I sat in a rear seat alone. After there had been a number of addresses delivered in various languages I was preparing to leave, when the chairman of the meeting announced that the author of 'Shall we gather at the river?' was present, and I was requested by name to come forward. Men applauded and women waved their handkerchiefs as I went to the platform. It was a tribute to the hymn; but I felt, after it was over, that I had perhaps done some little good in the world."

The year after it was written, on Children's Day, in Brooklyn, when the assembled Sunday schools of the city met in bewildering array, this song was sung by more than forty thousand voices. There was not a child from the gutter or a mission waif who did not know it.

An American lady writing from Cairo, who was allowed to visit the military hospital soon after some wounded men had been brought in from a skirmish, says: "The three hours we could stay were full of work for heart and hand. One young soldier from a Highland regiment especially excited my interest. He had lost a limb, and the doctor said he could not live through the night. I stopped at his side to see whether there was anything that I could do for him. He lay with closed eyes; and as his lips moved I caught the words, 'Mother, mother.' I dipped my handkerchief in a basin of iced water, and bathed his forehead where the fever flushes burned.

"'Oh, that is good!' he said, opening his eyes. Seeing me bending over him, he caught my hand and kissed it. 'Thank you, lady.' he said; 'it 'minds me o' mother.'

"I asked him if I could write to his mother. No, he said; the surgeon had promised to write; but could I, would I, sing to him? I hesitated a moment, and looked around. The gleam on the yellow water of the Nile, as the western rays slanted down, caught my eye and suggested the river the streams of which shall make glad the city of God. I began to sing in a low voice the Gospel hymn, 'Shall we gather at the river?' Eager heads were raised around us to listen more intently, while bass and tenor voices, weak and tremulous, came in on the chorus, –

> Yes, we'll gather at the river,
> The beautiful, the beautiful river;
> Gather with the saints at the river
> That flows by the throne of God.

"When the song was ended, I looked into the face of the boy – for he was not over twenty – and asked, 'Shall you be there?'

"'Yes, I'll be there, through what the Lord Jesus has done for me.' he answered, with his blue eyes shining, while a 'light that never was on sea or land' irradiated his face. The tears gathered in my eyes as I thought of the mother, in her far-off Scottish home, watching and waiting for tidings of her soldier boy, who was breathing away his life in an Egyptian hospital.

"'Come again, lady, come again,' I heard on all sides as we left the barracks. I shall go; but I shall not find my Scottish laddie, for by tomorrow's reveille he will have crossed the river."

Shall we Meet?

Words by Horace L. Hastings   Music by Elihu S. Rice

> Shall we meet beyond the river,
> Where the surges cease to roll?

While secretary and chorister of the Baptist Sunday-school at Logansport, Mr. Rice composed the music of this song and sent it to Robert Lowry, then editor of the musical department of the "Young Reaper," a Sunday-school paper published in Philadelphia. It was accepted and first published in that periodical. Years passed before the composer realized its popularity.

"The first notice I received," he says, "of the favourable reception of 'Shall we meet' by the musical public was from Mr. Sankey, in a very kind letter written in August, 1879, thirteen years after its first publication. While music has been written for those words by a number of eminent musical composers, I have the satisfaction of knowing that my music has received the choice and approval of Mr. Hastings, the author of the words."

Shall You? Shall I?

Words by James McGranahan   Music by James McGranahan

> Some one will enter the pearly gate
> By and by, by and by.

An active minister in the West in his boyhood attended our meetings in Madison Square Garden, and he says that his soul was thrilled by the singing there. He writes to me, also, of this personal experience:

"I was passing through a town where I was known. At the close of a service which I had attended the minister asked me to sing a solo. Picking up 'Gospel Hymns,' I sang,

> Some one will enter the pearly gate

By and by, by and by...
Shall you? Shall I?

"In the audience was a well-educated man, clearly under the influence of liquor. He afterward said that he forgot or failed to hear the very able sermon. But he heard the song; and for days after 'Shall you? Shall I?' kept ringing in his ears, until he finally had to give his heart to God. He is now a faithful minister in the Methodist church."

Singing all the Time

Words by E. P. Hammond   Music by George C. Stebbins

> I feel like singing all the time,
> My tears are wiped away.

"One day in a children's meeting in Utica, New York," E. P. Hammond writes me, "while I was explaining how Jesus loved us and gave himself for us, I noticed a bright-looking girl bursting into tears. She remained at the inquiry-meeting, and with others was soon happy in the love of Christ. The next day she handed me a letter of which this is a part:

'I think I have found the dear Jesus, and I do not see how I could have rejected Him so long. I think I can sing with the rest of those who have found Him, Jesus is mine. The first time I came to the meetings I cried, but now I feel like singing all the time.' This prompted me to write the hymn, but I had no thought of its ever being sung, although it almost seemed as if I could hear her singing:

> I feel like singing all the time,
> My tears are wiped away,
> For Jesus is a friend of mine,
> I'll serve Him every day.

"Mr. Spurgeon was very fond of this hymn. At the first meeting in his building one of his deacons said to me, 'This Tabernacle will seat six thousand grown people, but there are eight thousand crowded into it today.' Three thousand could not get in on account of the crowd. Every child had one of our hymn-books, and all united in singing this hymn which they loved so much. It has been sung in our meetings in nearly every state in the Union, and translated into many languages. "We sang it in our daily meetings in Jerusalem, near where Christ was crucified, and away in Alaska, two thousand miles north of San Francisco. Thousands of children sang it in Norway and Sweden, day after day.

"A little boy, who felt himself a great sinner in not having loved Jesus, was led by God's spirit to believe, and his burden was gone. Bright smiles took the place of tears, and with the happy throng he was soon joining in the song, 'I feel like singing all the time.' Little did I then think that years afterward I would find that same boy the pastor of a large church in Minneapolis, rejoicing that so many of his own Sunday-school were able to join in the same hymn which he sang when his heart was filled with a newfound love for Christ. It was largely through his influence that during one week of our meetings in Minneapolis, last spring, about seven hundred confessed conversion. I received in one day at Newark, New Jersey, more than two hundred letters from those who had just professed to have found Christ in our meetings. Many of those young converts, in giving what they believed to be the story of their conversion, often put in the words, 'Now I feel like singing all the time.'"

Something for Jesus

Words by S. D. Phelps   Music by Robert Lowry

> Saviour! Thy dying love
> Thou gavest me.

Now famous in many lands, this hymn was first published more than forty years ago in the "Watchman and Reflector," and from there it was copied by various other religious papers. Dr. Robert Lowry requested the author, Mr. Phelps, to furnish some hymns for the hymn-book, "Pure Gold," which he and W. H. Doane were preparing, and among others which Mr. Phelps contributed was "Saviour! Thy dying love." Dr. Lowry composed for it the tune with which it will always be associated. On the author's seventieth birthday-nine years before his death in 1898–Mr. Phelps received this congratulation from Dr. Lowry:

"It is worth living seventy years, even if nothing comes of it but one such hymn as 'Saviour! Thy dying love.' Happy is the man who can produce one song which the world will keep on singing after its author shall have passed away."

Professor W. F. Sherwin was holding a Sunday-school institute in Maine on one occasion. This hymn was used in the exercises, and a young lawyer was so much affected by the singing of the third verse that it was the means of changing all his plans for life. He consecrated himself to Christ's service, and thereafter devoted himself with his whole heart to evangelistic work.

"A large family joined my church lately," says a minister in Glasgow. "The mother told me that, while a stranger in the city, she had happened to drop into our chapel, when she was quite overcome. Her heart was lifted up as the people sang,

> Saviour! Thy dying love
> Thou gavest me
> Nor should I aught withhold,
> My Lord, from Thee.

Sometime We'll Understand

Words by Maxwell N. Cornelius D D.   Music by James McGranahan

> Not now, but in the coming years,
> It may be in the better land.

Mr. Cornelius was brought up on a farm in my own county in Pennsylvania. He left farming when he came of age, and learned the trade of a brick-mason. Later he became a contractor in Pittsburg. In erecting a house in that city his leg was broken. The physicians decided that it would have to be amputated, and they gave him a week in which to get ready for the ordeal. My own physician was sent for to assist at the operation. When the day arrived the young man said that he was ready, but asked for his violin, that he might play one more tune-perhaps the last one he would ever play.

Whatever the tune was, the melody was so sweet that it caused even the physicians to weep. He stood the operation well and came out safely, but was maimed for life. He now decided to go to college and get an education. After passing through college with honour he concluded to become a minister of the gospel. His first charge was at Altoona, Pennsylvania, but on account of his wife's health he soon removed to California, locating at Pasadena, where he built the largest Presbyterian Church in that place. Many who had subscribed to help to pay for the building failed in business, and he was left to meet the obligations as best he could. But in a few years he had the church cleared from all debt. Shortly afterward his wife died. He preached the funeral sermon himself.

At the conclusion he quoted the words of this hymn, which he had composed shortly before. Both the words of the hymn and the sermon were printed in a Western newspaper, where Major Whittle found them. Impressed by their beauty, he cut them out and carried them in his Bible for three months before he wrote the chorus:

> Then trust in God through all thy days;
> Fear not! For He doth hold thy hand;
> Though dark thy way, still sing and praise;
> Sometime, sometime we'll understand.

Soon after he handed the words to his friend, James McGranahan, who composed the tune to which the hymn is now sung.

While Mr. Moody and I were holding meetings in the great Convention Hall in Washington, in 1894, one evening he requested me to go to an overflow meeting in the Second Presbyterian Church. I sang "Sometime We'll Understand" as a solo, and I told how Major Whittle had found it. At the conclusion of the meeting a lady came forward to the platform, and said "That hymn was written by my pastor;" and for the first time I learned who had written the beautiful words of the hymn I loved so much. A year or two later I sang this hymn in the Church of the Covenant in Washington. The late Secretary of State, John Hay, was present. He was much moved by the song, and at the conclusion of the service came forward and thanked me. While we were talking a young lady with her husband came up to me and said that she was the daughter of Dr. Cornelius, the author of the hymn, and hoped that God would continually bless my singing of the song.

At one of our crowded meetings in the Free Assembly Hall in Edinburgh, Scotland, Mr. Moody called to the platform Lord Overtoun, who changed the meeting into a memorial service for the Prince of Wales' eldest son, the Duke of Clarence, who had recently died in England. After a number of addresses had been made by ministers and others, Lord Overtoun asked a member of my choir, Miss Jane Darling, if she had any song suitable to the occasion. I had gone to Dunfirmline to commence meetings there. Miss Darling took her seat at my little organ and sung in the most touching and pathetic manner the hymn, "Sometime We'll Understand." At the conclusion of the meeting Lord Overtoun sent a dispatch to the Princess of Wales, including in the message three of the verses of the hymn. The same evening he received a dispatch from the

Princess, thanking him for the verses. A few days later Miss Darling had the hymn beautifully engrossed upon parchment and forwarded it to the Princess.

Stand Up for Jesus

Words by George Duflield   Music by G. J. Webb

Stand up! Stand up for Jesus!
Ye soldiers of the cross.

In the "Great Work of God" of 1858, in Philadelphia, Dudley Tyng was the recognized leader. While standing by a piece of farm machinery on his place, the sleeve of his coat became entangled in the gearing. His arm was drawn into the machinery and torn off, and he died soon after. In the prime of his life he was taken away from the direction of that great revival movement. But his dying message to his associates in the work, "Stand up for Jesus," supplied the theme for this hymn. It was written by George Duffield, and was read at the close of a sermon which he delivered on the Sunday following the death of his friend. Set to the tune composed by Mr. Webb, this hymn has become famous and useful.

Substitution

Words by Mrs. A. R. Cousin   Music by Ira D. Sankey

O Christ, what burdens bowed Thy head!
Our load was laid on Thee.

Written in Melrose, Scotland, by the author of the immortal poem, "Immanuel's Land," this hymn was sent to me by a minister in Dublin; and in the letter conveying the verses he remarked: "It is said of you that you sing the Gospel, and I am sure that if you will sing the enclosed there will be no question as to the truth of that assertion." I then wrote the music and sang it in one of Mr. Moody's meetings, where it was blessed to the saving of two persons the first time it was sung, according to their own testimony.

A young officer in the British army turned away in horror from the doctrine of this hymn. His pride revolted, his self-righteousness rose in rebellion, and he said: "He would be a coward indeed who would go to heaven at the cost of another!" As the years rolled away this man rose to distinction and high rank in the army, and he also learned wisdom. In his last hours, as he lay on his deathbed, he repeatedly begged those near him to sing "O Christ, what burdens bowed Thy head;" calling it, "My hymn, my hymn!"

A gunner of the royal artillery was attending the Old Soldiers' Home in Woolwich during the spring of 1886. The chief attraction to him at first was the night-school. From this he was eventually led to join the Bible-class and attend the Sunday evening service in the Hall. Seeing that he looked very unhappy and that he lingered after the meeting, one night, a worker asked him if anything was troubling him. The tears came to his eyes at once, and he said: "I want to be a Christian, but I am afraid that I am too bad." He then told how on the previous Sunday evening, when this hymn was sung, he was so overpowered by the thought of what the Lord had endured for our sins that after the first verse he could not sing. The solemn words were fixed in his memory, and had troubled him all the week, until he came to the great Burden-bearer.

Sun of My Soul

Words by John Keble   Music by Peter Ritter, 1798

> Sun of my soul, Thou Saviour dear,
> It is not night if Thou be near.

This is taken from Mr. John Keble's evening hymn, which originally consisted of fourteen verses and was published in "The Christian Year" in 1827. It was based upon the words found in Luke 24:29, "Abide with us; for it is toward evening and the day is far spent." Keble was born. in Gloucestershire, 1792, and died in 1866. The old English tune to which the hymn is sung was written in 1798.

Sweet By and By

Words by S. Fillmore Bennett   Music by Joseph P. Webster

> There's a land that is fairer than day,
> And by faith we can see it afar.

Mr. Bennett, the author of this world-famed hymn, has this to say about its origin:

"In 1861 I became a resident of the village of Elkhorn, Wisconsin, the home of the composer, J. P. Webster; and shortly after became associated with him in the production of sheet music (songs) and other musical works. In the summer or fall of the year 1867 we commenced work on 'The Signet Ring.' One of the songs written for that book was 'Sweet By and By.' Mr. Webster, like many musicians, was of an exceedingly nervous and sensitive nature, and subject to periods of depression, in which he looked upon the dark side of all things in life. I had learned his peculiarities so well that on meeting him I could tell at a glance if he was in one of his melancholy moods, and I found that I could rouse him from them by giving him a new song or hymn to work on. On such an occasion he came into my place of business, walked down to the stove, and turned his back to me without speaking. I was at my desk writing. Presently I said:

"'Webster, what is the matter now?'

"'It is no matter,' he replied; 'it will be all right by and by!'

"The idea of the hymn came to me like a flash of sunlight, and I replied: 'The sweet by and by! Would that not make a good hymn?'

"'Maybe it would,' said he indifferently. Turning to the desk I penned the three verses and the chorus as fast as I could write. In the meantime two friends, Mr. N. H. Carswell and Mr. S. E. Bright, had come in. I handed the hymn to Mr. Webster. As he read it his eye kindled, and his whole demeanor changed. Stepping to the desk, he began writing the notes in a moment. Presently he requested Mr. Bright to hand him his violin, and then he played the melody. In a few moments more he had the notes for the four parts of the chorus jotted down. I think it was not over thirty minutes from the time I took my pen to write the words before the two gentlemen; Mr. Webster and I were singing the hymn in the same form in which it afterward appeared in 'The Signet Ring.' While singing it Mr. R. R. Crosby came in. After listening awhile, with tears in his eyes, he uttered the prediction: 'That hymn is immortal.' I think it was used in public shortly after, for within two weeks children on the streets were singing it."

"Next year the publishers of 'The Signet Ring' heralded its advent by distributing a large number of circulars upon which selections from the work were printed; among them 'Sweet By and By.' These circulars first brought the hymn to the notice of the public, and created the principal demand for the book. Toward the close of that year the hymn was published in sheet-music form. It is now in numerous collections of vocal music in America, and, as a newspaper account says, 'It is translated into various foreign languages and sung in every land under the sun.'

"Webster, Crosby and Carswell are dead. S. E. Bright, of Fort Atkinson, Wisconsin, and myself are the only remaining living witnesses to the birth of 'Sweet By and By.'"

Sweet Hour of Prayer

Words by W. W. Walford   Music by Wm. B. Bradbury

Sweet hour of prayer, sweet hour of prayer!
That calls me from a world of care.

This most useful hymn was set to music by William Batchelder Bradbury. He was born in October 6, 1816, and died in New Jersey, January 7, 1868. He published a large number of Sunday-school hymnbooks, which had a very large circulation in the United States. When quite a young man, I attended a musical convention conducted by Mr. Bradbury in the State of Ohio, and there received my first impressions as to the power of sacred song.

Sweet Peace, the Gift of God's Love

Words by Peter P. Bilhorn   Music by Peter P. Bilhorn

There comes to my heart one sweet strain,
A glad and a joyous refrain.

The author of this well-known and popular hymn, a gifted evangelist and Gospel singer, was born in Mendota, Illinois, in 1861. His father was killed near the close of the war, and at eight years of age he had to leave school to help his mother. Though the education of books was thus denied him, yet through wonderful ways of Providence he has been able to read in the great book of human nature, and his knowledge of men is as great as his influence and power for good over them. At the age of fifteen he moved with his family to Chicago, where his voice was a great attraction in concert-halls and among worldly comrades. He was standing by a piano in a German concerthall, one day in 1881, when a Christian worker entered and persuaded him to attend one of the revival meetings in Mr. Moody's church being conducted by Dr. Pentecost and Mr. Stebbins. He was interested, and for twelve nights he attended regularly. On the twelfth night he heard a sermon from the words, "Christ hath redeemed us," and he gave his heart to God. Shortly afterward he engaged in mission work in all parts of Chicago, wherever and whenever he could make himself useful, at the same time studying music under Professor George F. Root. After two years he went to work among the cowboys in the West, where he had many thrilling experiences. Since then Mr. Bilhorn has devoted his talents entirely to the work of singing the Gospel, and today he is ranked among the leaders of evangelistic work in song.

Take Me as I Am

Words by Eliza H. Hamilton   Music by Ira D. Sankey

Jesus, my Lord, to Thee I cry;
Unless Thou help me I must die.

Years ago, while revival meetings were being held in one of the large towns in Scotland, a young girl became anxious about her spiritual condition. Returning from one of the meetings, she went to her own minister and asked him how she might be saved.

"Ah, lassie," he said, "don't be alarmed! Just read your Bible and say your prayers, and you will be all right."

But the poor, illiterate girl cried out: "O Minister, I canna read, I canna pray! Lord Jesus, take me as I am!"

In this way the girl became a follower of Christ; and a lady who heard of the girl's experience wrote this hymn, "Take Me as I Am." I found the verses in a religious newspaper, and set them to the simple music by which they are now most generally known. At the same time Mr. Stebbins also found the verses and set them to music, and he sent them to me at the same time that I was sending my tune for the same words to him. In "Gospel Hymns" both tunes are published.

A minister in England writes to me about a Christian woman, a shoemaker's wife, who had a lodger that was an obstinate unbeliever. The good woman often tried to induce him to go to meetings, but in vain. Tracts which she placed on the table in his room she found crushed on the floor. She would smooth them out and again place them so as to attract his attention, but he would read nothing but his novels and newspapers. One spring the old man fell ill with bronchitis. The good woman acted as his nurse, for he had no relatives who cared for him. She used the opportunity, often speaking to him about his soul and reading the Word of God; but she could make no impression upon him. One day she was reading the hymn 'Jesus, my Lord, to Thee I cry,' and when she came to the refrain, the old man called out to her sharply: 'That's not in the book!' The woman answered, 'Why, yes, it is.' He declared again that he did not believe it was in the book. The good woman told him that he could read it for himself. He asked for his glasses, and read with wonder and amazement, again and again,

> My only plea – Christ died for me!
> Oh, take me as I am.

A few weeks afterward he said to the woman one morning, 'I am going home today, and I am so happy, so happy!' In an hour or two he passed away, repeating these words to the last."

"One afternoon when visiting the Royal Infirmary," a missionary in England writes, "I found a young girl very ill and without any prospect of recovery. I sat down by her and read the hymn, 'Jesus, my Lord, to Thee I cry.' She listened very attentively, but I did not know until the following week, when I visited her again, what a deep impression it had made upon her. On this second occasion I was told that she was much worse. Hearing I was there, she asked her mother to tell me that she wanted very much to see me. When I went to her she leaned forward and, with an eagerness which surprised me, repeated the words:

> My only plea–Christ died for me!
> Oh, take me as I am.

These comforting lines had been constantly on her lips during this last week of her life. That night the Lord took her home."

A party of policemen had gathered in a drawing-room in the West End of London. One was there who had been persuaded by his Christian comrades to attend for the first time a meeting of The Christian Policemen's Association. He went unwillingly and rather late, and did not expect to care for the meeting. But soon after he had entered the room a lady, Miss Beauchamp, sang "Take me as I am" as a solo. The repeated refrain set him to thinking. As he was? He had led a rough life, first as a blue-jacket and then as a policeman. He could not well be more wretched and miserable than he was that night, with a load of sins upon him and a dark, dreary future to look forward to. He had never thought that Jesus would take him as he was. He had always thought that he must be much better first, and had often tried to make himself better; but it had been a miserable failure. Now the words, "Take me as I am," sounded over and over again in his ears; and in his heart he repeated them, "Lord, take me as I am." He left before the end of the meeting, and so it was not until the following month that his friends heard of the great change that had come over him. Since that time his delight has been to proclaim the love of God as opportunity offered, on the street or to his comrades, seeking to turn other lost ones to the path of life.

While Mr. Moody and I were holding meetings at Plymouth, England, Professor Henry Drummond, who was assisting us, became very much interested in an infidel who came to the services – labouring with him for several days and visiting him in his home, twenty miles distant, but making no impression on him. Near the close of the mission the infidel came again. On reaching the building, which was located inside the barrack grounds, he found the door closed and the building full. And while he was standing on the green sward outside he heard the choir sing "Take me as I am." He told Professor Drummond afterward that God used this simple hymn to lead him into the Shepherd's fold.

Take Time to be Holy

Words by W. D. Longstaff   Music by Geo. C. Stebbins

Take time to be holy,
Speak oft with thy Lord.

Mr. Longstaff, of Sunderland, England, wrote this hymn after hearing a sermon at New Brighton on "Be ye holy as I am holy." "Take Time to be Holy" was first published in Gospel Hymns and Sacred Songs and Solos, in 1891. It has been much used in holiness-meetings, both in this country and Great Britain. Mr. Longstaff was the treasurer of Bethesda Chapel, in Sunderland, when we held our first meetings in that town, and was the first one to write anything in relation to our meetings in Great Britain.

Tell It Out

Words by Frances R. Havergal   Music by Ira D. Sankey

> Tell it out among the nations that the Lord is King;
> Tell it out! Tell it out!

Miss Havergal's sister Maria bears record that this hymn was written in England in 1872, when the author was unable to go to church one snowy morning. She asked for her prayer-book, always liking to follow the services of the day. On the return of her brother-in-law, Mr. Shaw, from church, he heard her touch upon the piano.

"Why, Frances, I thought you were upstairs!"

"Yes, but I had my prayer-book; and in the Psalms for Today I read, 'Tell it out among the heathen that the Lord is King.' I thought, 'What a splendid first line!' and then the words and music came rushing in to me. There! it's all written out."

I found Miss Havergal's tune rather difficult to sing, and therefore arranged the one which is now found in "Gospel Hymns," in "Sacred Songs and Solos," and in the new Methodist Episcopal hymnal.

Tell Me the Old, Old Story

Words by Miss Kate Hankey   Music by W. H. Doane

> Tell me the old, old story,
> Of unseen things above.

This excellent hymn by Miss Hankey, of London, has been translated into many languages, and has been set to several tunes. Dr. Doane has this to say regarding the music by which it has become popular, and the occasion on which he composed it: "In 1867 I was attending the International Convention of the Young Men's Christian Association, in Montreal. Among those present was Major-General Russell, then in command of the English forces during the Fenian excitement. He arose in the meeting and recited the words of this song from a sheet of foolscap paper – tears streaming down his bronzed cheeks as he read. I wrote the music for the song one hot afternoon while on the stage-coach between the Glen Falls House and the Crawford House in the White Mountains. That evening we sung it in the parlours of the hotel. We thought it pretty, although we scarcely anticipated the popularity which was subsequently accorded it."

Mr. Wm. Luff relates a striking story of conversion through the singing of this hymn at one of the Moody and Sankey meetings during our first Mission in London: — "A young stock-broker, the child of many prayers, was given to a life of gambling and drunken dissipation, bringing disgrace upon his wife and family, and costing his parents some thousands of pounds to save him from utter failure. On the Stock Exchange he was a leader in ridiculing the work of the evangelists from over the sea.

"One day the question was put to him, 'Is it fair to mock at what you have not heard? 'He owned it was not, and promised to attend one of the meetings. As he entered, this hymn was being sung; and he was all attention as the second verse pealed forth from the vast congregation:

> Tell me the story slowly
> That I may take it in,
> That wonderful redemption,
> God's remedy for sin.
> Tell me the story often,
> For I forget so soon;
> The early dew of morning
> Has passed away at noon.

"These words went to his heart. It was an exact description of his case. His early goodness had all passed away Hke the morning dew, and all was dry as the desert. While the succeeding verse was being sung he entirely broke down. But the words 'Remember, I'm the sinner whom Jesus came to save,' brought hope, then confidence, then joy; and that day he realized that Jesus was a sufficient Saviour for the vilest sinner. All things were changed, and from that time he sought with untiring energy the salvation of others 'whom Jesus came to save.'"

Ten Thousand Times Ten Thousand

Words by Henry Alford. D.D.   Music by Ira D. Sankey

> Ten thousand times ten thousand, in sparkling raiment bright,
> The armies of the ransomed saints, throng up the steeps of light.

This is considered the best of Dean Alford's hymns. It was written in 1866 and published in the "Year of Praise" in 1867. Beside the open grave of the author, January 17, 1871, the hymn was sung with intense emotion by his sorrowing friends.

That Will be Heaven for Me

Words by P. P. Bliss   Music by James McGranahan

> I know not the hour when my Lord will come
> To take me away to His own dear home.

Elizabeth Stuart Phelps' "The Gates Ajar," which aroused so much criticism a generation ago, suggested to Mr. Bliss the need of this hymn. The Scripture teaching that we shall be "with the Lord" he deemed sufficient for spiritual contentment, offsetting the "I know not" of speculation by the "I know" of faith. Mr. McGranahan was visiting Mr. Bliss at that time. Bliss handed the words to him, asking what he could get for a tune. McGranahan worked upon it a long time without success, making harmonies and trying to satisfy himself with something that would properly express the words. When suppertime came he did not care to eat. At bedtime they all went to their rooms, leaving him in the parlour at the piano. Finally, dissatisfied with the result, he threw himself on the floor and fell into a doze. Suddenly he awoke, and the tune, chorus and all, had come – different from the harmonies he had worked upon. When he sang it to Bliss in the morning he was delighted with it, and immediately adopted it for use.

A wealthy Quaker lady heard this hymn in Newcastle-on-Tyne, sung in connection with Mr. Moody's lecture upon "Heaven." She was so much impressed by it that she went home and induced her husband to attend the meetings. She soon became one of the most successful workers in our subsequent meetings there and in London, taking lodgings near so as to more efficiently work in the inquiry-meetings.

At the time Mr. Bliss and his wife were lost in the railroad accident at Ashtabula I was living in a hotel in Chicago. I had engaged a room near mine for him, and was awaiting his arrival, when a friend came into my room and, putting his hand on my shoulder, said, "Bliss is dead." The next Sunday we held a great memorial service in the Tabernacle, to give expression to our sorrow. While I was singing "That will be Heaven for Me" as a solo, the two small crowns of flowers which had been placed in front of the organ on the platform were taken away, as it was discovered that their two little children, Paul and George, who were supposed to have been lost with their parents, had been left at home at Towanda, Pennsylvania, and were safe.

The Anchored Soul

Words by W. O. Cushing   Music by Robert Lowry

> I have anchored my soul in the haven of rest,
> I sail the wild seas no more, no more.

The words of this hymn were written by W. O. Cushing, and the music by Robert Lowry. It has become very popular among sailors and seafaring men.

The Child of a King

Words by Hattie E. Buell   Music by John B. Sumner

> My Father is rich in houses and lands.
> He holdeth the wealth of the world in His hands!

Mr. Peter P. Bilhorn relates the following incident in connection with this hymn, which happened when he was engaged in evangelistic work among the cowboys in the West, in 1883. "We had started up the Missouri River for Bismarck, and on Sunday we stopped at a new town, named Blunt, to unload some freight. A crowd of men and boys came down to the wharf. I took my little organ, went on the wharf-boat, and sang a few songs – among others the glorious hymn, 'I'm the child of a King.' "I thought nothing more of the occasion until long afterward, when I sang the same song in Mr. Moody's church in Chicago. Then a man in the back part of the house arose, and said in a trembling voice: 'Two years ago I heard that song at Blunt, Dakota; I was then an unsaved man, but that song set me to thinking, and I decided to accept Christ, and I am now studying for the ministry.'"

The Christian's "Good-Night"

Words by Sarah Doudney   Music by Ira D. Sankey

> Sleep on, beloved, sleep, and take thy rest;
> Lay down thy head upon thy Saviour's breast.

The words of this hymn were occasioned by the death of a friend. They were handed to me at Bristol, England. I wrote the music soon afterward, and sang it at the funeral of Charles H. Spurgeon, the great

London preacher. It has since become very useful on two continents as a funeral hymn.

Each member of the Masonic Quartet of Pittsburgh recently received a cheque and a note of thanks for singing at the funeral of Captain S. S. Brown. An unusual story was also made public thereby. "In the last hours of the turf king's life," one of the daily papers says, "he had an interval in which his mind was clear. He called his daughter-in-law and asked if she would take on herself the task of seeing that 'The Christian's Goodnight' was sung at his funeral; and he told her, in a disjointed way, of a dream from which he had just awakened. He had thought himself dead, and there were four ministers taking part in his funeral. He named the ministers and said that one of them had broken down while making an address, and that another, naming this minister also, had taken up the address. Captain Brown said that he awoke as all were singing 'The Christian's Goodnight,' and that he had joined with them in the singing. The dying man smiled faintly at the picture he drew, but begged his daughter-in-law to remember her promise."

The Cross of Jesus

Words by Elizabeth Clephane   Music by Ira D. Sankey

> Beneath the cross of Jesus
> I fain would take my stand.

I composed the music to this hymn in the home of my dear friend, Dr. Thomas Barnardo, whose death is announced through the public press just at the time I am writing this note. The author of the hymn, Elizabeth Clephane, also wrote the widely-known hymn, "The Ninety and Nine," and these two were the only hymns from her pen which have become popular.

The first time this hymn was sung is still fresh in my memory. The morning after I had composed the music W. H. Aitkin was to speak at our mission in the great Bow Road Hall, in London, Mr. Moody having made an arrangement to speak at Her Majesty's Theatre. It was a lovely morning, and a great gathering had assembled at the meeting, which was held at eight o'clock. Before the sermon I sang "Beneath the cross of Jesus" as a solo; and as in the case of "The Ninety and Nine," much blessing came from its use for the first time. With eyes filled with tears, and deeply moved, the preacher said to the audience: "Dear friends, I had intended to speak to you this morning upon work for the Master, but this new hymn has made such an impression on my heart, and evidently upon your own, that I will defer my proposed address and speak to you on 'The Cross of Jesus.'" The sermon was one of the most powerful I have ever heard, and many souls that morning accepted the message of grace and love. Some years later Mr. Aitkin held many successful meetings in New York and other cities in this country, and he often used this hymn as a solo.

An odd incident occurred in connection with Mr. Aitkin's use of this hymn in St. Paul's Church, at Broadway and Wall Street, the money centre of America. A gentleman, having heard this piece sung frequently by great congregations of business men and Wall Street brokers in St. Paul's Church, called upon the publishers of the small book of words which had been distributed in the church, and said that he "wished to secure that beautiful English tune which Mr. Aitkin used so much in his meetings." When he was told that he could find it in any copy of "Gospel Hymns" he became quite indignant, and insisted that it was a fine classic which the great preacher had brought with him from England – nothing like the Moody and Sankey trash! Having secured a copy of Mr. Aitkin's hymn-book containing the "fine English tune" to the beautiful words of "Beneath the cross of Jesus," he went away happy, but only to find that it was written by the author of the music to "The Ninety and Nine."

The Eye of Faith

Words by J. J. Maxfield   Music by W. A. Ogden

I do not ask for earthly store
Beyond a day's supply.

This was a favourite hymn of Mr. Moody during our last campaign in Scotland. As we went from place to place the choirs which had sung at our meetings would often gather at the stations and sing this and other hymns at our parting.

The Gate Ajar for Me

Words by Mrs. Lydia Baxter   Music by S. J. Vail

> There is a gate that stands ajar,
> And through its portals gleaming.

Mrs. Lydia Baxter, born in Petersburg, New York, in 1809, was an invalid for many years. But her interest in the religious welfare of those around her was manifested in many ways. She wrote "There is a gate that stands ajar" about three years before her death in New York City in 1874, when she was considerably past the sixty-year mark.

In our meetings in Great Britain, 1873-74, this hymn was much used. It was sung at the watchnight service in 1873, the night before New Year's, in the Free Assembly Hall of Edinburgh. A young lady who was present – Maggie Lindsay, of Aberdeen, Scotland – was much impressed by the hymn, and those seated by her side heard her exclaim, "O, heavenly Father, is it true that the gate is standing ajar for me? If it is so, I will go in." That night she became a disciple of the Lord Jesus. The next day she called on her pastor, J. H. Wilson, minister of the Barclay Church, and told him of her decision. He was greatly pleased, and advised her to tell her school companions of her experience. This she did, and succeeded in leading several of them into the light. Scarcely a month later, on January 28, Maggie took a train for her home, but she never reached there alive. At Manual Junction a collision took place between a mineral train and the one on which she was riding. A number of passengers were killed, and Maggie, all crushed and broken, was found in the wreck. In one of her hands was a copy of 'Sacred Songs and Solos," opened at her favourite hymn, "There is a gate that stands ajar," the page of which was stained with her heart's blood. She was carried into a cottage near the station, where she lingered a few days and was frequently heard to sing on her dying couch the chorus of the hymn so dear to her, "For me, for me! was left ajar for me!"

In commemoration of this event, which touched me deeply, I wrote my first hymn, "Home at last," which I also set to music.

An affecting incident was related by one of the colporteurs of the Christian Colportage Association for England. "I called at a house in B–, where lived two aged people who were invalids had called several times before, but could never sell them any books or command their attention to hear about good things. On this occasion I began to sing, 'There is a gate that stands ajar.' When I came to the chorus, 'Oh, depth of mercy,' I saw a tear in the old lady's eye, and I stopped. But she said, 'Go on; that is a nice song.' I continued, but before I had finished she burst into tears, asking, 'Is that mercy for me?' I then talked to them both about Jesus and prayed with them. They bought the hymn-book containing the song, and earnestly begged me to come again as soon as possible. I have visited them every month. Last week, when I called I found the poor woman dying; but when her husband told her I had come, she said, 'I want to see him, tell him to come in.' She could hardly speak, but she said in a whisper: 'Do sing my favourite.' I knew which one she meant, and sang very softly,

> 'Oh, depth of mercy! Can it be
> That gate was left ajar for me?'

She tried to join me in singing, but fell back, quite exhausted. I could not talk much with her, she was so weak; but she held my hand with a firm grasp, still repeating the words, 'Oh, depth of mercy I can it be?' I have just heard that she has passed away, happy in the Saviour's love, and singing as well as she could that beautiful hymn."

Lord Shaftesbury once told the following story: "A young woman had wandered away from home and parents. One day, while listening to the Gospel, she was so impressed that she resolved to return home. She started, and on reaching the house found the door unfastened, and she walked upstairs to her mother. 'Mother,' she asked, 'how was it that I found the door open?' "'My girl,' replied the mother, 'that door has never been closed since you have been away; I thought that some night my poor girl would return.'"

The Half Was Never Told

Words by P. P. Bliss   Music by P. P. Bliss

> Repeat the story o'er and o'er,
> Of grace, so full and free.

This was suggested to Mr. Bliss by his reading notes, written by his friend and sometime fellow labourer in gospel work, James M. Brookes, of St. Louis, upon the Queen of Sheba's visit to King Solomon. This was one of my most popular solos.

The Handwriting on the Wall

Words and Music by Knowles Shaw   Arr. by Ira D. Sankey

> At the feast of Belshazzar and a thousand of his lords,
> While they drank from golden vessels, as the Book of Truth records.

This hymn was written by Knowles Shaw on the experience of King Belshazzar of Babylon. I arranged it to music from a tune written by the author of the words, and frequently sang it as a solo.

The Harbour Bell

Words by Job H. Yates   Music by Ira D. Sankey

> Our life is like a stormy sea
> Swept by the gales of sin and grief.

John H. Yates, a humble layman who lived at Batavia, New York, wrote this hymn after reading the following incident in a newspaper: "We were nearing a dangerous coast, and the night was drawing near. Suddenly a heavy fog settled down upon us. No lights had been sighted, and the pilot seemed anxious and troubled, not knowing how soon we might be dashed to pieces on the hidden rocks along the shore. The whistle was blown loud and hard, but no response was heard. The captain ordered the engines to be stopped, and for some time we drifted about on the waves. Suddenly the pilot cried, 'Hark!' Far away in the distance we heard the welcome tones of the harbour bell, which seemed to say, 'This way, this way!' Again the engines were started, and, guided by the welcome sound, we entered the harbour in safety."

On receiving this hymn from Mr. Yates, in 1891, I at once set it to music. It has been found useful in meetings for sailors and fishermen.

The King is Coming

Words by Ira D. Sankey   Music by Ira D. Sankey

> Rejoice! Rejoice! Our King is coming!
> And the time will not be long.

During one of my trips to Great Britain, on "The City of Rome," a storm raged on the sea. The wind was howling through the rigging, and waves like mountains of foam were breaking over the bow of the vessel.

A great fear had fallen upon the passengers. When the storm was at its worst we all thoght that we might soon go to the bottom of the sea. The conviction came to me that the Lord would be with us in the trying hour, and, sitting down in the reading room, I composed this hymn. Before reaching England the tune had formed itself in my mind, and on arriving in London I wrote it out and had it published in "Sacred Songs and Solos." It has been much employed in England in connection with sermons on the second coming of Christ, and was frequently used by Mr. Moody.

The Light of the World is Jesus

Words by P. P. Bliss   Music by P. P. Bliss

> The whole world was lost in the darkness of sin,
> The light of the world is Jesus.

Both the words and music of this hymn were written by P. P. Bliss in the summer of 1875, at his home in Chicago. It came to him altogether, words and music, one morning while passing through the hall to his room, and was at once written down.

The Lily of the Valley

Words by C. W. Fry   Arr. by Ira D. Sankey

> I've found a friend in Jesus,
> He's everything to me.

A young Jewess had been converted in London through her German governess. She had been forbidden to read the New Testament by her parents, who were ardent Jews, but while reading Isaiah 53 she found the Messiah, and was soon expelled from her home. She then went to Germany, and herself acted as governess for several years. When she heard of Mr. Moody's work at Northfield, she decided to go there. Having been entertained in London for a few weeks by Mr. Denny, a prominent layman, this gentleman asked me one day in London, as he was about to sail for America, if I would see her safely across the ocean, which I promised to do. In Louisville she first saw Mr. Moody. On leaving Louisville she went to New York and applied to the Presbyterian Board of Foreign Missions for appointment as a foreign missionary. There being some delay in accepting her application, she decided to go with Hudson Taylor, whom she had met at Northfield. On arriving in China she adopted the garb of the Chinese women, and became a faithful and useful worker. After two years she was married to a missionary from Scotland. They are still engaged in missionary work in Northern China.

"Auntie, please sing 'Lily of the Valley,' said a little girl of six, as she stood by the piano in company with a number of other children on a Sunday evening. In a few minutes all present were singing:

> I've found a friend in Jesus, He's everything to me;
> He's the fairest of ten thousand to my soul;

And the little one, who knew only the chorus, joined in heartily with the rest, her clear voice ringing out sweetly amid those of the older children. When her auntie would play on the piano she would always run to her and beg for one or another of her favourite hymns, but her favourite was, "Lily of the Valley," and she never tired of hearing it. The following winter was a very severe one, and this little girl was stricken with diphtheria.

Nothing would soothe her but to have her mother sing to her. Over and over again the mother would sing all the songs she knew, but specially "The Lily of the Valley." One morning, soon after dawn, the child seemed to be a little brighter, and tried to raise her hand, as though she wished to speak. Tenderly the mother asked what she wanted and the girl whispered, "Sing 'The Lily of the Valley' once more."

With tears streaming down her cheeks the mother attempted to sing the first verse and the chorus. A smile broke over the little one's face, and as her head dropped back on the pillow her spirit went out into the bosom of Him, who is indeed the "Lily of the Valley, and the fairest of ten thousand."

Bitter indeed were their tears when they realized that their darling was no more, but their sorrow was lightened by the knowledge that she was free from pain, and they will always treasure with her memory the hymn she loved so well.

Mr. Fry is one of the leaders of the Salvation Army in London. In addition to writing the words, he also set the hymn to music, and later arranged it to slower time and published it in Gospel Hymns.

The Mistakes of my Life

Words by Mrs. Urania Locke Bailey   Music by Robert Lowry

> The mistakes of my life have been many,
> The sins of my heart have been more.

While we were holding meetings in Boston, in 1876, Mr. Moody was entertained by one of the leading lawyers of the city, who frequently before the meetings would ask what solo I had selected. If I had none, he would say, "Please sing, 'The mistakes of my life have been many'; for one of the greatest mistakes I have ever made was to ignore God in all my affairs. But at last he took away my only child, a beloved son. That led me to the feet of Jesus, and I bowed to kiss the hand that had laid the rod upon me. Then I told the Lord that I would devote my fortune to His service. In keeping with that promise I erected a college for young women, located at Wellesley Lake, near Boston." This good man has now passed on to his reward. Shortly before he died Mr. Moody and I purchased a perpetual scholarship in Wellesley College, as a prize to be sought after by the young women of Northfield Seminary.

Written about the year 1871, this hymn was much used and became very popular in our meetings in Great Britain.

The Model Church

Words by John H. Yates   Music by Ira D. Sankey

> Well, wife, I've found the model church,
> And worshiped there today.

I found this poem in a newspaper, wrote the music for it, and sang it for the first time at a meeting for ministers and Christian workers at Atlanta, Georgia, conducted by Mr. Moody. It has been repeatedly used as a solo in meetings gathered for the discussion of the subject, "How to reach the masses." Once, in Buffalo, I had the pleasure of meeting Mr. Yates of Batavia, New York; and I urged him to devote more of his time to writing Gospel hymns. He has since written several popular songs, one of the most successful being "Faith is the Victory," which I published in "New Hymns and Solos," and is now included in the enlarged edition of "Sacred Songs and Solos."

A poor little girl, living in an alley of the slum district of Chicago, was used in a remarkable way for the conversion of a commercial traveler. He had received instructions, his trunks filled with samples had been sent to the depot, and hurried good-byes had been said. With grip sack in hand, he took a short-cut to the station through one of the filthy alleys of the city. He saw a great number of half-clad children, whose only home was a wretched basement or illy-ventilated tenement. As he passed, one little waif was singing at the top of her voice:

"There'll be no sorrow there."

"Where?" said the thoughtless salesman.

"In heaven above, where all is love, there'll be no sorrow there, "
Sang the little girl.

The answer, the singer, the far-away heaven with no sorrow there, lodged in his heart. The fastflying train soon left behind the hurry and the bustle of city life, but the answer of the little singing waif was taken up and repeated by the rapid revolution of the car-wheels. He could not forget the singer and the song, nor could he rest until he cried for mercy at the Cross. It was one of the many fulfillments of the promise, "A little child shall lead them."

The Morning Land

Words by Ellen K. Bradford   Music by E. H. Phelps
                                               (Arr. by Ira D. Sankey)

'Some day,' we say, and turn our eyes
Toward the fair hills of Paradise.

This hymn was written by the author of the music of, "Over the Line," and first published in sheet form in England, where I found it, and by permission of the publishers arranged it for use in the "Sacred Songs and Solos" and "Gospel Hymns." It has been sung as a duet at funerals all over the world.

The Ninety and Nine

Words by E. C. Clephane   Music by Ira D. Sankey

There were ninety and nine that safely lay
In the shelter of the fold.

It was in the year 1874 that the poem, "The Ninety and Nine," was

211

discovered, set to music, and sent out upon its world-wide mission. Its discovery seemed as if by chance, but I cannot regard it otherwise than providential. Mr. Moody had just been conducting a series of meetings in Glasgow, and I had been assisting him in his work as director of the singing. We were at the railway station at Glasgow and about to take the train for Edinburgh, whither we were going upon an urgent invitation of ministers to hold three days of meetings there before going into the Highlands. We had held a three months' series in Edinburgh just previous to our four months' campaign in Glasgow. As we were about to board the train I bought a weekly newspaper, for a penny. Being much fatigued by our incessant labours at Glasgow, and intending to begin work immediately upon our arrival at Edinburgh, we did not travel second or third-class, as was our custom, but sought the seclusion and rest which a first-class railway carriage in Great Britain affords. In the hope of finding news from America I began perusing my lately purchased newspaper. This hope, however, was doomed to disappointment, as the only thing in its columns to remind an American of home and native land was a sermon by Henry Ward Beecher.

I threw the paper down, but shortly before arriving in Edinburgh I picked it up again with a view to reading the advertisements. While thus engaged my eyes fell upon a little piece of poetry in a corner of the paper. I carefully read it over, and at once made up my mind that this would make a great hymn for evangelistic work – if it had a tune. So impressed was I that I called Mr. Moody's attention to it, and he asked me to read it to him. This I proceeded to do with all the vim and energy at my command. After I had finished I looked at my friend Moody to see what the effect had been only to discover that he had not heard a word, so absorbed was he in a letter which he had received from Chicago. My chagrin can be better imagined than described. Notwithstanding this experience, I cut out the poem and placed it in my musical scrap-book- which, by the way, has been the seedplot from which sprang many of the Gospel songs that are now known throughout the world.

At the noon meeting on the second day, held at the Free Assembly Hall, the subject presented by Mr. Moody and other speakers was "The Good Shepherd." When Mr. Moody had finished speaking he called upon Dr. Bonar to say a few words. He spoke only a few minutes, but with great power, thrilling the immense audience by his fervid eloquence.

At the conclusion of Dr. Bonar's words Mr. Moody turned to me with the question, "Have you a solo appropriate for this subject, with which to close the service?" I had nothing suitable in mind, and was greatly troubled to know what to do. The Twenty-third Psalm occurred to me, but this had been sung several times in the meeting. I knew that every Scotchman in the audience would join me if I sang that, so I could not possibly render this favourite psalm as a solo. At this moment I seemed to hear a voice saying: "Sing the hymn you found on the train!" But I thought this impossible, as no music had ever been written for that hymn. Again the impression came strongly upon me that I must sing the beautiful and appropriate words I had found the day before, and placing the little newspaper slip on the organ in front of me, I lifted my heart in prayer, asking God to help me so to sing that the people might hear and understand. Laying my hands upon the organ I struck the key of A flat, and began to sing.

Note by note the tune was given, which has not been changed from that day to this. As the singing ceased a great sigh seemed to go up from the meeting, and I knew that the song had reached the hearts of my Scotch audience. Mr. Moody was greatly moved. Leaving the pulpit, he came down to where I was seated. Leaning over the organ, he looked at the little newspaper slip from which the song had been sung and with tears in his eyes said: "Sankey, where did you get that hymn? I never heard the like of it in my life." I was also moved to tears and arose and replied: "Mr. Moody, that's the hymn I read to you yesterday on the train, which you did not hear." Then Mr. Moody raised his hand and pronounced the benediction, and the meeting closed. Thus "The Ninety and Nine" was born.

A short time afterward I received, at Dundee, a letter from a lady who had been present at the meeting, thanking me for having sung her deceased sister's words. From correspondence that followed I learned that the author of the poem was Elizabeth C. Clephane, a resident of Melrose, Scotland, one of three sisters, all members of a refined Christian family. She was born in Edinburgh in 1830. Her sister, in describing Elizabeth, says: "She was a very quiet little child, shrinking from notice and always absorbed in books. The loss of both parents, at an early age, taught her sorrow. As she grew up she was recognized as the cleverest of the family. She was first in her class and a favourite with the teacher. Her love for poetry was a passion. Among the sick and suffering she won the name of 'My Sunbeam.' She wrote 'The Ninety and Nine' for a friend, who had it published in 'The Children's Hour.' It was copied from thence into various publications, but was comparatively little noticed. She died in 1869."

When Mr. Moody and I returned from England, in 1875, we held our first meeting on a Sunday afternoon in front of the old Congregational church in the village of Northfield, Massachusetts, Mr. Moody's home. On reaching the church we found it overflowing, and more people surrounding the church outside than were inside. Mr. Moody, when entering the pulpit, said: "I always speak to the largest crowd, and as it is outside, I will speak from the front of the church." The congregation retired to the open air, and the small cabinet organ was carried to a position on a small porch in front of the church, where it was placed with just room enough for me to take my seat. After a few of the congregational hymns had been sung, Mr. Moody announced that I would sing "The Ninety and Nine."

Nearly opposite the church, across the river, a man was seated on his porch. He had refused to attend the service in the village, and was quite angry because his family and neighbors had all gone to the meeting. But the singing of this song reached him, and two weeks later he attended a prayer meeting at a small school-house near his home, where he rose and said that he had heard a song which greatly troubled him, sung by Mr. Sankey at the meeting held in the open air at Northfield, and that he wished the Christians to pray for him. This they did, and he became converted. He then removed to Northfield and joined Mr. Moody in his work in connection with the schools, where he continued for many years.

On the occasion of laying the corner-stone for the new Congregational church in Northfield, Mr. Moody asked me to stand on the corner-stone and sing "The Ninety and Nine" without the organ accompaniment, as he hoped that this church would be one whose mission it would be to seek the lost ones. While I was singing, Mr. Caldwell, the man who had heard the song across the river, lay dying in his cottage near Mr. Moody's home. Calling his wife to his bedside, he asked her to open the south window, as he thought he heard singing. Together they listened to the same song which had been used to lead him into the way of life. In a little while he passed away to join the Shepherd in the upper fold.

Mrs. Barbour once remarked: "When you hear the 'Ninety and Nine' sung, you know of a truth that down in this corner, up in that gallery, behind that pillar which hides the singer's face from the listener, the hand of Jesus has been finding this and that and yonder lost one, to place them in His fold. A certain class of hearers come to the services solely to hear Mr. Sankey, and the song throws the Lord's net around them."

At the close of our meetings at Newcastle-on-Tyne one of the most efficient workers in connection with our services, Mrs. Claphin, decided to go to the Continent for a season of rest. When passing through London she purchased a large number of the penny edition of "Sacred Songs and Solos," for distribution on the way. At the Grand Hotel, in Paris, she left a number of them on the reading-table, with a prayer for God's blessing upon those who might find them there. A few weeks later she visited Geneva, Switzerland, and while attending a prayer-meeting there one evening, the minister of the church told a touching story about a young English lady, who was a member of his church. She had received a letter from a long lost brother, who was ill at the Grand Hotel in Paris. The young lady asked her physician if he would allow her to go to see her brother. The physician said: "You will die if you do." She replied: "I will die if I don't." A few days later she started for Paris, and on reaching the Grand Hotel she was taken to the room where her dying brother lay. After a warm greeting he took from under the pillow a copy of "Sacred Songs and Solos," and pointing to "The Ninety and Nine," said: "This hymn was the means of bringing me to Christ." Mrs. Claphin, who was in the audience and heard this story related, thanked God for having put it into her heart to distribute the little hymn-books.

A friend sends me the following: "One day I was talking with a woman of the most abandoned sort, who had hardened her heart by many years of drunkenness and sin. Nothing I could say made any impression on her. When I was about to give up, our old Scotch cook, who was fond of poetry, began to sing:

> But none of the ransomed ever knew
> How deep were the waters crossed;
> Nor how dark was the night that the Lord passed through,
> Ere he found His sheep that was lost.

She was in the kitchen, and was not aware that any one was within hearing. Her rich Scotch brogue lent charm to the verse, and it seemed a message from God. For the poor woman to whom I had been talking, and who was so hardened a moment before, burst into tears, and falling on her knees, began to pray to the Good Shepherd to receive her. She was converted, and has often testified to the fact that the song led her to Christ."

Mr. Blane, of South Africa, relates: "I knew a young man who was the only unconverted member of his family. At home he was constantly hearing of Christ, and being asked to accept Him as his Saviour. He determined to rid himself of all home restraint, and to enjoy himself by making a tour of the Continent. He set out, and for some time all went well. "At one of the hotels at which he stayed there was an old Christian woman. As was her constant habit, having first obtained the consent of the proprietor, she went from room to room, leaving upon the table of each a little tract or book. She entered this young man's room, and with a prayer to God for guidance, took out a small copy of Sankey's hymns, opening it at the one beginning,

> There were ninety and nine that safely lay
> In the shelter of the fold.

Under the guidance of the Holy Spirit she took her pencil and drew a stroke under the words of the third line, 'One was out on the hills away.' Soon the young man entered his room, and at once the book caught his eye. He went over and read the penciled line. Like a flash the image of his home came up before him, and all the dear ones there, until his stony heart was broken. Throwing himself upon his knees, he cried for mercy and besought the Father to receive him for Christ's sake. Soon the answer came, and he rose to his feet a new man in Christ Jesus."

Mr. Thomas Leigh, of Liverpool, who assisted in our meetings in that city, writes me as follows: "At your first mission in Liverpool an old man, between seventy and eighty, was converted through your singing 'There were ninety and nine.' He lived for a number of years afterward, and was a bright worker and gave a clear testimony. During the remainder of his life he went by the name of 'Ninety and Nine.'"

From South America, only last November, came this testimony from a former co-worker: "Many years ago, in 1884, I had the pleasure of meeting you. I was then a member of your London choir and helped in speaking to souls at the after-meetings of those wonderful gatherings you and dear Mr. Moody held in London in that year. Now, more than twenty years after, I am out here, where God in His grace has given me the privilege of witnessing for Him for the last sixteen years. "I cannot tell you the blessing that the translations of your hymns into Spanish have been here. I send you a copy of our hymn-book, in which I have collected a large number of songs, the great majority having against them 'S. S.,' signifying 'Sacred Songs and Solos.' These are translations, adaptations or tunes of your collection. I am sure God has graciously used these hymns in blessing many souls. Only this afternoon, while I was out visiting some new converts, I heard of the case of a woman converted through the singing of a Spanish translation of 'There were ninety and nine.' Some time ago a man, who was a bad character, was spoken to by a colporteur, and he had a desire to read the Bible. He lost his work for a day and a half while he hunted in the different book-shops for a Bible. At last he got one, and commenced reading it. He came to our open air meetings, followed us into one of our halls, and was soon converted. He was so thankful to the Lord for what He had done for him that he asked us to come and have meetings in his house. The result has been that at least twelve of his relatives and neighbors have been converted. "Not long ago a woman came into the meeting in his house in a careless, laughing way. The hymn I have referred to was being sung. The Spirit of God convicted her then and there, and she burst into tears and cried to God for mercy, saying that she was 'that lost sheep, out on the mountains.' She found peace, and now her husband is converted, and they are bright and earnest Christians."

An aged woman in Coupar-Angus, said to be 103 years of age, said she wearied for the next coming of a young friend who visits her, that she might hear once more the song of the "Ninety and Nine."

The Shining Shore

Words by the David Nelson   Music by George F. Root

My days are gliding swiftly by,
And I, a pilgrim stranger.

Mr. Nelson was a surgeon in the army during the War of 1812. Afterward he entered the ministry, preached in Tennessee and Kentucky, and later moved to Missouri, where he opened a plantation. There he heard an address on the evils of slavery that changed his views. "I will live on roast potatoes and salt before I will hold slaves!" he declared. He advocated colonization of the Negroes. This brought down upon him the wrath of his slave-holding neighbors, who drove him from his home and pursued him through the woods and swamps for three days and nights. Finally he came out on the banks of the Mississippi River opposite Quincy, Illinois. By signs he made known his condition to friends there, and then hid in the bushes to await the approach of night. As he lay there in danger of being captured every moment, the land of freedom in plain sight, with the swiftly gliding waters between, the lines of this hymn began to assume form in his mind, and he wrote them down on the back of a letter he had in his pocket. The voices of the vengeful pursuers were heard in the woods about him. Once they strode by the very clump of bushes in which he was concealed, and even poked their guns in to separate the branches; but they failed to notice him. Several members of the Congregational church of Quincy came over in the evening in a canoe, and began fishing near his hiding-place. When they had located this exactly they gave a signal, and drawing near to the shore, met him as he rushed down to the water's edge. They got him safely to the Illinois side, but were discovered and followed by the slaveholders, who demanded his surrender. But they were informed that Mr. Nelson was now in a Free State, and that nothing should molest him. In Illinois he was employed by the Home Missionary Society, and continued to take an active part in the anti-slavery agitation of those times. He died in 1844.

As to the music of this hymn Mr. Root says: "One day, I remember, as I was working at a set of graded part-songs for singing classes, mother passed through the room and laid a slip from one of the religious newspapers before me, saying; 'George, I think that would be good for music.' I looked at the poem, which began, 'My days are gliding swiftly by,' and a simple melody sang itself along in my mind as I read. "I jotted it down and went on with my work. That was the origin of the music of 'The Shining Shore.' Later, when I took up the melody to harmonize it, it seemed so very simple and commonplace that I hesitated about setting the other parts to it. I finally decided that it might be useful to somebody, and I completed it, though it was not printed until some months afterward. In after years I examined it in an endeavor to account for its great popularity – but in vain. To the musician there is not one reason in melody or harmony, scientifically regarded, for such a fact. To him hundreds of others, now forgotten, were better."

This was a favourite hymn of Henry Ward Beecher.

The Smitten Rock

Words by George C. Needham   Music by Ira D. Sankey

From the riven Rock there floweth
Living water ever clear.

"When Mr. Sankey lived at Cohasset, Massachusetts, in the summer of 1876, after the great Boston meetings, he very naturally desired to bring the Gospel to the people living in that neighbourhood. Accordingly he invited me," wrote Mr. Needham on one occasion, "to spend a week with him in a series of evangelistic meetings. Before the breakfast-hour one morning, while Mr. Sankey was playing on his organ, I remarked: 'I wish we had a good hymn on The Smitten Rock, as I hope to speak on that subject tonight.' Mr. Sankey replied with enthusiasm:

'Here is a new hymn which came to me last night in my sleep; I believe the Lord gave it to me. I wish I had words for it. Why don't you write a piece on The Rock?'

I replied, 'Why, I can't write such a hymn as you want, and you know that I don't understand music; how to fit words to your music would puzzle an unmusical man.'

"The enthusiastic soloist, still playing, said: 'You'll find pen and paper on the table; this is a stirring tune and I want the words; try your hand at it.'

I immediately sat down and asked the Lord's special blessing, and then wrote the hymn as it now appears. Mr. Sankey took the paper, with the ink scarcely dry on it, sang it through with the chorus – the new air and the words exactly fitting, without alteration or amendment. "'I think the Lord gave you the words as truly He gave me the tune,' was Mr. Sankey's first remark. And then we commended the little piece and its music to the great Master, praying that the unction of the Holy One might rest upon it. Mr. Sankey sang the hymn for the first time in public that evening, after I had given my address on The Smitten Rock."

The Solid Rock

Music by William B. Bradbury   Words by Edward Mote

> My hope is built on nothing less
> Than Jesus' blood and righteousness.

"I went astray from my youth," said the author this hymn. "My Sundays were spent on the streets in play. So ignorant was I that I did not know there was a God." He was a cabinet-maker, and was converted under the preaching of John Hyatt. The refrain came into the author's mind one morning in 1834, as he was walking up Holborn Hill, London, on his way to work. Four stanzas were completed that day and two more on the following Sunday. In 1852 Mr. Mote became the pastor of a Baptist church in Horsham, Sussex, where he continued to minister for more than twenty years. In his eighty-first year his health declined. "I think I am going to heaven," he said; "yes, I am nearing port. The truths I have preached I am now living upon; and they will do to die upon. Ah! The precious blood! The precious blood which takes away all our sins; it is this which makes peace with God." And so he passed peacefully away, his hope "built on nothing less than Jesus' blood and righteousness."

The Sweet Story of Old

Words by Mrs. Jemima Luke   Music by J. C. Englebrecht

> I think when I read that sweet story of old,
> When Jesus was here among men.

"In the year 1841 I went to the Normal Infant School in Gray's Inn Road to obtain some knowledge of the system," writes Mrs. Luke. "Mary Moffat, afterwards Mrs. Livingstone, was there at the same time, and Sarah Roby, whom Mr. and Mrs. Moffat had rescued in infancy when buried alive, and had brought up with their own children. Among the marching pieces at Gray's Inn Road was a Greek air, the pathos of which took my fancy, and I searched Watts and Jane Taylor and several Sunday-school hymn-books for words to suit the measure but in vain. Having been recalled home, I went one day on some missionary business to the little town of Wellington, five miles from Taunton, in a stage coach. It was a beautiful spring morning; it was an hour's ride, and there was no other inside passenger. "On the back of an old envelope I wrote in pencil the first two of the verses now so well known, in order to teach the tune to the village school supported by my step-mother, and which it was my province to visit. The third verse was added afterward to make it a missionary hymn. My father superintended the Sunday-school in which we taught, and used to let the children choose the first hymn. One Sunday the children started their new hymn. My father turned to his younger daughters and said, 'Where did that come from? I never heard it before.' 'Oh, Jemima made it,' they replied. Next day he asked for a copy, and sent it, without my knowledge, to 'The Sunday-School Teachers' Magazine.' But for this it would probably never have appeared in print." Mrs. Luke adds regarding her composition: "It was a little inspiration from above, and not 'in me,' for I have never written other verses worthy of preservation."

The Wondrous Cross

Words by Isaac Watts   Arr. Music by Ira D. Sankey

When I survey the wondrous cross
On which the Prince of Glory died.

This beautiful hymn was founded on Paul's word in Galatians 6:14, "God forbid that I should glory, save in the cross of our Lord Jesus Christ."

The author occupies one of the highest positions among all the hymn writers who ever lived. Wesley and Watts stand on the highest pedestal of fame together. Watts was the son of a schoolmaster, and was born at Southampton, 1674. He belonged to a family of non-conformists, who were very pious and godly people. He was educated by a clergyman in his home city, and later by an Independent minister in London.

He became minister to an Independent congregation in London, where he continued to preach for fourteen years. In the year 1712 he paid a visit to some friends in Hertfordshire, for the purpose of regaining his health, which, on account of excessive study, had suffered. While here. Sir Thomas and Lady Abney became so interested in him and took such a liking to him that they insisted upon his staying with them in their beautiful home. He accepted their kind offer, and for thirty-six years he lived in their house, being a constant source of joy and blessing to his benefactors. It was here he wrote many of the most useful and popular hymns now used by the Christian churches throughout the world. He died 1748. Just before passing away he said:

"If God has no more service for me to do through grace, I am ready; it is a great mercy to me that I have no manner of fear or dread of death. I could, if God please, lay my head back and die without alarm this afternoon or night. My chief supports are from my view of eternal things, and my sins are pardoned through the blood of Jesus Christ."

In this happy frame of mind the great hymnist entered into his last rest. At least a score of different melodies have been written to the words, but Lowell Mason's "Hamburg" is no doubt the most popular.

There is a Fountain

Words by the William Cowper   Music by Dr. Lowell Mason

There is a fountain filled with blood,
Drawn from Immanuel's veins.

Born of a personal experience when the author was forty years old, this hymn of faith for more than a century has been eminently useful in the practical work of evangelizing the world.

Along the streets of Glasgow, shortly after our first visit to Scotland, a little boy passed one evening, singing "There is a fountain filled with blood." A Christian policeman joined in the song, and when he had finished his beat he asked the boy if he understood what he was singing. "Oh, yes," said the little fellow, "I know it in my heart, and it is very precious." A few evenings afterward someone asked the policeman: "Do you know that a woman standing where we are, was awakened and saved the other night by hearing, 'There is a fountain,' sung by a policeman and a boy?"

A lieutenant in the Union army, having received his death-wound in a gallant charge at the head of his regiment, was visited in the hospital by the chaplain, who inquired how he felt. He said he had always been cheerful, and was now ready to meet God in peace. "Chaplain," he added, "I was passing through the streets of New York once on a Sunday night, and I heard singing. I went in and saw a company of poor people. They were singing 'There is a fountain filled with blood.' I was overpowered with the impression the hymn made upon me, and I gave my heart to God. Since then I have loved Jesus, and I love him now." That was his last speech.

There is a Green Hill Far Away

Words by Cecil F. Alexander   Music by George C. Stebbins

> There is a green hill far away,
> Without a city wall.

While holding meetings with Mr. Moody, at Cardiff, Wales, in 1883, I visited the ruins of Tintern Abbey with Professor Drummond. While there I sang this song, which the professor said to me was one of the finest hymns in the English language. A number of years later I sang it on the green hill believed to be Calvary, outside the walls of Jerusalem.

Mrs. Alexander was the wife of the Most Reverend W. Alexander, D. D., Archbishop of Armagh. She first published "There is a green hill far away" in her "Hymns for Little Children" in 1848. It is a popular children's hymn in England. Mr. Stebbins set it to a new tune in 1884. Mrs. Alexander wrote about four hundred hymns and poems for children.

There'll Be No Dark Valley

Words by the W. O. Cushing   Music by Ira D. Sankey

> There'll be no dark valley when Jesus comes,
> There'll be no dark valley when Jesus comes.

I arranged this hymn from the words which Mr. W. O. Cushing wrote for me, of which, however, I used only the first line, "There'll be no dark valley when Jesus comes." It has of late become quite a favourite throughout America.

One night during the Boxer revolt when the Chinese had set fire to many buildings and it seemed as though all the missionaries and native Christians in a besieged city would be destroyed; the children belonging to the Junior Christian Endeavour Society held a meeting in a chapel. While the cracklings of the flames, the sharp report of the Chinese guns, and the cries of men and women running to and fro were rending the air, these little disciples of Jesus were singing: "There'll be no dark' valley when Jesus comes."

A missionary, working in the slums of a city in Ireland, writes me as follows: "I feel constrained to thank you from the bottom of my soul for all the great blessings I have received from singing your songs. I am a worker in the slums of –, and I find that your songs reach the hearts of fallen men and women before anything else. I have just returned home from our meeting, and the message I sang tonight was your sweet song: 'There'll be no dark valley when Jesus comes.' "I want to thank you in particular for this song, because it presents death to us in such a glorious way. The old Welsh people used to speak and sing of death as something very fearful – a dark river, great waves and so on – and I remember my dear mother singing all the Welsh hymns referring to death, until I shuddered. But, praise the Lord, I know now that it is different. Your little song has confirmed this belief in me not only, but in many, many more souls."

There's a Light in the Valley

Words by P. P. Bliss   Music by P. P. Bliss

Through the valley of the shadow I must go,
Where the cold waves of Jordan roll.

"Some years ago I was in the dark," a young lady of London told me, "and was seeking the Lord day and night; but I could get no rest or peace for my soul. For two or three weeks the title of 'There's a Light in the Valley' kept ringing in my ears. I had never carefully read through the hymn, but in my constant pleadings with the Lord I always begged for this light of the valley to be given to me. And one night Christ gave the light I had been asking for. "I cannot describe my joy when I could say, 'There is a light in the valley for me.' I scarcely slept that night, for the words would come to me again and again. It is now my privilege, sometimes, to help sing them for others, and then they seem to bring a fresh wave of my Saviour's love to me, as they did on that blessed night."

Throw Out the Life-Line

Words and Music by E. S. Ufford   Arr. by Geo. C. Stebbins

Throw out the Life-Line across the dark wave,
There is a brother whom some one should save.

The author of this famous hymn, while living in Massachusetts near the ocean, one day saw a vessel wrecked near the shore, and this suggested the idea of the song. Mr. Stebbins shortly afterward, about 1889, obtained it from the author, and made a number of changes in

Mr. Ufford's harmony. From Mr. Stebbins I secured it for publication in "Gospel Hymns" and in "Sacred Songs and Solos." It became one of the most useful of evangelistic hymns, and was often sung with effect at our meetings in Great Britain.

A Christian commercial traveler has just sent me this word: "A few of us were holding a street meeting at Warsaw, Indiana, last August. 'Throw out the Life-Line' had been sung, and a man spoke as follows: "'I live at North Tonawanda, on the Niagara River. Some time ago my son was walking toward home when he heard a scream from the river. He rushed down and saw a young lady struggling in the water, being swept down the river. He hurriedly took off his coat, vest and shoes, jumped in, swam to the lady, took hold of her and called to some men, who were farther down the river, to throw out a life-line. The men heard the voice, saw the man and woman being swept down the river, and hastily threw out a line to them. But it was just about three feet too short. My son and the woman were swept over the falls and both were drowned.' There were two or three hundred people at this street meeting, and the speaker made the application that we should be sure that our life-line is long enough to reach the people we are after. It was a very effective service, and resulted in at least one conversion."

Professor Drummond told me this story, and made his own application of it: "On the coast of Spain a great storm was raging, and a wrecked vessel came drifting near the light-house. The cries of the perishing seamen were heard in the darkness. The lighthouse keeper, in making his report to the government – which was required by law in the case of a wreck said: "'We rendered all possible aid from the top of the light-house with the speaking trumpet; notwithstanding, the next morning twenty corpses were found on the shore and the vessel had disappeared.' This is too often the case in our preaching. We get into a high pulpit and shout at the top of our voices, but we seldom take the life-line in our hands and go down to those who are perishing in the waves of sin, to rescue them ere it is too late."

A man on an Atlantic steamer told me another story, which in its way illustrates the song: "One stormy night at sea a cry was raised on board a steamer, 'Man overboard; man overboard!' A number of the alarmed passengers ran to the captain and begged him to stop the vessel. He roughly told them to mind their own business and not to bother him. As he said this a seaman ran up to the bridge and cried that the man who had gone overboard was the captain's brother. This made a great difference to the captain. He at once reversed the vessel, rushed to the stern, seized a life-line, and threw it as far as he could toward the drowning man, hoping that he might be able to lay hold of it. Fortunately the man seized the line, and, tying it around his body, cried: 'Pull away, pull away!' The captain cried, 'Have you hold of the line?' A faint answer came back, 'The line has hold of me.' In a little while the man was drawn on board and saved."

Till He Come

Words by E. H. Bickersteth   Music by Dr. Lowell Mason

'Till He come! Oh, let the word
Linger on the trembling chords.

The author, E. H. Bickersteth, says this hymn was written to present one aspect of the Lord's Supper which is passed over in many hymnals, "Ye do show forth the Lord's death till He come."

'Tis Midnight

Words by Wm. B. Tappan   Music by Virgil C. Taylor

'Tis midnight; and on Olive's brow
The star is dimm'd that lately shone.

The author of the words of this hymn, William Bingham Tappan, was born at Beverly, Mass., October 29, 1794. He was a Congregational minister and was engaged for many years in the service of the American Sunday-school Union. The hymn was first published in the author's "Gems of Sacred Poetry," in 1822, under the title, "Gethsemane." Mr. Tappan died in his native state in 1849.

Today the Saviour Calls

Music by Lowell Mason   Words by S. F. Smith

Today the Saviour calls;
Ye wand'rers, come.

For inducing immediate acceptance of the offer of salvation through faith in Christ this hymn has been of great value. In one of his sermons Mr. Moody refers to my singing it on a night never to be forgotten:

"For four or five nights in succession I had been preaching in Chicago on the subject of 'The Life of Christ,' and we had followed Him from the cradle to the judgment hall of Pilate. I have always felt that on that night I made one of the greatest mistakes of my life – How often I have wished that I could call back what I said to the congregation at the close of the meeting on that memorable night of the Chicago fire! That night I spoke from the text, 'What shall I do with Jesus?' and as I closed I said: 'Now I want you to take this question home with you, think it over, and next Sunday night I want you to come back here and tell me what you are going to do with Jesus.' What a mistake! I gave them a week to decide; but I never met that audience again. Even then the huge bell of the court-house near by was tolling out what proved to be the death-knell of the city. How well I remember the hymn Mr. Sankey sang as a solo at the closing moment of that meeting, as his voice rang out:

> Today the Saviour calls; for refuge fly;
> The storm of justice falls, and death is nigh.

It seemed almost prophetic. It was the last verse sung in that beautiful hall. We closed the meeting and went out into the streets, never to meet again. It is estimated that a thousand lives were lost that night. As many of them were lost near Farwell Hall, it may have been that some who heard me say that night, 'Take a week to decide the question,' were among the lost ones."

To the Work

Words by Fanny J. Crosby   Music by W. H. Doane

> To the work! To the work! We are servants of God,
> Let us follow the path that our Master has trod.

Fanny Crosby wrote the words of this hymn in 1869, and it was set to music by W. H. Doane two years later. I sang it for the first time in the home of Mr. and Mrs. J. B. Cornell at Long Branch. The servants gathered from all parts of the house while I was singing, and looked into the parlour where I was seated. When I was through one of them said: "That is the finest hymn I have heard for a long time; won't you please sing it over again?" I felt that this was a test case, and that if the hymn had such power over those servants it would be useful in reaching other people as well; so I published it in "Gospel Hymns" in 1875, where it became one of the best work-songs for our meetings that we had.

Trust and Obey

Words by J. H. Sammis   Music by D. D. Towner

> When we walk with the Lord,
> In the light of his Word.

"Some years ago," says Professor Towner, musical director of the Moody Bible Institute, "Mr. Moody was conducting a series of meetings in Brockton, Massachusetts, and I had the pleasure of singing for him there. One night a young man rose in a testimony meeting and said, 'I am not quite sure – but I am going to trust, and I am going to obey.' I just jotted that sentence down, and sent it with the little story to J. H. Sammis, a Presbyterian minister. He wrote the hymn, and the tune was born. The chorus,

> Trust and obey,
> For there's no other way
> To be happy in Jesus
> But to trust and obey,

Was written before the hymn was."

Trusting Jesus, That is All

Words by E. P. Stites   Music by Ira D. Sankey

> Simply trusting every day,
> Trusting through a stormy way.

The words of this hymn were handed to Mr. Moody at Chicago, in 1876, in the form of a newspaper clipping. He gave them to me, and asked me to write a tune for them. I assented, on condition that he should vouch for the doctrine taught in the verses, and he said he would.

"About two years ago," writes a minister, "I visited a woman who was suffering from an incurable disease; but great as was her agony of body, her distress of mind was greater still. One day she said: 'The future is so dark, I dare not look forward at all.'

"To my question, 'Can't you trust yourself in God's hands?' she replied:

'No, I can't leave myself there.'

"I repeated the hymn, 'Simply trusting' ev'ry day,' and especially dwelt on the refrain, 'Trusting as the moments fly, trusting as the days go by.' 'Ah,' she said, 'I can trust him this moment; is it like that?' I then sang the hymn to her, and the change that came over her was wonderful. She never lost this trust, and she had the page in her hymn-book turned down, that she might have the hymn read to her. After many months of intense suffering she passed away, 'simply trusting,' to the land where there shall be no more pain."

Under His Wings

Words by W. O. Cushing   Music by Ira D. Sankey

> Under His wings I am safely abiding;
> Though the night deepens and tempests are wild.

As Mr. Moody used to approach the seminary building at Northfield, Massachusetts, to conduct the morning worship, the young ladies there would join in the singing of this hymn as he entered the room. It was one of their popular hymns, as it was also of the Estey Quartet made up of the leading singers of the seminary.

The music of this hymn was among my later compositions.

A young man in a hospital in Western Massachusetts was once visited by a minister, and after he had prayed, the invalid asked him to sing his favourite song, "Under His Wings," saying that it had been the means of his conversion. The hymn was sung, and in a short time the listener had passed away to the shelter under his Master's wings.

Verily, Verily

Words by James McGranahan   Music by James McGranahan

> O what a Saviour that He died for me!
> From condemnation He hath made me free.

"About twenty years ago," writes James Sprunt, of London, "Mrs. S— one evening left her home, near Blandford Square, to visit some of her friends. She was disappointed to find that they were not at home. She called upon others, but they also had gone out. Vexed in mind and weary in body she was returning to her home. Passing the doors of Omega Hall, she was invited to the service then being held inside. She entered, and enjoyed the service, especially the singing of 'O what a Saviour, that He died for me!' This was good news to her soul. By the Spirit of God she had been taught her lost condition. What was she to do? She had been told in the Hall to repent and believe the Gospel, to accept Christ as her Saviour, and to rest her soul on the finished work of Calvary's cross. She heard all this, but did not obey. But when she retired that night her mind could not rest. During her sleep she dreamed that she was in the meeting and had again joined in the hymn, 'O, what a Saviour, that He died for me!' and with the dreamy singing she awoke to say, not in a dream and not in unbelief, but with true faith in God's Son, 'From condemnation He hath made me free.'"

The following story is an apt illustration of the teaching of this hymn:

In the garrison town of Woolwich, some years ago, a soldier was about to be brought before the commanding officer of the regiment for some misdemeanour. The officer entering the soldier's name said:

"Here is John again. What can we do with him? He has gone through almost every ordeal."

The sergeant-major apologised for intruding, and said: "There is one thing which has never been done with him yet, sir."

"What is that, sergeant-major? "

"Well, sir, he has never yet been forgiven."

"Forgiven!" said the colonel; "here is his case entered."

"Yes, but the man is not yet before you, and you can cancel it."

After the colonel had reflected for a few minutes, he ordered the man to be brought in, wlien he was asked what he had to say relative to the charges brought against him.

"Nothing, sir," was the reply, "only that I am sorry for what I have done."

After making some suitable remarks, the colonel said, "Well, we have resolved to forgive you."

The soldier was struck with astonishment; the tears started from his eyes; he wept. The colonel, with the adjutant and the others present, felt deeply when they saw the man so humbled. The soldier thanked the colonel for his kindness and retired. The narrator had the soldier under his notice for two years and a half after this, and never, during that time, was there a charge brought against him, or fault found with him. Mercy triumphed! Kindness conquered! The man was won!

This is just the method God adopts with us in the everlasting Gospel. We are guilty. The charges are brought against us. The case is entered. But the Lord delighteth in mercy. He seeks to melt us by His love. He is ready to forgive. He sends to us, saying, "Only acknowledge thine iniquities;" and then offers us pardon — a pardon through the life of His only-begotten Son. A pardon, not of one sin, but of all our sins; a pardon that will bring peace to the conscience on earth, and entitle us to eternal rest in heaven.

Waiting and Watching for Me

Words by Marianne Hearn   Music by P. P. Bliss

> When my final farewell to the world I have said,
> And gladly lie down to my rest.

At one of our Boston meetings, after I had sung this hymn as a solo, Mr. Moody related the following anecdote:

When we were in Chicago, a St. Louis merchant stopping at the Grand-street Hotel on some business had a friend who had got to drinking. He heard that we were interested in trying to reach and reform drinking men, and he thought he would try to get him to come into the meeting. The man had not been into a meeting for twenty years. The last six months he had been studying the Gospel of John, and trying to prove that it ought not to be in the Bible, and he had settled it in his own mind that it ought not to be there. He went to the meeting, and there he heard this hymn sung: "Waiting and Watching," and he wondered if anyone was waiting and watching for him. He went out of the meeting, but he could not get that "Waiting and Watching "out of his head. He went to the hotel and ate his dinner, and all the time he kept saying to himself, "I wonder if anybody is waiting and watching for me;" when night came he went to sleep, and he kept tossing on his bed all night, and finally he got up and knelt down by the bed and prayed for the first time in his life. He prayed that Christ would have mercy on him. He said, "Lord Jesus Christ, take me in Thy arms." God heard him, and now he is one of the very best workers we have. He was converted, and we left him in Chicago hard at work for Jesus, and I don't know how many souls he has led to Christ.

At one of Mr. Moody's meetings in Farwell Hall, Chicago, this testimony was given on one occasion: "For many years past I have been an infidel, and often lectured to audiences in opposition to the Bible. Today, in the presence of all you who see me, I declare that I am a converted man. I owe the softening of my hitherto stony heart to a Gospel hymn sung by Mr. Bliss, the refrain of which is, 'Will anyone then, at the beautiful gate, be waiting and watching for me?' It reminded me so tenderly of my Christian wife, parents, brothers, sisters and children who have gone before me that it quite broke me down; and now Christ and the Word have become my best hope and stronghold."

An aged Christian woman — a ripe old saint — a few years ago "fell asleep in Jesus." She had some few years before parted with lier favourite daughter, whose name was Maggie. Just before she breathed her last, Maggie had said to her mother: "Mother, when you come to heaven, I shall be at the gate waiting for you. I shall be the first to bid you welcome." And her spirit soared to the realms of bliss.

And now the dear old mother was passing away. She looked forward with joy to welcome her loved ones; for faith in Jesus Christ takes all tlie sting from death. And she could not help thinking of her dear Maggie, and of her parting words, "I shall be at the gate of heaven waiting for you."

Her eldest daughter was nursing her in her last moments. The end was fast approaching; but she was quite conscious.

"Mother," asked her daughter, "shall I sing your favourite hymn?"

"Yes," said the dying saint, "'Waiting and watching for me.'"

And she sang the first stanza of Marianne Farningham's popular hymn:

> When my final farewell to the world I have said,
> And gladly lie down to my rest:
> When softly the watchers shall say 'She is dead,'
> And fold my pale hands o'er my breast:
> And when, with my glorified vision, at last.
> The walls of that City I see.
> Will any one then at the beautiful gate
> Be waiting and watching for me?

Just as the singer was repeating the words:

> Will any one then at the beautiful gate,

her mother sprang up as if she saw her beloved daughter close at hand, and exclaimed:

"There's Maggie at the gate!"

These were her last words. Her spirit departed "to be with Christ, which is far better."

Welcome! Welcome! Welcome!

Words by Horatius Bonar   Music by Ira D. Sankey

> In the land of strangers,
> Whither thou art gone.

Written for me by Dr. Bonar, in 1883, this hymn became the favourite song of the choir of over fifteen hundred voices, led by Percy S. Foster, at our meetings in the great Convention Hall in Washington during the winter of 1894.

"An editor of a paper in the South," says one who was connected with the Florence Mission at the time this incident occurred, "lost all through drink and dissipation, and one day left his wife and five children to look after themselves. Without bidding them good-bye he left home, determined not to return until he was a man and could live a sober life. In New York he sank still lower. One night he pawned some of his clothing; but soon he was again penniless and had no place to sleep. He then wrote a note to his wife, bidding her good-bye, saying they would never see each other again, as he had decided to die that night. He was walking toward East River when the sound of music attracted his attention. He looked up and saw the sign, 'The Florence.' That was the name of his oldest daughter. He listened; a lady was singing a song his wife used to sing on Sunday afternoons at home, words that went to his heart,

> In the land of strangers,
> whither thou art gone,
> Hear a far voice calling,
> "My son, My son!
> Welcome! Wanderer, welcome!
> Welcome back to home!
> Thou hast wandered far away:
> Come home, come home!

"The song, coupled with the name that was his daughter's, led him to think we were praying for him. He came in, drunk as he was, and asked us to do so. He became a convert and an earnest Christian worker, and has held a position of responsibility in business for many years, he and his family having been reunited."

We Shall Meet By and By

Words by J. Atkinson   Music by Hubert P. Main

> We shall meet beyond the river, by and by, by and by;
> And the darkness shall be over, by and by, by and by.

John Atkinson, D. D., a Methodist minister, wrote this hymn on the death of his mother, in 1867. This is another instance of a hymn being written out of a deep and special heart-felt experience, and like gold, the best comes from the greatest depth.

What a Friend We Have in Jesus

Words by Joseph Scriven   Music by Charles C. Converse

> What a friend we have in Jesus,
> All our sins and griefs to bear.

Thousands have been cheered in time of trouble, and so led nearer to Christ, by this sweet and simple hymn; for very few hymns have been more widely published or more frequently sung. The author was born in Dublin in 1820, and came to Canada when he was twenty-five. There he lived a useful life until his death in 1886. The young lady to whom he was to be married was accidentally drowned on the eve of their wedding day. This led him to consecrate his life and fortune to the service of Christ. Though a graduate of Trinity College and a man of refinement, he chose humble duties. One afternoon he was seen walking down the streets of Port Hope, where he lived, dressed as a plain workingman and carrying a saw-horse and a saw on his mission of help. A citizen, noticing that a friend recognized him, said:

"Do you know that man? What is his name and where does he live? I want some one to cut wood, and I find it difficult to get a sober man to do the work faithfully."

"But you can't get that man," was the reply.

"That is Mr. Scriven. He won't cut wood for you."

"Why not?" queried the gentleman.

"Because you are able to pay for it. He only saws wood for poor widows and sick people."

"Until a short time before his death it was not known that he had a poetic gift. A neighbor, sitting up with him in his illness, happened upon a manuscript copy of "What a friend we have in Jesus." Reading it with great delight and questioning Mr. Scriven about it, he said that he had composed it for his mother, to comfort her in a time of special sorrow, not intending that anyone else should see it. Some time later, when another Port Hope neighbor asked him if it was true that he composed the hymn, his reply was: "The Lord and I did it between us."

Returning from England in 1875, I soon became associated with P. P. Bliss in the publication of what later became known as "Gospel Hymns No. 1." After we had given the completed compilation to our publishers I chanced to pick up a small paper-covered pamphlet of Sunday school hymns, published at Richmond, Virginia. I discovered this and sang it through, and determined to have it appear in "Gospel Hymns." As the composer of the music was my friend C. C. Converse, I withdrew from the collection one of his compositions and substituted for it, "What a friend we have in Jesus." Thus the last hymn that went into the book became one of the first in favour.

As published in the small Richmond hymnal, the authorship of the words was erroneously attributed to the great Scotch preacher and hymn-writer, Dr. Horatius Bonar. We were in error, also, in assigning the words to him. Some years afterward Dr. Bonar informed us that he was not the author, and that he did not know who wrote it. It was not until six or eight years after the hymn first appeared in our collection that we learned who the author really was.

What Must it be to be There?

Words by Mrs. Elizabeth Mills   Music by George C. Stebbins

We speak of the land of the blest,
A country so bright and so fair.

"You see that I am still in the land of the dying," wrote Philip Phillips, The Singing Pilgrim, shortly before his death at Delaware, Ohio. "Why I linger so long is to me a problem. The precious Saviour is more to me than I ever expected when I was well. Often during the night seasons I have real visions; I am walking on the banks of the Beautiful River, and getting glimpses of the bright Beyond. The lines that come most often to me are these:

We speak of the land of the blest,

A country so bright and so fair,
And oft are its glories confest,
But what must it be to be there?

"Blessed be God! I shall soon know. What a singing time we will have when we get there!"

What Shall the Harvest Be?

Words by Emily S. Oakley   Music by P. P. Bliss

Sowing the seed by the daylight fair,
Sowing the seed by the noonday glare.

In the winter of 1876 Mr. Moody and I were holding meetings in Chicago in a large building owned by John V. Farwell, one of Mr. Moody's first and most valued friends in that city. It was our custom to hold temperance meetings on Friday afternoons. At one of these meetings the following testimony was given:

"At the breaking out of the war in 1861 I enlisted in the army and was soon appointed a first lieutenant. I was not yet eighteen and had never been away from home influences. I had never tasted liquor and did not know one card from another. The regiment to which I was assigned was principally officered by young men, but many of them were old in dissipation. This new life was attractive to me, and I entered upon it with avidity. I was soon a steady drinker and a constant card-player. I laughed at the caution of the older heads, and asserted with all the egotism of a boy that I could abandon my bad habits at any time I wanted to. But I soon found that my evil desires had complete control over my will.

In 1870, being a physical wreck, I resigned, and determined to begin a new life. Time and again I failed, and at last I gave up all hope and abandoned myself to the wildest debauchery, speculating with reckless indifference on how much longer my body could endure the strain. In anticipation of sudden death I destroyed all evidence of my identity, so that my friends might never know the dog's death I had died. It was while in this condition that I one day wandered into this Tabernacle and found a seat in the gallery. There I sat in my drunken and dazed condition, looking down upon well-dressed and happy people. "I concluded that it was no place for me, and was just about to go out, when out of a perfect stillness rose the voice of Mr. Sankey singing the song, 'What Shall the

Harvest be?' The words and music stirred me with a strange sensation. I listened till the third verse had been sung:

> Sowing the seed of a lingering pain,
> Sowing the seed of a maddened brain,
> Sowing the seed of a tarnished name,
> Sowing the seed of eternal shame;
> Oh, what shall the harvest be?

"These words pierced my heart. In desperation I rushed downstairs and out into the snowy streets. I soon found a saloon, where I asked for liquor to drown my sorrow. On every bottle in the bar-room, in words of burning fire, I could read 'What shall the harvest be?' When I took up my glass to drink I read, written on it, 'What shall the harvest be?' and I dashed it to the floor and rushed out again into the cold, dark night. The song still followed me wherever I went, and finally drew me back to the Tabernacle two weeks later. I found my way into the inquiry room and was spoken to by a kind-hearted, loving brother. With his open Bible he pointed me to the Great Physician who had power to cure me and heal me of my appetite, if I would only receive him. Broken, weak, vile and helpless, I came to him, and by his grace I was able to accept him as my Redeemer; and I have come here today to bear my testimony to the power of Jesus to save to the uttermost."

We were all deeply touched by this testimony, and there was scarcely a dry eye in the audience. A week later this man came into our waiting-room and showed me a letter from his little daughter, which read about as follows:

"Dear Papa: Mamma and I saw in the Chicago papers that a man had been saved in the meeting there who was once a lieutenant in the army, and I told mamma that I thought it was my papa. Please write to us as soon as you can, as mamma cannot believe that it was you."

This letter was received by the man at the general post-office. The mother and their two children were sent for, and with the help of Mr. Moody a home was soon secured for them and employment for the man. He was asked to go to many places to give his experience, and he soon became so effective in his addresses that his friends prevailed upon him to study for the ministry. Eventually he became a pastor of a large church in the Northwest, where he laboured for a number of years till his death, in Evanston, Illinois, in 1899. His name was W. O. Lattimore. He wrote a hymn for me, entitled, "Out of the darkness into light," which I set to music.

The author of "What shall the harvest be?" who was born at Albany, was a frail, delicate woman, always an invalid, never having known, as she once said, an hour of health in all her life.

We Shall Sleep, But Not Forever

Words by Mrs. M. A. Kidder   Music by S. J. Vall

> We shall sleep, but not forever,
> There will be a glorious dawn.

Mrs. Kidder is believed to be the author of about one thousand hymns, some of which have become very popular. I set a number of her pieces to music. This hymn and, "Is my name written there?" are perhaps her most widely known compositions. She died in Chelsea, Mass., November 25, 1905, in her eighty-sixth year.

When Jesus Comes

Words by P. P. Bliss   Music by P. P. Bliss

> Down life's dark vale we wander,
> Till Jesus comes.

One day in 1872 Mr. Bliss heard a conversation between two of his friends, who were speaking on the subject of the return of our Lord. One of the ladies quoted a line from a work of Anna Shipton, "This may be the day of His coming," and spoke of the joy and comfort the thought gave her. Mr. Bliss was much impressed, more deeply than ever before, as to the reality of this subject; and a few days after as he was coming downstairs from his room, still occupied with the thought of looking for Christ's appearing, he commenced singing, "Down life's dark vale we wander," the words and music coming to him as he took the successive steps down the stairs. He at once wrote it down just as we have it today in the popular hymn-books.

The hymn was often sung at our meetings in Great Britain.

When the Mists have Rolled Away

Words by Annie Herbert   Music by Ira D. Sankey

> When the mists have rolled in splendour
> From the beauty of the hills.

I sang this hymn for the first time in The Free Trade Hall, in Manchester, in 1883, at one of Mr. Moody's meetings. The service was held at eight o'clock on a gloomy winter morning. The hall was densely crowded and filled with mist, so much so that the people could hardly be discerned at the farther end of the hall. I felt the need of something to brighten up the meeting, and then and there decided to launch this new song. It was received with much enthusiasm, and at once became a favourite of Mr. Moody's, and continued to be so until his death.

When the Roll is Called up Yonder

Words by J. M. Black   Music by J. M. Black

> When the trumpet of the Lord shall sound, and time shall be no more,
> And the morning breaks, eternal, bright and fair.

"While a teacher in a Sunday-school and president of a young people's society," says the author of this hymn, "I one day met a girl, fourteen years old, poorly clad and the child of a drunkard. She accepted my invitation to attend the Sunday-school, and joined the young people's society. One evening at a consecration-meeting, when members answered the roll call by repeating Scripture texts, she failed to respond. I spoke of what a sad thing it would be, when our names are called from the Lamb's Book of Life, if one of us should be absent; and I said, 'O God, when my own name is called up yonder, may I be there to respond!' I longed for something suitable to sing just then, but I could find nothing in the books. We closed the meeting, and on my way home I was still wishing that there might be a song that could be sung on such occasions. The thought came to me, 'Why don't you make it?' I dismissed the idea, thinking that I could never write such a hymn. "When I reached my house my wife saw that I was deeply troubled, and questioned me, but I made no reply. Then the words of the first stanza came to me in full. In fifteen minutes more I had composed the other two verses. Going to the piano, I played the music just as it is found today in the hymn-books, note for note, and I have never dared to change a single word or a note of the piece since."

Where Is My Boy Tonight?

Words by Robert Lowry   Music by Robert Lowry

> Where is my wandering boy tonight
> The boy of my tenderest care?

The author of this hymn, which has done more to bring back wandering boys than any other, became a follower of Christ at the age of seventeen. After a score of years in different pastorates he accepted the professorship of letters in his alma mater, Bucknell University, together with the pastorate of another church. This double service he performed for six years, and then moved to Plainfield, New Jersey, where he lived until his death, in 1899, at the age of seventy-three. Dr. Lowry will continue to preach the Gospel in his hymns long after his sermons have been forgotten. Many of his hymns were written after the Sunday evening service, when his body was weary but his mind refused to rest.

A mother came to me in Boston and asked me if I would try to find her wandering boy in California when I should go there with Mr. Moody to hold meetings. I promised to do what I could. For several weeks, as opportunity presented itself, I searched the cheap boarding-houses for the young man. At last I found him in the slums of the city and asked him to come to our meetings. He refused, saying that he was not fit to be seen there; but after much persuasion he came. One evening I sang: "Where is my wandering boy," and prefaced it with a few remarks, saying that I knew of one dear mother in the East who was praying for her wandering boy tonight. This, together with the song, touched the young man's heart, and he found his way into the inquiry room, where, with my open Bible, I was enabled by God's grace to lead him into the light. I wrote to his mother and told her that her boy had been found, and that he was now a professed Christian. She sent me money to pay his railway fare back to Boston, and in a short time he had reached home and received a hearty welcome. He soon found employment, and became a useful citizen, and has since been a follower of Christ.

"I heard Chancellor Sims relate," states H. B. Gibbud, "that he was once traveling with a man from the West who was on his way to visit his father, whom he had left years before when he was a boy. There had been trouble between them, and the father had told the son that he could go. In his anger the boy said that he would, and that he would never return. He had gone West, where he became a wealthy ranch owner; but he had never written to his father and had held the anger in his heart toward him all those years. Then he told the Chancellor how it was that he was now returning. A train on which he had been traveling had been snowed in, and people living near had made up a load of provisions and taken them to the imprisoned passengers. Then it was discovered that Mr. Sankey was on board, and at the people's request he came out on the steps and sang: 'Where is my wandering boy?' That song touched this man's heart, led him to God, and he was now going east to seek reconciliation with his parents."

A wayward boy was brought by a friend to the evening service of J. H. Byers, of Stanberry, Missouri. Having learned something of his condition, Mr. Byers asked the leader of the choir to sing as a solo: "Where is my wandering boy tonight?" which he did with great feeling. The boy was converted, the next evening he united with the church, and he has continued to be an active, praying worker ever since. The young man's parents were devoted Christians. On the same night and until the next afternoon, for what was an unknown reason to them, they were led to pray most earnestly for their lost boy. During the time when the prayer-meeting was being held, they were comforted, and believed that they would hear good news. In a few hours they received a telegram that their boy was saved. At the meeting where this hymn was sung there were present the parents of two other boys who had left their homes, and as the solo was sung they prayed that their boys might be saved and brought home. In a few days letters were received from those boys, telling their parents that they were saved on the night when the solo was sung and the prayers were sent up for them.

While the Days are Going By

Words by George Cooper   Music by Ira D. Sankey

There are lonely hearts to cherish,
While the days are going by.

This, one of the most popular hymns to which I have set music, was written by George Cooper. I found it as a poem in a periodical in 1881, and immediately wrote the chorus and composed the tune. It has been much used and greatly blessed in Gospel meetings.

Whiter than Snow

Words by James Nicholson   Music by Wm. G. Fisher

> Lord Jesus, I long to be perfectly whole,
> I want Thee forever to live in my soul.

"In the spring of 1893," relates Mr. Bradley, a Methodist minister in Utah, "a lady who had come from Ireland as a Mormon immigrant several years before was brought under very pungent conviction of sin, which lasted for several days. She attended our services several times, but seemed to get no relief. On the following Monday morning, while she was about her work as usual, the burden had become almost unbearable. As she worked she began to sing, 'Lord Jesus, I long to be perfectly whole;' and when she came to the closing words,

> To those who sought Thee,
> Thou never saidst no.

a feeling came over her like a flash, she says, that He would not say 'No' to her. From that moment the burden was lifted and she was filled with joy."

Mr. Fischer, the composer, was a resident of Philadelphia, and in 1876 was the leader of the Moody and Sankey choir in the great building at Thirteenth and Market streets, in that city.

Whosoever Will

Words by P. P. Bliss   Music by P. P. Bliss

> 'Whosoever heareth,' shout, shout the sound!
> Send the blessed tidings all the world around.

Henry Moorehouse, the English evangelist, preached seven sermons on John 3:16 in Chicago during the winter of 1869-70. Those sermons made a very deep impression on Mr. Bliss, Mr. Moody and others, and from that time a new and clearer view of the love of God was experienced by many who went forth to preach – perhaps not less about the law, but surely more about the boundless love of God in Jesus Christ. As an outcome of this experience the hymn was written at that time. In singing it, Bliss put special emphasis on the word "whosoever." So he helped many a man to believe in the magnificent offer of salvation, and – like Richard Baxter, the famous London preacher – to praise the Lord, "... I thank God," he said, "for the word 'whosoever.' If God had said that there was mercy for Richard Baxter, I am so vile a sinner that I would have thought he meant some other Richard Baxter; but when he says 'whosoever,' I know that it includes me, the worst of all Richard Baxters."

Mr. Moody said: — "I thank God for the whosoevers' of the invitations of Christ. 'God so loved the world that He gave His only-begotten Son, that whosoever believe th on Him should not perish, but have everlasting life;' and 'Whosoever will, let him take the water of life freely.'

"I was in Ohio a few years ago, and was invited to preach in the State prison. Eleven hundred convicts were brought into the chapel; and all sat in front of me. After I had got through the preaching, the chaplain said to me: 'Mr. Moody, I want to tell you of a scene which occurred in this room. A few years ago, our commissioners went to the Governor of the State, and got him to promise that he would pardon five men for good behaviour. The Governor consented, with this understanding — that the record was to be kept secret; and that at the end of six months the five men highest on the roll should receive a pardon, regardless of who or what they were. At the end of six months the prisoners were all brought into the chapel; the commissioners came up, and the president stood up on the platform, and putting his hand in his pocket, brought out some papers, and said, "I hold in my hand pardons for five men." Every man was as still as death; many were deadly pale, and the suspense was awful; it seemed as if every heart had ceased to beat. The commissioner went on to tell them how they had got the pardons; but the chaplain interrupted him. 'Before you make your speech,

read out the names. This suspense is awful.'

"So he read out the first name, Reuben Johnson will come and get his pardon' ; and he held it out. But no one came forward. He said to the Governor, 'Are all the prisoners here?' The Governor told him they were all there. Then he said again, 'Reuben Johnson will come and get his pardon. It is signed and sealed by the Governor. He is a free man.' No one moved. The chaplain told me he looked right down where Reuben was; he was well-known; he had been nineteen years there. Many were looking round to see him spring to his feet. But he himself was looking round to see the fortunate man who had got the pardon. Finally the chaplain caught his eye and said, 'Reuben, you are the man.' Reuben turned round and looked behind him to see where Reuben was. The chaplain said the second time, 'Reuben, you are the man' ; and the second time he looked round, thinking it must be some other Reuben.

"Well, the chaplain could see where Reuben was; and he had said three times, 'Reuben, come and get your pardon.' At last the truth began to steal over the old man; he got up and came along down the hall, trembling from head to foot. And when he had received the pardon he looked at it, went back to his seat, buried his face in his hands, and wept. When the prisoners got into the ranks to go back to the cells, Reuben got into the ranks too: and the chaplain had to call to him, 'Reuben, get out of the ranks: you are a free man; you are no longer a prisoner.' And Reuben stepped out of the ranks. He was free!

"That is the way men make out pardons. They make them out for good character or good behaviour. But God makes out pardons for men who have not got any character; for men who have been very, very bad. He offers a pardon to every sinner in England if he will take it. I do not care what he is nor what he is like. He may be the greatest libertine that ever walked the streets; or the greatest black-guard who ever lived; or the greatest drunkard, or thief, or vagabond: but I come to such with glad tidings, and preach the Gospel to every creature.'"

Why Not Tonight?

Words by Eliza Reed   Music by Ira D. Sankey

> Oh, do not let the Word depart,
> And close thine eyes against the light.

A tram-car man was passing along the broadway at Deptford, England, where some Christians were singing at an open-air meeting.

> Oh, do not let the Word depart,
> Nor close thine eyes against the light,
> Poor sinner, harden not thy heart,
> Thou would'st be saved – Why not tonight?

He felt the force of the appeal and hastened home to pray. Though he knelt down and plead earnestly, no light, or peace, or rest came. A fortnight passed away in this state of uncertainty, and on the following Sunday he was so miserable that he could not go to his work on the tram-car. In the evening he went to a chapel and remained for the prayer-meeting. The leader of the open-air meeting, in which the hymn was sung a fortnight before, happened to be present, and he saw the young man weeping and covering his face with his handkerchief. Praying the Lord to give him a word for this troubled soul, the leader asked: "Are you trusting Christ?" "No, but I am seeking Him," the man replied. And there he found Him, to the joy of his soul. Thus, in the providence of God, the Christian worker who was the cause of producing the anxiety, without knowing at the time any of the circumstances, was also the means of removing it. This is but one of the numerous instances of the usefulness of "Why not Tonight?" in evangelistic meetings.

Windows Open Toward Jerusalem

Words by P. P. Bliss   Music by P. P. Bliss

> Do you see the Hebrew captive kneeling,
> At morning, noon and night, to pray?

While attending a Sunday service at the State Prison in Joliet, Illinois, where he had gone to sing, P. P. Bliss heard H. G. Spafford of Chicago, who wrote "It is well with my soul," address the prisoners, and use Daniel in Babylon as an illustration of Gospel truth, asking the question in closing, "Are your windows open toward Jerusalem?" This suggested the hymn to Mr. Bliss.

About a month before his death Mr. Bliss came to Chicago to attend a convention called by Mr. Moody, and there, at a morning meeting, where over a thousand ministers were present, he sang, "Are your windows open toward Jerusalem?" with intense spiritual feeling. One minister cried out: "God bless Mr. Bliss for that song!" His face fairly shone as he sang, and half of those present were in tears under the influence of the song. Mr. Moody, filled with emotion, leaned his head forward upon the desk. It was the last time he heard his beloved friend and brother sing.

I often used to sing this song as a solo in connection with Mr. Moody's lectures on the prophet Daniel.

Wonderful Words of Life

Words by P. P. Bliss   Music by P. P. Bliss

> Sing them over again to me,
> Wonderful words of Life.

"While visiting an old man, who suffered much from rheumatic gout," narrates a Methodist minister of Birmingham, England, "I was led to start up,

> Sing them over again to me,
> wonderful words of Life.

When I had finished and while the tears were coursing down his cheeks, he exclaimed, 'Oh, sing them over again to me, those wonderful words of life! For they take my pain away.' And so I repeated that God-sent message to the poor old sufferer, who soon afterward passed away to the land where there is no more pain.

"On another occasion this hymn became very useful to me. I was preaching to a crowded audience at Dartmouth on a Sunday evening, when a young man fell from his seat near the pulpit, and the service was in danger because of the confusion. I started singing, 'Wonderful Words of Life,' in which the whole congregation joined heartily. By the time we had sung the hymn through the young man had recovered consciousness and found his seat again, listening earnestly to my sermon on the theme, 'In God's Word there are spirit and life.' Those present thought his case a living illustration of the song and sermon."

Work for the Night is Coming

Words by A. L. Walker   Music by Dr. Lowell Mason

> Work, for the night is coming,
> Work through the morning hours.

This splendid work-hymn was written by Anna L. Walker, a resident of Canada, and first published in her "Poems," in 1868. It was suggested to her by the words of Jesus: "The night cometh, when no man can work." The music was written by Dr. Lowell Mason. It was often used in our meetings both in Great Britain and America.

Ye Must be Born Again

Words by W. T. Sleeper   Music by George C. Stebbins

A ruler once came to Jesus by night,
To ask Him the way of salvation and light;

"One evening in November, 1886," says the superintendent of a boys' school, "I was walking along a street in St. Joseph, Missouri, when I saw before me a great crowd gathered around a door. On coming nearer I saw that it was at the entrance of the hall of the Young Men's Christian Association. In the doorway stood some young men, singing. Just as I came near enough to hear they began to sing:

A ruler once came to Jesus by night,
To ask Him the way of salvation and light;
The Master made answer in words true and plain,
Ye must be born again.

"When they came to the chorus the sword of the Spirit entered my soul. It seemed to me that I was brought face to face with the Lord Jesus. There on the street, while that song was being sung, I asked him to teach me how to be born again – and he did it. I accepted an invitation to the service for the evening, and after that service, for the first time in my life, I publicly acknowledged Christ as my Saviour. "I have always considered that it was through the influence of that hymn that my soul was awakened. Many times have I thanked God for the song, as well as for the courage he gave to his disciples to sing it in that public way."

Many years ago an English evangelist sent me this incident: "We were holding evangelistic meetings," he said, "in a town in Perthshire, and there was one who helped us more effectually than we were at first aware of. I hardly know how we became acquainted with 'Blind Aggie;' for, besides being old and blind, she was a great sufferer and could seldom creep beyond her doorstep. We were strangers in the place and no one told us of her; yet in the providence of God one of our party was led to visit her little room, discovering what a saint she was and how deeply interested in all she had heard about our intended meetings. She helped us mightily by prayer, and as far as she could by individual work. Lodging in the same flat with blind Aggie was a seamstress – a poor, giddy, foolish girl – in whom she took a deep interest. With great difficulty she persuaded this girl to attend one of our meetings. While the girl was at the meeting Aggie was praying for a blessing upon her; and when she returned Aggie asked many questions, but to her sorrow could not find that any impression had been made on the young woman's heart. "The good old woman induced the thoughtless girl to go again, and when she returned the second time it was late, and blind Aggie had already gone to bed. But the girl burst into the old woman's room crying:

'Oh, Aggie, where are you? I must tell you!'

'Well, dear, what is it? Come and tell me.'

'Oh, but I want a light first, I canna tell ye in the dark.'

Though Aggie never had use for a candle, she told the girl where to find one. After it was lighted the girl burst forth from a full heart:

"'Oh, Aggie, woman, I didna laugh this time! They sang a hymn, and it kept saying, 'Ye must be born again,' and it just laid hold on me, Aggie, and oh! I'm born again! Jesus has taken me, Aggie!'"

"On a Sunday evening," relates a young lady of Dunfermline, Scotland, "I went with a companion to take a walk in the public park, when our attention was drawn to an open-air meeting. While we were standing there listening, the hymn 'Ye Must be Born Again' was given out and sung. Two lines of the last verse,

A dear one in heaven thy heart yearns to see
At the beautiful gate may be watching for thee,

took a firm hold on me, and I felt that I must be born again, for I never could get there of myself. That night I went to the meeting and decided for Christ, and ever since that hymn has been very dear to me."

Yet There is Room

Words by Horatius Bonar   Music by Ira D. Sankey

'Yet there is room!' The Lamb's bright hall of song,
With its fair glory, beckons thee along.

Dr. Bonar wrote this hymn at my request. I had been singing Tennyson's great poem, "Late, late, so late, and dark the night and chill," at our meetings in Great Britain, in 1873-74, and, on asking permission of the owners of the copyright to use it in my collection of songs, was refused. I then requested Dr. Bonar to write a hymn that should cover much the same ground. "Yet there is room" was the result. It was one of the first hymns for which I wrote music. It always had a very solemnizing effect on the meetings, especially when the last lines were sung: "No room, no room – oh, woful cry, 'No room.'"

At Dundee a careless, thoughtless young woman was one day invited by an acquaintance to accompany her to a meeting. She declined to go, saying that she did not care to hear Moody and Sankey. On being further pressed, she consented and went. She was not impressed by anything she heard in the course of the meeting. Indeed, she thought there was "nothing in it," and wondered why people should make so much ado about what seemed so commonplace. The last hymn, "Yet there is Room!" was being sung by Mr. Sankey alone. He had reached the last stanza —

> Ere night that gate may close, and seal thy doom.
> Then the last, low, long cry "No room! no room!"
> No room, no room; oh, woful cry, "No room!"

These last words of Dr. Bonar's hymn fell upon the ear of the young woman like a sudden thunderclap. She left the meeting, but the words went with her. "No room! no room!" still rang in her ears. Conscience awoke at the sound of this warning bell. Nor could she rest, until she found rest in the great Redeemer.

Yield Not to Temptation

Words by H. R. Palmer   Music by H. R. Palmer

> Yield not to temptation,
> For yielding is sin;

Mr. Palmer says: "This song was an inspiration. I was at work on the dry subject of 'Theory' when the complete idea flashed upon me, and I laid aside the theoretical work and hurriedly penned both words and music as fast as I could write them. I submitted them to the criticism of a friend afterward, and some changes were made in the third stanza, but the first two are exactly as they came to me. The music was first written in A flat; but I soon saw that B flat was better, and for many years it has appeared in that key. I am reverently thankful it has been a power for good."

A friend contributes this incident: "Twenty years ago, when the State prison at Sing Sing, New York, had women as well as men within its walls, a lady used to visit the women's department. Every Sunday afternoon the inmates were permitted to come out and sit in the corridor to hear her talk, and to sing hymns with her. One day some of the women rebelled against an order of the matron, and a terrible scene followed. Screams, threats, ribaldry and profanity filled the air. It was said, by those who knew, that an uprising among the women prisoners was worse and more difficult to quell than one among the men. The matron hastily sent to the men's department for help. Suddenly a voice rose clear and strong above the tumult, singing a favourite song of the prisoners,

> Yield not to temptation,
> For yielding is sin;
> Each victory will help you
> Some other to win.
> Fight manfully onward,
> Dark passions subdue;
> Look ever to Jesus,
> He'll carry you through.

There was a lull; then one after another joined in the sacred song, and presently, with one accord, all formed into line and marched quietly to their cells."

A minister who at the time was labouring there, writes me that when Dr. Somerville, of Scotland, and Mr. Varley, of England, were in New Zealand, in the seventies, in connection with Young Men's Christian Association work, many young men found strength for life's temptations in the first lines of this hymn, which for months was sung at every meeting held.

"Some twenty-four years ago," writes James A. Watson, of Blackburn, England, "the Presbyterian church of England was preparing to issue a new book of praise, 'The Church Praise,' now in use. I was asked to send in a suitable list of hymns for the young. Among the number I sent 'Yield not to temptation,' but to my regret, when I got a draft copy of the proposed hymn-book, that hymn was not in it. Three or four Sundays afterward I was requested by the teacher of the infant class in the St. George's School, where I have been superintendent for over forty years, to visit a dying boy. I found him unconscious. All that his widowed mother could tell me about him was that he had kept saying: 'He'll carry me through.' When I asked her if she knew what he meant, she told me that she did not. She did not attend church or school. I told her that it was the chorus of a hymn, and pointed out how the good Shepherd was carrying her little boy through the valley, how he was gathering her lamb in his loving arms. I also told her that the Saviour would carry her through her trouble, would comfort, strengthen and keep her, and at last bring her to the happy land where death-divided ones will meet to part no more. I was so much impressed by the incident that I wrote to the convener of the hymn-book committee, and pleaded for the insertion of the hymn in the new book. The committee put it in, and for twenty-three years the young people of our Presbyterian church have been able to sing it when wanted, all through the comfort it had been to a little dying boy, the only son of a widow, on a back street of Blackburn."

Index of Hymns